THE ULTIMATE COCKTAIL BOOK

© FOLEY PUBLISHING CORP.

D1444227

Cover by LeRoy Neiman

Printed in The United States of America

First Printing May 1990
10 9 8 7 6 5 4 3 2 1

© Copyright 1990 by Raymond Peter Foley

Published by FOLEY Publishing

ISBN 0-9617655-1-8

DEDICATION

To Walter Mannheimer for his encouragement, knowledge and help...

To LeRoy Neiman for his contribution and acknowledgement of Bartenders in his Art and his Heart!

And especially to

Jaclyn Marie

INTRODUCTION

As a Bartender for over 20 years and Publisher of BARTENDER MAGAZINE for 11 years, I now have the honor of presenting *The Ultimate Cocktail Book*.

I started collecting cocktail recipe books over 20 years ago and my collection now consists of over 750 different books from 1862 to the present day. Many new products and cocktails have been created since 1862. With the influx of new products in the 90's, many new cocktails have become as popular as the old standards. We have included in this guide the old standards as well as the more popular cocktails of the 80's and into 1990.

I have also selected the finest ingredients to be represented in *The Ultimate Cocktail Book*. After all, when preparing a great steak, you must start with a great steak. Likewise, by using the best liquor you create the ultimate cocktail. The proof is in the taste. Use premium brands at all times. They represent your cocktail, your establishment and you.

We have not included drink recipes with items you'll have difficulty finding (i.e., Italian blue olives, Chinese sesame syrup, New Zealand kumquat mix, etc.).

Drinks are listed alphabetically by Liquor in the Table of Contents and by Name in the Index.

Enjoy *The Ultimate Cocktail Book*. But please remember not to drink in excess. *Moderation* is the key word. Good judgment for yourself and your guests is most important to any successful party. Drinking and driving do not mix! The cocktail recipes herein are for your pleasure. Enjoy in moderation.

CHEERS-

Raymond P. Foley

ACKNOWLEDGMENT

to the Bartenders and Suppliers
who made this *The Ultimate Cocktail Book*

I would like to thank the following who have made this *The Ultimate Cocktail Book:*

Carillon Importers, Ltd., with special thanks to Michel Roux, Richard McEvoy, Jerry Ciraulo and Ernie Capria;

The House of Seagram, with special thanks to Tom McInerney, Peter Angus and Mark Gothberg;

Hiram Walker, Inc., with special thanks to William Wilde, Phil Denomme, Tony Bongiovanni, Bill Donan, Randy Herbertson and Bob Suffredini;

The Paddington Corporation, with special thanks to Roger Slone, Paul Tynan, Tony Foglio, Keith Greggor and David Margolis;

Bacardi Imports, Inc., with special thanks to Ed Sardina, Ian Gomar, Kim Smith and Laura Rogers;

Maidstone Wine & Spirits, Inc., with special thanks to Dennis Brophy and Gary Clayton;

Asbach International Wine & Spirits, with special thanks to Peter Nelson;

Austin, Nichols & Co., Inc., with special thanks to Bruce Schwartz and Pam Levine;

Domecq Importers, Inc., with special thanks to Gabe Sagaz;

Anheuser-Busch, Inc., with special thanks to Lynn Patton and Tracy Toenjes;

Schweppes USA Ltd., with special thanks to Peg Fort;

Premiere Wine Merchants, Inc., with special thanks to Janet Unger;

and *Libbey Glass, Inc.*, with special thanks to Ed Pohlman and Allyson Lennon Roose.

To all those I have worked with over the last twenty years, especially those at the Manor Restaurant, West Orange, New Jersey, and a special thanks to William Boggier; Millie and Anthony Rinaldi; Ann Guidice; The Knowles Family: Harry, Doris, Kurt, and Wade; and, of course, Mike Cammarano.

A special thanks to the late Harry Knowles, Sr., who wouldn't let me quit.

To my Bartending Partner, John Cowan.

To the Multiple Sclerosis' U.G.L.Y. Bartenders throughout the United States.

And a special thanks to the following members of BARTENDER MAGAZINE'S "Bartender Hall of Fame"™:

Eli Grober, Jimmy Zazzali, Tommy Ragonese, Cathy Bush, Herman Herschbach, Mark Magnusson, Ross Carlino, Jimmy Caulfield, Hugh Keniff, Joe Burke, Walt Coleman, Rene Bardel, Richard Grecco, Bobby Batugo, Charles Chop, John Chop, Walter Mellen, Hoppy Degutman, Ronald Terzuole, Harry Fendt, Joe Luby, James Kelly, Harry Ayala, Angelo Cammarata, William Bedics, Michael Critz, Ernie Anderson, Stanley Trowbridge, Sylvia Schmidt, Anthony Rinicella, Thomas Killeen, Tom Core, John Wannemacher, Kitty Fitzke, John Boyle, John Neckland, Raphael Caloia, William Estanich, Gerald Kratzer, Fred Edwards, Carol Schwanke, R. M. Haas, Jerry Gasber, Al Checchi, Jack Fitzpatrick, John Hannan, Bill Kehoe, Pat Heenan, Ronald Beth, William Aldon, Hugh McNally, Joanne Ash, Lay Mastry, Kathy Benson, Betty Coach, Gus Contos, Charles Barker, Matthew Wojciak, Ed Chambers, Bru Mysak, Peter Carlton, Vincent Laporta, Joe Cole, Joseph Kleha, Bob Frisch, Ernest Hardin, Deborah Gutherie, Frank Cigoy, Dave Delaney, Peter Glegorivich, Thomas McEvoy, Matilda Bloom, Orlean Carlson, Geri Gillen, Joe Sicillano, Mike Costa, David Skaggs, Fermin Gomez, Tom Tolstoy, Albert Repetty,

Joe Demartini, Gail Coward, Martha Van Holsbeke, Kenneth Sauer, Fran Means, Lena Drosdal, Bonnie Ferraro, Cindy Meyer, Sonny Skrakowski, David Vanel, Charles Peters, Mary Beddo, Jose Ruiseco, Maria Howard, Robert Julien, Jeffrey Staughton Gale, Ada King, John King, Leonard Daniels, Joseph Gates, Faye McCall, Bob Murphy, Saverio Ciavarella, Tom Mathers, Grant Faulkner, Jose Ancona, Gonzolo Gutierrez, Gary Martin, Bill Sherer, Margie Putnam, Ella Zoesch, Nick Maras, Joseph McClure, Louis Yakich, George Dutchman, Robert Donatta, Ed Murati, W. J. Ohlsen, Bart Perry, Michel McCourt, Billie Epperson, Michael Looper, Ted Chmielewski, Marian Haats, Romualdo Vincente, Gabe Ferroni, James Elliott, Buzz Bozzini, David Baciqulupi, Russell Muncy, Anthony Cordero, Mark Andersen, Tom Chaskey, Carl Storlazzi, Billy Reilly, Edward Olling, Joe Ponce, Thomas Riordan, Sol Prignano, Sandra Gutierrez, Ted Weesner, Victor Lee, Nick Stipelcovich, Bernie Wieloch, Tommy Leonard, Joseph Hajjar, Olga Morgan, Herb Reinardy, Lee Steffanich, William Collier, Roy Stewart, George Coyle, Joseph Damiani, Andrew Wasko, Max Schelle, Thomas O'Hara, Salvatore Sommese, Frederick Roome, Donald Pangrazio, Charles Clarke, Jerimiah Mires, Violet Bakich, Mary Davidson, Fred Cosentino, Robert Paganico, Guy Tirabassi, Dan Muttutat, Marye Anderson, Jerome Hafner, Rosemary Butler, Louie Steamer, Lyndon C. Brewerton, Wilson Albert, David Kujawski, Ronald Morris, Vincent P. Riley, Carolyn McCrimmon, J. Russel Settle, Sherry Paris, Denise Faulkner, Richard Flannigan, Ken Strone, John Rotolo, Kathryn Corr, Barney L. Micek, Ivan Harry Schryver, III, Mark Rapp, Ralph Roselli, Andrew S. Sabilia, Tim Myles, Frank McCaffrey, Zobby Miktarian, Walter Eugene Helfrich, Robert H. Clay, Michael G. Karlovich, Patty Quinn . . .

and Kerry French.

ACKNOWLEDGMENT
About the Artist
LeRoy Neiman

The art of LeRoy Neiman vividly chronicles the vitality, depth, and emotion of the art of Bartending. The very principle we urge all of you to reflect in the way you work—the fact that Bartending is an art as well as a profession to be treated with respect, dignity and pride—Neiman reflects in his art with consummate skill, insight and sensitivity.

To refer to him as the most popular artist in America today is almost an understatement. Over the years, LeRoy Neiman has firmly established himself as the artist of and for the people. He renders the excitement, color, movement and emotion of people and places common enough for all to relate to and identify with.

Throughout the 1950's, Neiman was living in Chicago's near North Side in the Night Club Belt where he drew on the activities of its people for his material. Critics at the time referred to his work as a revival of the historically popular saloon painting, capturing the sights and emotions of this universal and timeless relaxation of man. His work, The Chicago Key Club, was exhibited at the Corcoran American Exhibition of Oil Painting, 25th Biannual, Washington, DC, in 1957. Also in 1957, his oil painting The Pump Room won the popular prize in the Chicago Artist Show at the Navy Pier, voted on by some 25,000 visitors. In 1958, Neiman's painting The Bartender won the Municipal Art Award in the Chicago Artist Show. Neiman also began his feature Man at His Leisure in PLAYBOY MAGAZINE in 1958 with The Pump Room. The years the feature ran allowed Neiman to expand his interest in capturing Man at His

Leisure from the popular saloons of Chicago to the world's most expensive and glamorous social and sporting events.

It is not simply coincidence that caused Neiman to focus his early work on Bartenders. Growing up in St. Paul, Minnesota, Neiman recalls that during the depression there was little else for the fathers to do than to spend time in neighborhood bars. Amid all of this stood the Bartender, a distinctive figure and neighborhood hero. In contrast to his customers, the Bartender was always cleanly dressed in his pressed white shirt, wearing his Sunday finest every day of the week. He maintained his dignity and a sense of style and class by not drinking and being in control throughout his customers' downhearted imbibing and stimulated revelry.

We would once again like to thank LeRoy Neiman for sharing his talent and generosity with BARTENDER MAGAZINE, *The Ultimate Cocktail Book* and its readers.

Photo by Paul Chapnick

CONTENTS

B.C.
BEACH BALL COOLER
BLUE LEMONADE
CAJUN KING MARTINI
CILVER CITRON
CITRON CELEBRATION
CITRON CHI CHI
CITRON CODDER
CITRON COOLER
CITRON MADRAS
COOL CITRON
FLORIDA JOY
GOLFER
LEMONDROP
PERFECT RON
PILOT HOUSE FIZZ
PINK BABY
PINK LEMONADE
RAINBOW
RIGHT IDEA
SALTY GROG
SUPER LEMON COOLER
SWEDISH BLACKBERRY
TEANECK TOT
  (COOLER)
TROPICAL ORCHARD
TWISTED BULL
WHITE CITRON

ASBACH URALT...85
AMBROSIA
ASBACH BEAUTY
ASBACH COLA
ASBACH SODA
ASBACH SOUR
BLACK FOREST
  SPECIAL
BLUE BRACER
BRANDTINI
BRANDY ALEXANDER
BRANDY AND SODA
BRANDY CASSIS
BRANDY COLLINS
BRANDY FIZZ
BRANDY FLIP
BRANDY FLOATER
BRANDY HIGHBALL
BRANDY MANHATTAN
BRANDY OLD
  FASHIONED
BRANDY SLING
CARROL COCKTAIL
CLASSIC
DRY STINGER
DUTCH TREAT
FRENCH 75
FROUPE
HARRY LIME
HARVARD
HERMAN'S SPECIAL

HEUTCHEN
LADY BE GOOD
LAJOLLA
MARIPOSA
MCBRANDY
MIKADO
MISSISSIPPI PLANTERS
  PUNCH
NICKOLASKA
OLYMPIC COCKTAIL
PEPPERMINT FIZZ
PHOEBE SNOW
PRINCE OF WALES
QUAKER
RUEDESHEIM ICED
  COFFEE
RUEDESHEIMER COFFEE
SIDECAR
SLOE BRANDY
SNOWBALL
SOUTH PACIFIC
STINGER
UNPUBLISHED
  HEMINGWAY

BACARDI RUM....93
ACAPULCO
APPLE COOLER
APPLE PIE COCKTAIL
APPLE RUM RICKEY
APPLE RUM SWIZZLE
BACARDI AND COLA
BACARDI AND TONIC
BACARDI ALEXANDER
BACARDI ANCIENT
  MARINER
BACARDI BLACK
  RUSSIAN
BACARDI BLOODY
  MARY
BACARDI BLOSSOM
BACARDI BUCK
BACARDI CHAM-
  PAGNE COCKTAIL
BACARDI COCKTAIL
BACARDI COLLINS
BACARDI DAIQUIRI
BACARDI EGGNOG
BACARDI FIRESIDE
BACARDI FIZZ
BACARDI FROZEN
  DAIQUIRI
  BANANA
  ORANGE
  PEACH
  PINEAPPLE
  STRAWBERRY
BACARDI GIMLET
BACARDI
  GRASSHOPPER

BACARDI HOT
  BUTTERED RUM
BACARDI IRISH
  COFFEE
BACARDI NIGHTCAP
BACARDI OLD
  FASHIONED
BACARDI ON-THE-
  ROCKS OR MIST
BACARDI PINA
  COLADA
BACARDI RICKEY
BACARDI RUM PUNCH
BACARDI SOUR
BACARDI TOM &
  JERRY
BALI HAI
BANANA MAN
BARRACUDA
BAT BITE
BEACH PARTY
BEACHCOMER
BEACHCOMER'S
  SPECIAL
BISHOP COCKTAIL
BOLERO COCKTAIL
BONBINI
BONGO DRUM
BROADWAY COOLER
BUCK-A-ROO
CALIFORNIA
  COOL-AID
CALIFORNIA
  LEMONADE
CALYPSO COOL-AID
CARIBBEAN COCKTAIL
CARIBBEAN JOY
CASA BLANCA
CHICAGO STYLE
CHOCOLATE CREAM
CIDERIFIC
CLAM VOYAGE
COCONUT PUNCH
COFFEE CREAM
COOLER
CONTINENTAL
CORKSCREW
COW PUNCHER
CRICKET
DERBY DAIQUIRI
DUNLOP COCKTAIL
EYE OPENER
FLORIDA SUNRISE
FRENCH DAIQUIRI
GARTER BELT
GRAPE PUNCH
HARD HAT
HAWAIIAN NIGHT
HEAT WAVE
LUCKY LADY

MAI-TAI
MIAMI SPECIAL
OLD SAN JUAN
  COCKTAIL
OLD SAN JUAN SIPPER
PINA VERDE
PINK PANTHER
PLANTER'S PUNCH
RACER'S EDGE
RED HOT MAMA
RUDOLPH'S NOSE
RUM-TA-TUM
SAN JUAN COCKTAIL
SAN JUAN COLLINS
SAN JUAN SUNSET
SCORPION
SLOE SUNSET
TAILGATE
TEXAS SUNDOWNER
TROPICAL STORM
YELLOW BIRD
ZOMBIE

**BAILEYS ORIGINAL
IRISH CREAM ... 109**
50-50 BAR
AFTER 5
AFTER 8
AFTER SIX SHOOTER
"B" ORIGINAL
B-52
BAIL-OUT aka IRISH
  BULLDOG
BAILEYS ALEXANDER
BAILEYS BLIZZARD
BAILEYS CHOCOLATE
  COVERED CHERRY
BAILEYS COCONUT
  FRAPPE
BAILEYS COFFEE
BAILEYS COMET
BAILEYS CREAM
  DREAM
BAILEYS CUDDLER
BAILEYS DREAM SHAKE
BAILEYS EGGNOG
BAILEYS FIZZ
BAILEYS FLOAT
BAILEYS HOT MILK
  PUNCH
BAILEYS IRISH COFFEE
BAILEYS ITALIAN
  DREAM
BAILEYS MINT KISS
BAILEYS MIST
BAILEYS MOCHA
  CREAM
BAILEYS PRALINE
  SUPREME

BAILEYS ROMA
BAILEYS SHILLELAGH
BARNUM & BAILEY
BARNUMENTHE &
  BAILEYS
BERRY BAILEYS
BIT O'HONEY
BUSHWACKER
CAFE ROMA
CALIFORNIA SHOT
COFFEE BEANS
DUBLIN HANDSHAKE
EMERALD ISLE
EYES R SMILIN
FIFTH AVENUE
HOT MINT KISS
HOT SLIPPERY NIPPLE
IRISH COCONUT
IRISH DREAM
IRISH ITALIAN
  CONNECTION
IRISH RULE
NUTCRACKER SWEET
NUTTY IRISHMAN
O'CASEY SCOTCH
  TERRIER
ORGASM NO. 1
ORGASM NO. 2
PAINT THINNER
PEACHES N' CREAM
POND SCUM
RUSSIAN QUAALUDE
SCHNAPPY
  SHILLELAGH
SCREAMING ORGASM
SLIPPERY NIPPLE
SUPER BOWL
  COCKTAIL/REFEREE'S
  REVENGE
THREE LEAF CLOVER
TIDY BOWL
TINKER'S TEA
TOOTSIE ROLL

BOMBAY GIN....119
BOMBAY GIN
  MARTINI
APPARENT
BERMUDA ROSE
BLUE LADY
BOMBAY GRAND
BRONX COCKTAIL
CLARIDGE
CREST OF THE WAVE
CROSS BOW
EVERYTHING
FALLEN ANGEL
GIN ALEXANDER
GIN AND CRAN
GIN AND SIN

GIN AND TONIC
GIN CASSIS
GIN COCKTAIL aka
  DUBONNET
  COCKTAIL
GIN DRIVER
GIN JULEP
GIN OLD FASHIONED
GIN RICKEY
GIN SCREWDRIVER
GIN SIDECAR
GIN SOUR
GIN SOUTHERN
GIN SPIDER
GIN STINGER
GOLDEN BILL
GOLDEN GIRL
GREEN DRAGON
GUIDO
JOHN BULL
MINT COOLER
MOONSHOT
ORANGE BLOSSOM
ORANGE SUNSET
PINK LADY
POLO
SALTY DOG
SEE-THRU
SINGAPORE SLING
SLIM GIN
SURE GIN FIZZ
TOM COLLINS
TROPICAL GIN
VELVET CROWN
WHITE LADY
YELLOW FELLOW

B&B/BENEDICTINE.127
B&B ALEXANDER
B&B AMERICANO
B&B AND TEA
B&B AND TONIC
B&B CAFE
B&B COLLINS
B&B FLOAT
B&B MANHATTAN
B&B MIST
B&B STINGER
BEWITCHED
BRIGHTON PUNCH
CHAMPAGNE CUPID
EROS
FRENCH GOLD
FRENCH SPRING
JE TAIME
MIDNIGHT ENCOUNTER
WIDOW'S KISS
B AND TEA
BENEDICT

BARBERRY COAST
BEANBERRY
BELLINI
BERRY BERRY
BERRY GOOD
BLACK ANGEL
BLACK BAT
BLACK PEARL
BLACKBERRY BRANDY
BOTCH-A-ME
BURRBERRY
CALYPSO CIDER
CHOCOLATE MINT
 CREAM
CHOCOLATE MINT
 FREEZE
CINNAMON COLA
CINNAMON STICK
COCOMINT
CONTINENTAL STINGER
COOL ON THE ROCKS
CRAN MINT
CRANBERRY KIR
CRANBERRY
 SNOWBLOWER
FROZEN AMARETTO &
 APPLE
FUZZ-BUSTER
FUZZY NAVEL
GIRL SCOUT COOKIE
GOLDEN PEACH
GRASSHOPPER
GRETEL
HEAD
ITALIAN SPEAR
JELLY BEAN
KAHUNA
KOKO CODDLER
KOKO SUNSET
LIFT
MAD MOGUL
MAI BERRY
MEXICAN CRANBERRY
MULLBERRY
NANTUCKET
NIGHTCAP
PEACH BLOSSOM
PEACH CREAMY
PEACH ON THE BEACH
PEACH PIRATE
PEACH ROYAL
PEACHY
PEACH SOUR
PEPPERMINT PATTI
PEPPERMINTINI
PINK SQUIRREL
PINK VELVET
PRALINE N CREAM
PRALINE CAJUN
 COOLER

ROOT BEER RUSSIAN
ROOT BEER SUNRISE
ROOTY-TOOTY
ROYAL KIR
SCHNAPP HAPPY
SNOWFLAKE
SON OF A PEACH
SPARK PLUG
SPEARMINT TROPICAL
ST. MORITZ
SWEET SUNSHINE
SWISS CHOCOLATE
 TROPICANA
SWISS PEACH
TRAVELING WILDBURYS
TRIPLE ORANGE
WHIPPER SCHNAPPER
WILD IRISH BERRY

JAMESON PREMIUM
IRISH WHISKEY...169
B.A.S.I.L.
BLACK AND TAN
BLACKTHORN
BOG
BRAINSTORM
COMMANDO FIX
DANCING
 LEPRECHAUN
EVERYBODY'S RUSH
HUDSON'S STING
IRISH BROGUE
IRISH COLLINS
IRISH COW
IRISH CRESTA
IRISH HIGHBALL
IRISH ROVER
IRISH SHILLELAGH
IRISH SPRING
JAMESON HOT TODDY
JAMESON IRISH
 COFFEE
JAMESON
 MANHATTAN
KERRY COOLER
LEPRECHAUN
MINGLING OF THE
 CLANS
ONE IRELAND
PADDY COCKTAIL
RED DEVIL
SERPENT'S TOOTH
SHAMROCK
TIPPERARY

J&B SCOTCH ...175
BAGPIPE
BAIRN
BALMORAL
BEADLESTONE

BLACK JACK
BLOODY JOSEPH
BLOODY MARY,
 QUEEN OF SCOTS
BLUEBLAZER
BOBBY BURNS
BUTTERSCOTCH
 COLLINS
CHURCHILL
DRY ROB ROY
DUNDEE
GENTLE JOHN
GIBRALTAR
GODFATHER
HEATHER COFFEE
HIGHLAND COFFEE
HIGHLAND FLING
HOPSCOTCH
IRON LADY
J&B INTERNATIONAL
 STINGER
J&B ROB ROY
J&B SCOTCH BOUNTY
J&B ULTIMATE SOUR
J&BEACH
KERRY BLUE
L.S.D.
LOCH LOMOND
MARLON BRANDO
NORTH SEA
OLD FASHIONED J&B
PLANTATION SCOTCH
PUNCH
RED FIZZ
ROYAL MILE
RUSTY NAIL aka NAIL
 DRIVER
SCOTCH BRU
SCOTCH COBBLER
SCOTCH COLLINS
SCOTCH MIST
SCOTCH SIDECAR
SCOTCH SMASH
SCOTCH SOLACE
SCOTCH SOUR
SCOTCH SPARLKE
SCOTCH STAR
SCOTCH TODDY
SCOTIA'S SECRET
SCOTTISH COFFEE
SCOTTISH SHORT -
 BREAD COFFEE
SCOTTY DOG
SIRROCO COCKTAIL
SOUR NAIL
SWEET PEAT
WALKMAN
WHIZZ BANG
WOODWARD

HOT TODDY
HURRICANE COCKTAIL
INK STREET
METS MANHATTAN
MILLIONAIRE
 COCKTAIL
MONTE CARLO
 COCKTAIL
NEW YORKER
 COCKTAIL
OLD FASHIONED
 COCKTAIL #1
OLD FASHIONED
 COCKTAIL #2
SEAGRAM'S V.O.
 COLLINS
SEAGRAM'S V.O.
 HIGHBALL
T.N.T. COCKTAIL
V.O. COOLER
V.O. DRY MANHATTAN
V.O. GOLD RUSH
V.O. GOLD SPLASH
V.O. GOLDFINGER
V.O. LEMONADE
V.O. MANHATTAN
 DANE
V.O. MANHATTAN
 ROSE

V.O. PERFECT
 MANHATTAN
V.O. SOUR
WALDORF COCKTAIL
WARD EIGHT #1
WARD EIGHT #2
WHITE SAND COOLER
ZAZARAC COCKTAIL

ANGELIC
ATLANTA BELLE
BEEHIVE
BIG BOY NOW
BIONIC TURKEY
BOURBON AND COLA
BOURBON AND
 GINGER
BOURBON COLLINS
BOURBON DELIGHT
BOURBON MILK
 PUNCH
BOURBON OLD
 FASHIONED
BOURBON SLOE GIN
 FIX
BRASS KNUCKLE
COLONEL "T"
COMMODORE

CRANBOURBON
DIXIE
DIZZY LIZZY
DUBONNET BOURBON
 MANHATTAN
FIVE-LEAF CLOVER
FLORIDA PUNCH
HOT APPLE COBBLER
JOHNNY
KENTUCKY COCKTAIL
KENTUCKY GENT
MACHO KAMACHO
MINT JULEP
MINTY JULEP
PERFECT BOURBON
 MANHATTAN
PRESBYTERIAN
SHRAPNEL
SLOE BIRD
SOUR TURKEY
SOUTHERN SOUR
STEVE'S SOUR
TURKEY CRUSH
TURKEY SHOOT
TURKEY SHOOTER
W.T. FIZZ
WARD 101

EDITOR'S NOTE:
 You will find the following
abbreviations throughout the
drink recipes.
btle. . . . . bottle
drps. . . . . drops
dshs . . . . dashes
med. . . . . medium
scp. . . . . scoop
scps. . . . . scoops
splsh. . . . . splash
tbs. . . . . tablespoon
tsp. . . . . teaspoon

FACTS ON LIQUOR AND PROOF

THE MEANING OF PROOF

Proof spirit, underproof, and overproof are terms difficult to explain in easy language since they are arbitrary standards set up by governments for collection of revenue.

Proof spirit is defined by law to be spirit which at 51° F weighs 12/13 of an equal measure of distilled water. At 51° F it has a specific gravity of .92308. It is a mixture of about 57% pure alcohol and 43% of water.

An underproof mixture of alcohol and water contains less than 100% of the mixture called proof spirit. So in 100 gallons of 20 underproof whiskey there is 80 gallons at proof strength and 20 extra gallons of water.

Overproof whiskey contains more alcohol and less water than proof spirit.

A proof chart shows these differences.

BRITAIN & CANADA		AMERICAN		ALCOHOL % BY VOLUME
	75.25 Overproof	200	Proof	100%
50	Overproof	172	Proof	86%
30	Overproof	149	74.5%	
	Proof	114.2	Proof	57.1%
12.5	Underproof	100	Proof	50%
30	Underproof	80	Proof	40%
50	Underproof	57	Proof	28.5%
100	Underproof	0	Proof	0%

CHARTS & MEASURES

MEASUREMENTS

	Metric	Standard
1 Dash	0.9 ml.	1/32 ounce
1 Teaspoon	3.7 ml.	1/8 ounce
1 Tablespoon	11.1 ml.	3/8 ounce
1 Pony	29.5 ml.	1 ounce
1 Jigger	44.5 ml.	1 1/2 ounces
1 Wineglass	119 ml.	4 ounces
1 Split	177 ml.	6 ounces
1 Miniature (nip)	59.2 ml.	2 ounces
1 Half Pint	257 ml.	8 ounces
1 Tenth	378.88 ml.	12.8 ounces
1 Pint	472 ml.	16 ounces
1 Fifth	755.2 ml.	25.6 ounces
1 Quart	944 ml.	32 ounces
1 Imperial Quart	1.137 liter.	38.4 ounces
1 Half Gallon	1.894 liter	64 ounces
1 Gallon	3.789 liter	128 ounces

Dry Wine and Champagne

Split (1/4 bottle)	177 ml.	6 oz.
"Pint" (1/2 bottle)	375.2 ml.	12 oz.
"Quart" (1 bottle)	739.0 ml.	25 oz.
Magnum (2 bottles)	1.534 liter	52 oz.
Jeroboam (4 bottles)	3.078 liter	104 oz.
Tappit-hen	3.788 liter	128 oz.
Rehoboam (6 bottles)	4.434 liter	
Methuselah (8 bottles)	5.912 liter	
Salmanazar (12 bottles)	8.868 liter	
Balthazar (16 bottles)	11.829 liter	
Nebuchadnezzar (20 bottles)	14.780 liter	
Demijohn (4.9 gallons)	18.66 liter	

DEPARTMENT OF THE TREASURY
BUREAU OF ALCOHOL, TOBACCO AND FIREARMS
DISTILLED SPIRITS

BOTTLE SIZE	EQUIVALENT FLUID OUNCES	BOTTLES PER CASE	LITERS PER CASE	U.S. GALLONS PER CASE	CORRESPONDS TO
1.75 liters	59.2 Fl. Oz.	6	10.50	2.773806	1/2 Gallon
1.00 liter	33.8 Fl. Oz.	12	12.00	3.170064	1 Quart
750 milliliters	25.4 Fl. Oz.	12	9.00	2.377548	4/5 Quart
500 milliliters	16.9 Fl. Oz.	24	12.00	3.170064	1 Pint
200 milliliters	6.8 Fl. Oz.	48	9.60	2.536051	1/2 Pint
50 milliliters	1.7 Fl. Oz.	120	6.00	1.585032	1, 1.6, & 2 Oz.

DEPARTMENT OF THE TREASURY
BUREAU OF ALCOHOL, TOBACCO AND FIREARMS
WINE

BOTTLE SIZE	EQUIVALENT FLUID OUNCES	BOTTLES PER CASE	LITERS PER CASE	U.S. GALLONS PER CASE	CORRESPONDS TO
4 liters	135 Fl. Oz.				1 Gallon
3 liters	101 Fl. Oz.	4	12.00	3.17004	4/5 Gallon
1.5 liters	50.7 Fl. Oz.	6	9.00	2.37753	2/5 Gallon
1 liter	33.8 Fl. Oz.	12	12.00	3.17004	1 Quart
750 milliliters	25.4 Fl. Oz.	12	9.00	2.37763	4/5 Quart
375 milliliters	12.7 Fl. Oz.	24	9.00	2.37753	4/5 Pint
187 milliliters	6.3 Fl. Oz.	48	8.976	2.37119	2/5 Pint
100 milliliters	3.4 Fl. Oz.	60	6.00	1.58502	2, 3, & 4 Oz.

CALORIES & CARBOHYDRATES

	Calories	Carbo-hydrates
Beer (12 oz. bottle or can)	144	11.7
Champagne —		
Brut (4 Fl. oz.)	92	2.1
Extra Dry	97	2.1
Pink	98	3.7
Gin, 80 proof (1 oz.)	65	0.0
Gin, 86 proof (1 oz.)	70	0.0
Gin, 90 proof (1 oz.)	74	0.0
Gin, 94 proof (1 oz.)	77	0.0
Gin, 100 proof (1 oz.)	83	0.0
Rum, 80 proof (1 oz.)	65	0.0
Rum, 86 proof (1 oz.)	70	0.0
Rum, 90 proof (1 oz.)	74	0.0
Rum, 94 proof (1 oz.)	77	0.0
Rum, 100 proof (1 oz.)	83	0.0
Vodka, 80 proof (1 oz.)	65	0.0
Vodka, 86 proof (1 oz.)	70	0.0
Vodka, 90 proof (1 oz.)	74	0.0
Vodka, 94 proof (1 oz.)	77	0.0
Vodka, 100 proof (1 oz.)	83	0.0
Whiskey, 80 proof (1 oz.)	65	0.0
Whiskey, 86 proof (1 oz.)	70	0.0
Whiskey, 90 proof (1 oz.)	74	0.0
Whiskey, 94 proof (1 oz.)	77	0.0
Whiskey, 100 proof (1 oz.)	83	0.0
Wine, aperitif (1 oz.)	41	2.3
Wine, port (1 oz.)	41	2.3
Wine, sherry (1 oz.)	41	2.3
Wine, white or red table (1 oz.)	29	1.2

NON-ALCOHOLIC

Club soda (1 oz.)	0	0.0
Cola (1 oz.)	12	3.1
Cream soda (1 oz.)	13	3.4
Fruit flavored soda (1 oz.)	13	3.7
Ginger ale (1 oz.)	9	2.4
Root beer (1 oz.)	13	3.2
Tonic water (1 oz.)	9	2.4

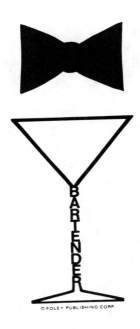
© FOLEY PUBLISHING CORP.

HOME BAR RECOMMENDATIONS & TIPS

Location

Choosing the proper location is essential. Select an open area that is easily accessible. A kitchen counter or a sturdy table near the kitchen counter is well suited. It should be convenient to the refrigerator and sink. The kitchen also becomes a gathering point for many partiers. Cleaning up water and spills is a lot easier on your kitchen floor, than your carpet.

If your kitchen is too small, a location near your kitchen on a sturdy table and, if you're worried about your carpet, spread a small rug beneath.

When setting up for a party of 25 or more, it's best to use the diagram below known as the "Diamond Plan."

The "Diamond Plan" gives the best guest flow and has two focal points: food and liquor.

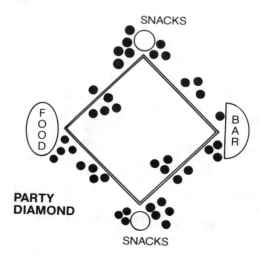

SNACKS

FOOD

BAR

PARTY
DIAMOND

SNACKS

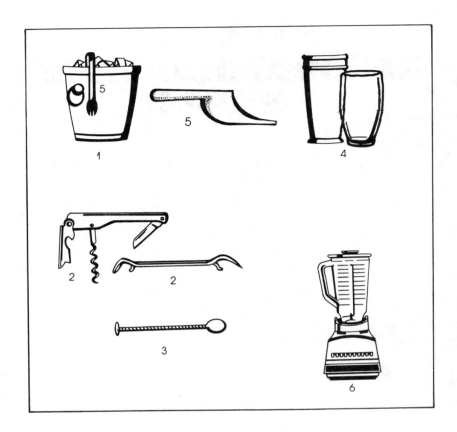

Bar Tools

The following should be displayed on your bar top (or table):

1. **Ice Bucket.** Try to find one with a vacuum seal, and large enough to hold at least three (3) trays of ice.

2. **Wine/Bottle Opener.** A good wine opener or waiter type. Church key or bottle opener that can open cans as well as snap off bottle tops.

3. **Bar Spoon.** One long spoon for stirring drinks or pitchers of drinks.

4. **Cocktail Shaker and Mixing Glass.** Mixing glass for use in stirring drinks. Shaker fits over glass to shake drinks.

5. **Ice Scoop/Tongs.** Use to pick up ice cubes from an ice bucket and place in glass. A must for every home bar. Never use your hands. If necessary, a large mouth spoon can be used.

6. **Blender.** Blending Margaritas, Pina Coladas and Daiquiris.

Bar Tools (continued)

Can also be used for crushing ice and making three or more drinks at once.

7. **Napkins/Coasters.** To place drink on or hold drink.
8. **Stirrers/Straws.** For mixing and sipping drinks.
9. **Pitcher of Water.** A large pitcher for water only.
10. **One Box of "Superfine" Sugar.**
11. **Three Large Bowls.** One for cut fruit, two for garnish. (olives, onions, etc.)
12. **Knife and Cutting Board.** Use to cut more fruit.
13. **Jigger/Measuring Glass.** All drinks should be made with a measuring glass or jigger. Drinks on the rocks or mixed drinks should not contain more than 1½ oz. of alcohol. Doubles should not be served.
14. **Muddler.** To muddle your fruit.
15. **Pourer.**
16. **Strainer.**

STOCKING THE BAR FOR HOME

The traditional bartender's formula for setting up a simple home bar is:
- Something white (Vodka, Gin, Rum or Tequila)
- Something brown (Scotch, Canadian Whiskey or Bourbon)
- Something sweet (a Liqueur)
- Wine and/or Vermouth if you want an apperitif or plan on making martinis.

In stocking your home bar for the first time, don't attempt to buy all types of exotic liquors and liqueurs. Your inventory should be based on items you and your friends will use most. Keep in mind that people will bring their favorite brands as gifts.

We're into the 90's and premium liquor is the call. Folks might be drinking less, but they're drinking the best. Buy the best, it's only pennies more and saves a lot of excuses and embarrassment. Treat yourself and your guests to the best!

BAR TABLE SET-UP

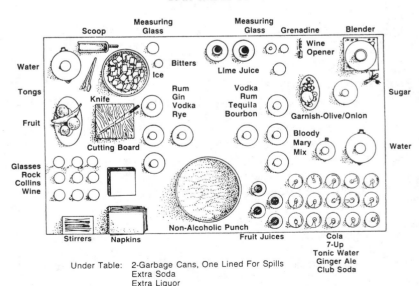

Under Table: 2-Garbage Cans, One Lined For Spills
Extra Soda
Extra Liquor
Extra Glasses

BASIC BAR STOCK AND PARTY TABLE

Product	Basic Stock (Quantities in Liters)	20	30	40	50
White Wine					
Domestic	2	4	4	5	6
Imported	1	2	2	2	3
Red Wine					
Domestic	2	1	2	3	3
Imported	1	1	1	2	2
Rose Wine	1	1	2	2	2
Champagne					
Domestic	1	2	3	4	6
or					
Imported	1	2	3	3	4
Vermouth - Martini & Rossi					
Extra Dry	1	1	2	2	2
Rosso (Sweet)	1	1	1	2	2
Liquors:					
Vodka					
Absolut	1	2	2	3	4
Peppar	1	1	1	1	2
Citron	1	1	1	2	3
Rum					
Bacardi	1	1	3	3	3
Gin					
Bombay	1	1	2	3	3
Scotch					
J&B	1	1	2	3	3
Whiskey					
Seagram's V.O.	1	1	1	2	2
Bourbon					
Wild Turkey 101	1	1	2	2	2
Tequila					
Sauza	1	2	2	3	3
Brandy					
Asbach	1	1	2	3	3

Product	Basic Stock	Number of Guests			
		20	30	40	50
Beer (12 oz. bottles):					
Budweiser	6	48	72	72	72
Bud Light	6	48	72	72	72
Aperitifs:					
Campari	750 ml.	1	1	1	2
Dubonnet					
Red	750 ml.	1	1	1	2
Blonde	750 ml.	1	1	1	1
Lillet	750 ml.	1	1	1	2
Cordials/Specials:					
Grand Marnier	750 ml.	1	1	1	1
Hiram Walker					
Creme de Menthe					
White	750 ml.	1	1	1	1
Green	750 ml.	1	1	1	1
Hiram Walker					
Peach Schnapps	750 ml.	1	1	1	1
Kahlua	750 ml.	1	1	1	1
Hiram Walker					
Creme de Cacao					
White	750 ml.	1	1	1	1
Dark	750 ml.	1	1	1	1
Baileys Original					
Irish Cream	750 ml.	1	2	3	3
Sambuca Romana	750 ml.	1	2	3	3
Hiram Walker					
Amaretto	750 ml.	1	2	2	2
Jameson Irish					
Whiskey	750 ml.	1	1	1	1
La Grande Passion	750 ml.	1	1	1	1
Liquore Galliano	750 ml.	1	1	1	1
B&B	750 ml.	1	1	1	1

1. This chart is based on 1¾ oz. per drink, this is a basic.
2. Product will vary on age (usually the younger the crowd, 21 - 35, the more beer and mixed drinks). So increase by ½ the amount of Absolut Vodka, Bacardi Rum, Sauza Tequila, Hiram Walker Schnapps and Anheuser-Busch Beer.

3. Geographical location is also important in selecting your liquor stock for your guests. Consult your local Bartender or liquor clerk to find the most popular product in your area.

Other Supplies

Product	Basic Stock	Number of Guests			
		20	30	40	50
Soda (2 Liters):					
Club	1	3	3	4	4
Ginger Ale	1	2	2	2	3
Cola	1	3	3	3	4
Diet Cola	1	3	3	3	4
7-Up	1	3	3	3	4
Tonic	1	3	3	4	4
Juice (Quart):					
Tomato	1	2	3	3	3
Grapefruit	1	2	3	3	3
Orange	1	2	3	3	3
Cranberry	1	2	2	3	3
Miscellaneous:					
Ice (trays)	2	8	10	15	20
Napkins (doz.)	1	4	4	6	8
Stirrers (24/box)	1	2	2	3	3
Rose's® Grenadine	1	1	1	1	1
Superfine Sugar (box)	1	1	1	2	2

Other Miscellaneous:
1 Quart Milk
2 Large Bottles of Mineral Water
2 Bottles of Rose's® Lime Juice
1 Bottle of Angostura Bitters
1 Bottle Worcestershire Sauce
1 Bottle McIlhenny Tobasco Sauce
1 Small Jar Horseradish for Bloody Marys
1 Can Cream of Coconut (Coco Lopez)

CUTTING FRUIT

Different kinds of fruit are used to garnish different kinds of drinks. REMEMBER to wash all fruit and vegetables before cutting.

Lemon twist
1. Cut off both ends. 2. Using a sharp knife or spoon, insert between rind and meat-carefully separating. 3. Cut skin into ¼" strips.

Pineapple
1. Cut off top and bottom. 2. Cut pineapple in half. 3. Cut in half again. 4. Cut ½" slices. 5. Cut wedges.

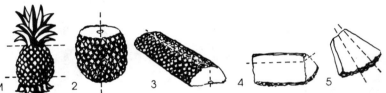

Celery
1. Cut off bottom of celery, also you may cut off top. 2. If leaf is fresh, you may use this as garnish. 3. Cut celery stalk in half.

Oranges
1. Cut orange in half. 2. Slice orange into half moon cuts. 3. Half moon cut.

Limes
1. Cut ends of lime. 2. Slice lime into half. 3. Cut in half moons.

Wedges(Lemon/limes)
1. Slice lime in half. 2. Cut halves flat down and half again. 3. Cut to ¼ to ½" wedges.

LIBBEY GLASS

There has been a lot written — and even more said — in professional circles about the importance of using the right glass for the right drink. Just how important is adherence to the classic standards of usage? What are the best glasses to have on hand if you can't afford, or don't have the space, to inventory them all? What are the hot looks in contemporary glassware and how can you use them to justify higher tariffs in your establishment? This chapter will answer these and many other questions about the selection and usage of glassware today.

Q: **What will happen if you serve a straight-up Martini in a water glass?**

A: **Nothing will happen to the Martini. If you mixed it right, it will have the clear color and taste of a Martini, especially if you throw in an olive or a twist. It might even be chilled to perfection. The problem is it won't look like a Martini to many of your customers.**

Over the years a number of our most popular cocktails — the Martini, Manhattan, Old Fashioned, Whiskey Sour, Tom Collins and Margarita to name a few — have become synonymous with the glasses in which they are traditionally served. The right glass for the right drink.

How important is it for you, a professional bartender, to adhere to these presentations today? After all, the 1920s and 30s — when these standards were established—are long gone.

The answer to that question depends largely on the preferences and expectations of your clientele. If you tend the bar in a private country club that caters to a mature and upscale crowd, chances are its very important that a traditional cocktail, or wine or beer selection for that matter, be offered to the customer in the "right" glass. On the other hand, if your establishment is populated by a young college crowd, you might be able to bend the rules a little.

The important thing to remember is that *any* bar patron — young or mature, white collar or blue, male or female — appreciates and *will pay a higher tariff* for a well prepared and attractively presented beverage. The little touches — a sparkling clean glass, fresh garnishes, a napkin — do make a difference.

Bear in mind that anyone can purchase a bartender's guide, stop by the neighborhood liquor store, mix up a cocktail in the kitchen and serve it in "whatever's handy." Once that same person becomes a *customer* at your establishment, however, his standards and expectations change considerably. Why? Because, he's *paying* you for a professional product and professional service.

If The Drink Fits Pour It

There are reasons — other than good looks — why straight-up Martinis and Manhattans are served in 3 to 6 ounce stemmed cocktail glasses. For one, the stems keep hands from warming the drink. But, perhaps even more important, is the fact that those drinks *fit* into those glasses without spilling over — from a glass that's too small — or looking lost — in a glass that's too large. A good rule of thumb: A drink should almost fill its glass. No patron feels good about paying top dollar for a drink that looks skimpy — even if it isn't — because it's served in a glass that's too big. On the other hand, putting a customer in the position of having to artfully gulp off the first ounce or two, rather than run the risk of dribbling the concoction onto a silk tie or "dry clean only" dress, is equally unappreciated.

Martinis, Manhattans and Stingers fit nicely into

stemmed cocktail glasses. Highballs fit nicely into highball glasses; Tom Collins into collins glasses; Whiskey Sours into sour glasses...and that alone makes a good case for sticking to the traditional glass. If you can't resist the urge to be creative OR if your customers expect you to be (tulip-garnished Martinis, on-the-rocks, served in little flower pot-shaped glasses), just make certain that the drink fits the glass.

To Stem or Not To Stem

The guideline for stem usage is a simple one, but one that should be kept in mind: *Use stems for chilled cocktails (or wines) that are served straight-up (without ice).* The stem keeps the hands off the bowl and prevents the drink from warming too quickly. Other than that one rule, stems can be used in any number of creative presentations, especially to dress up a drink (or even a premium beer, "designer" water or iced tea) and give it a more upscale appearance. Remember: The use of stemware in unexpected or creative contexts can translate to higher tariffs.

One of the most versatile of all stems is the 8½ to 14 ounce round wine glass. Designed for red wine service, it can be used for almost anything from cocktails to brandy to beer. And it looks spectacular!

Another must-have stem is the all-purpose 8 ounce wine glass which can be used to fine effect for red or white wine to Bloody Marys to Daiquiris and Pina Coladas to beer and beyond.

Other stems we recom-

Red Wine
Glass
#8414

All Purpose
Wine Glass
#8470

mend to round out your service:

Cocktail glass. Solid stems are not just for show, they keep hands from warming the drinks. Available in 3 to 6 ounce capacities, the 4½ ounce size is good for classic straight-up Martini, Manhattan and Stinger service.

Sour glass. A short stemmed glass traditionally used to serve sours, these can also hold Daiquiris and be used interchangeably with cocktail glasses in a pinch. The 4½ ounce version is the most popular.

White wine glass. The stem of a wine glass is used to maintain the product at the proper room temperature. The most popular sizes are from 6½ to 10 ounces. These can also be used for frozen Daiquiris and other specialty drinks.

Red wine glass. These have wider bowls—rounder to permit the red wine, usually served at room temperature to breathe — and to keep the aroma trapped.

Cocktail Glass
#3771

Sour Glass
#3775

White Wine
Glass
#8466

Red Wine Glass
#8471

Flute or tulip champagne glass. The most popular sizes are small — from 4½ to 6 ounces. The major advantage — aside from a decidedly upscale appearance — are tapered bowls which help prevent the bubbles from escaping too quickly. For any sparkling service, including ducks and ciders.

Saucer champagne glass. The traditional choice for champagne and sparkling service. It can also be used to enhance ice cream drink and ice cream dessert presentations. Avoid the hollow stemmed varieties which are difficult to clean and can be unsanitary.

Sherry glass. Serve sherry, port and aperitifs in these small, 2 to 3½ ounce, stems. *Cordials,* at 1 ounce, and 2 ounce *brandy glasses* are also available.

Brandy snifters. Brandy snifters range in size from 5½ to 22 ounces and

Flute/Tulip
Champagne Glass

#3795

#8477

Saucer Champagne Glass
#3777

Sherry Glass
#3788

larger. Small sizes can also be used for serving Cognac, liqueurs, and premium whiskeys whose bouquets deserve the special treatment. The larger sizes provide the maximum possible "noseful" desired by serious brandy drinkers. All snifters feature large bowls on short stems, designed to be cupped by the hand to warm the liquid.

Rocks Glasses and Tumblers

Rocks, highball glasses and other tumblers are primarily designed for serving medium to large capacity drinks on ice. We recommend that you start with the following:

Highball glass. These versatile glasses, available in a wide variety of capacities, are used for more drinks than any other glasses (for Gin and tonics, Scotch and waters, Rum and colas, etc.). Most are clear and fairly tall. The most popular sizes range from 8 to 12 ounces.

Brandy Snifters

#3708

#3702

Tall Hi Ball Glass #2310

Highball Glass #132

Collins glass. These are really just taller, often frosted, versions of the highball glass. They are traditionally used for collins service and also lend a cool, tropical look to Sloe Gin Fizzes, Singapore Slings, Sunrises and other fruity concoctions.

Rocks glasses. These are also known as *old-fashioned glasses.* The most popular sizes hold from 6 to 10 ounces and are used exclusively for on-the-rocks presentations. Larger double rocks sizes range between 12 to 15 ounces.

Coolers. These taller and somewhat larger capacity tumblers have been gaining popularity in recent years for extra volume highballs and non-alcoholic beverages. They hold a lot of ice and can accomodate fairly large treatments.

Hurricane glasses. Use these large (usually 16 to 23½ ounces) tall, curved, footed glasses for Bloody Marys and tropical fruit drinks.

Collins Glass
#126

Double Rocks Glasses
#816CD

Rocks Glasses
#916CD

Coolers
#96

Hurricane Glasses
#3616

Beer Service "Heads" For Variety

Up until a few years ago, beer service was pretty cut and dried: Simply pour into a mug or hourglass pilsner and set 'em up. Those days are gone. The growing popularity of premium beers — both domestic and imported — means that beer drinkers are not only more sophisticated about what kind of beer, ale or stout they drink, but also about what they drink it from. The traditional pilsner and mug are still fine for tap service, as well as for many non-premium domestic brands. But, if your establishment caters to the growing number of beer connoisseurs, here are some new shapes in beer service you might want to pick up on:

Stems. Traditional beer goblets are very stout and European looking. For a more contemporary, lighter look try serving premium brands in sheer rim 10 or 12 ounce wine stems or in balloon wines.

Flare pilsners. These sophisticated pilsners —

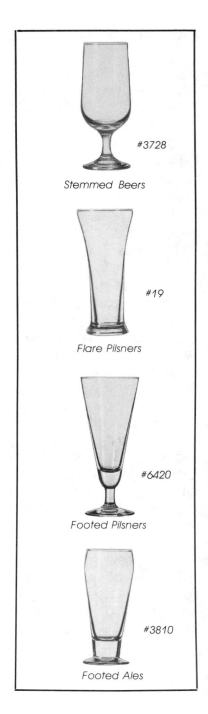

#3728

Stemmed Beers

#19

Flare Pilsners

#6420

Footed Pilsners

#3810

Footed Ales

minus the hourglass shape — flare up from the bottom in 10 to 12 ounce sizes. Perfect for premium domestic brands.

Footed pilsners. The short stems and foot on these flare-shaped pilsners give them a decidedly upscale and continental appearance. They are well-suited to premium imports.

Footed ales. Available in 10 and 12 ounce sizes, these attractive glasses feature a very heavy base and a unique bowed-out shape well-suited to the full-bodied flavor of imported ales and stouts.

For Special Drinks: Specialty Glasses

The classics aside, there is more latitude for creativity behind the bar today than ever before. There has also never been such an exciting selection of domestically-produced and widely available specialty glasses from which to choose.

Glasses in the shapes of owls, cowboy boots, flower pots, snowmen, and so on can fuel your imagination from one season of the year

Napoli
#1619

La Femme
#1620

Specialty Glasses
#383

Catalina
#3821

Boot
#97036

to the next. There is no end to the number of tasty and creative concoctions you can dream up and serve in specialty glasses to the delight of both your customers and your management. *Remember: Well-dressed drinks served in spectacular or whimsical glasses can command higher check averages.*

Must-have specialty glasses? We can think of a few:

Irish coffee glass/cup. In most parts of the country, the fall and winter months are made for merchandising hot beverages — Irish coffee and other coffee drinks, spiked or unspiked apple ciders, chocolates and toddies. Some of these items are available "heat-treated" for maximum durability.

Parfait glasses. These 7½ to 8 ounce footed glasses are used for drinks and desserts containing fruit or ice cream. They can also be used for Bloody Marys and highballs.

Crested glasses. Consider having a house glass or specialty glass crested

#390

Specialty Glasses

#2435

#5295

Irish Coffee Glass

#17106

Solitaire Parfait

(printed) with the logo, name and address of your establishment. For special occasions or promotions, give them away to your customers (you can work in their cost to the price of a specialty drink) as a form of take-away advertising.

Best Bets in Glassware for the Home Bar

The popularity of entertaining at home has grown dramatically in recent years and many of today's hosts are no longer content to serve cocktails and other beverages in "whatever's handy." On the other hand, few people have the space to store all of the different kinds of glasses they might like to have. This section will help you separate the "must haves" from the "nice to haves" for the home bar.

Perhaps the easiest way to stock a home bar with the most popular shapes and sizes of glassware is to invest in an entertainment set of domestically manufactured and packaged barware. Typical sets, widely available and affordably priced, will usually consist

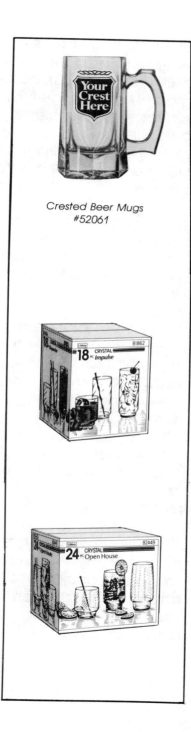

Crested Beer Mugs
#52061

of 18, 24 or 32 pieces and include beverage/highball glasses, tumbler/cooler glasses, and on-the-rocks/-old-fashioned glasses. Such a set will easily handle most of your iced beverage service needs and should be considered "must haves."

The only other thing you'll really need is an 8 to 10 ounce all-purpose wine stem. This versatile addition to the home bar can be used for serving red or white wine —even sparkling wines —as well as a wide range of straight-up and chilled cocktails (Martinis, Manhattans, Sours, Daiquiris, etc.) liqueurs and brandies. Consider it a "must have."

If the selection recommended above is still too much glassware for your cramped quarters or pragmatic disposition, consider the 8½ to 14 ounce stemmed balloon wine glass for all of your serving needs. This spectacular looking and versatile glass can be used for everything from red or white wine to beer to

Stemmed Cocktail

Brandy Snifter

Cordial

42

cocktails and brandy.

If space permits, you might wish to consider the following list of "nice to haves" to round out your selection of home barware:

Double rocks/old-fashioned glass. Also known as English highball glasses, these are the glasses of choice for on-the-rocks doubles. Because of their large capacity — usually about 13 ounces — they can also be used for most highballs as well as for Bloody Marys and other voluminous garnished cocktails.

Champagne flutes. The perfect choice for all festive occasions; made for sparkling service. The tall profile and small mouths of these stems keep the bubbles from evaporating too quickly.

Brandy snifters. Available in a wide range of sizes, these glasses feature large bowls and short stems designed to be cupped in the hand to warm the liquor.

They are also fine for Cognac and premium whiskey service.

Beer pilsners or mugs. Cordial or liqueur glasses.

There you have it! Our best for home bar glassware. No matter what selection or "mix" you finally decide on, remember that all of your glassware should be sparkling clean and in perfect condition when you use it. Your guests will often overlook your choice of glasses but not unsightly chips, spots or lint.

Beer Mug

Champagne Flute

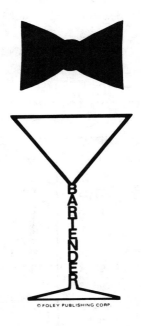

© FOLEY PUBLISHING CORP.

COCKTAIL —
WHERE DID IT
COME FROM?

Cocktail. According to *Jack's Manual* by J. A. Grohuska, 1933, the word cocktail first appeared in *The Balance*, an American periodical, under date of May 13, 1806, it read: "Cocktail is a stimulating liquor composed of spirits of any kind, sugar, water, and bitters — it is vulgarly called 'bitter sling' and is supposed to be an excellent electioneering potion." This is the earliest reference to the cocktail that we have been able to find in print.

The above is the first time the word cocktail can be traced in print. However, our search does not stop there. Listed below are the stories and their sources of just where the word cocktail originated.

So read on . . . The stories of where the word cocktail first originated will go on forever. Which do you believe?

1. From *Jack's Manual* by J. A. Grohuska, Alfred A. Knoff, New York, 1933:

Linguists have been misled by the word 'cocktail' into imagining that it was once in some way connected with the plumage of the domestic rooster. But this is not so. The true and incontrovertible story of the origin of the cocktail is as follows:

Somewhere about the beginning of the last century, there had been for some time very considerable friction between the American Army of the Southern States and King Axolotl VIII of Mexico. Several skirmishes and one or two battles had taken place, but eventually a truce was called and the King agreed to meet the American general to discuss terms of peace with him.

The place chosen for the meeting was the King's pavilion, and thither the American general repaired, and was accommodated with a seat on the bench, as it were, next to King A, himself. Before opening negotiations, however, His Majesty asked the general, as one man to another, if he would like a drink and being an American, he of course said yes. The King gave a command, and in a few moments there appeared a lady of entrancing and overwhelming beauty, bearing in her slender fingers a gold cup encrusted with rubies and containing a strange potion of her own brewing. Immediately an awed and ominous hush fell upon the assembly, for the same thought struck everyone; namely, that as there was only one cup, either the King or the general would have to drink from it first, and the other would be bound to feel insulted. The situation was growing tense and the cup bearer seemed also to realize the difficulty, for, with a sweet smile, she bowed her shapely head in reverence to the assembly and drank the drink herself. Everything was saved and the conference came to a satisfactory ending; but before leaving, the general asked if he might know the name of the lady who had shown such tact. "That," proudly said the King, who had never seen the lady before, "is my daughter Coctel."

"Your Majesty," replied the general, "I will see that her name is honored forevermore by my Army."

Coctel, of course, became cocktail, and there you are! There exists definite, unquestionable proof of the truth of this story, but no correspondence upon the subject can in any circumstances be entertained.

2 . *The Cocktail Book, A Sideboard Manual for Gentlemen*, L. C. Page and Company, Boston, 1913, "The Real Tale of the Cock's Tail:"

In a famous old tavern not far from the Philipse Manor House, the site of what is now Yonkers on the Hudson, and the very centre of the most popular sport of the times, was blended the first delightful cocktail. If the descendants of William Van Eyck, its jolly host, may be believed, no better place could be found along the length of the river, for William's stories were as good as the liquor that washed them down, and his liquors as honest and true and as sparkling withal as his daughter, Mistress Peggy, who gave them forth with such demure grace as made their serving doubly welcome to the thirsty gallants who thronged the bar and taproom.

Now Master Van Eyck loved but three things well — his daughter, his cellar, and old Lightening, his great fighting bird, the acknowledged champion from New York to Albany. Indeed 'twere hard to tell which loved he the most, though his daughter was truly the idol of his heart.'

Mistress Peggy's lovers were many, and many were the strong potions quaffed, even when the driest throats were long since drowned in good liquor, because of her bewitching beauty, which gave added flavour and bouquet to the concoctions for which the bar was famous. But so well did she justify her father's confidence and her own good name that, though the gay bucks from town quarrelled and even fought for her favour, the most fortunate could not boast of the lightest thing to her discredit. On especial occasions she was wont to make for her father, and certain good friends of hers and old Lightening's, a most delicious beverage, the composition of which was secret, but which was so popular that it lacked naught but appropriate naming to give it more than local fame.

Young Master Appleton, mate of the clipper-ship Ranger, had long been Mistress Peggy's ardent lover, and had even gone so far as to obtain mine host's reluctant consent that, when he could boast of a command, his daughter should be his and she would. Now Peggy, when she admitted to her coquettish self that she had a heart, knew that eventually she would be forced, in order to still its clamourings, to surrender it unconditionally into the keeping of the certain bold sailor; but womanlike put off capitulating as long as she might. The time came, however, when the knowledge of his pro-motion gave Master Appleton the courage he had lacked to force the citadel which her coquetry had heretofore so jealously guarded; and, when of a sudden Peggy's heart refused longer to be maligned by her mouth, and spoke eloquently from out of bright eyes grown almost serious — before she could summon her and to the fray — she was conquered, and, close embraced, was calling him dear whom, but the day before, she had flouted with reckless audacity.

Except when in training for a main, Van Eyck's champion game-cock held his court in an apart-ment builded for him and adapted to his Majesty's special wants. None found favour in his master's eyes, nor forsooth in the eyes of Mistress Peggy, who failed in admiring and respectful homage to old Lightening. Worshipful attendance upon this pam-pered hero of many bloody victories, together with honest admiration for the daughter of his host, was looked upon as the surest way of gaining Master Van Eyck's personal approval and the first step in advancing from favoured customer to friend.

It was here that Peggy surrendered to her lover.

And here it was that after a proper and reasonable time spent in the sweet dalliance due to such occasions, she mixed for him this most delightful of all drinks in order that he might face with proper spirit her bluff old father's temporary ire at the loss of his daughter. Just as the right proportions of bitters, root wine, and mellowest of old whiskey had been put to cook in a glass half-full of bits of purest ice, an interruption occurred, and the clarion voice of the brave old warrior bird was heard as if in celebration of the momentous event which had happened under his very eyes. As he plumed and shook himself after his effort, one of his royal tail feathers floated gently down towards his mistress.

"Lightening names the drink!" she cried, as she seized the feather and with it deftly stirred the glass's contents. And, again, with a sweeping curtsey, holding the glass aloft:

"Drink this Cocktail, sir, to your success with my father, and as a pledge to our future happiness!"

Thus was the drink named. And, in after days, when Master Appleton kept the tavern, its sign was the sign of the Cock's Tail, which ever proved an emblem of good fortune to him and his good wife, their children and their children's children.

3 . *The Bon Vivant's Companion or How to Mix Drinks*, compiled for his friends by George A. Zabriskie, Armond Beach, Florida, 1948 (not to be confused with Jerry Thomas, 1928, Bon Vivant's Companion); "Where Cocktails Came From:"

A Frenchman, Dr. Tardieu, declares that in the course of certain scientific investigations he discovered that cocktails, generally considered of American origin, are really the ancient French coquetele, popular for several centuries in regions of Bordeaux. Dr. Tardieu will be expected by Americans to produce evidence profoundly convincing. No mere ipse dixit will suffice. It is not the first time that foreigners have impugned the American beginnings of the cocktail. Robert Keable declared that the mixings were invented by the court physician of the festive Roman Emperor Commodus. None will deny that Commodus would have drunk cocktails if he had'em, but Mr. Keable's statement is not supported by Gibbon or any other dignified authority.

The most persistent American tradition regarding the cocktail fixes its birth in 1779 in Betsy Flanagan's Inn on the road between Tarrytown and White Plains, (NY) where American soldiers with gin, and French soldiers with vermouth, blended these beverages in token of brotherhood, stirring the resultant mess with the tail feathers of Mrs. Flanagan's rooster. Yet it may be that all this happened in Peggy Van Eyck's Cock's Tail Tavern in Yonkers, as another story runs. The grave antiquarian, Issac Markens, preferred to believe that the decoction first saw light as early as 1652 in the Tavern of Peter Cock, which stood where No. 1 Broadway is now.

Another delver into things historic, Appleton Morgan, rejected these theories and insisted that the name "cocktail" was applied to a mixed drink because of the color and shape of the arch formed when expert bartenders tossed the liquors from one tumbler to another.

Whatever the truth, the name of the drink was established early enough for its use by Hawthorne in "The Blithedale Romance," by Fenimore Cooper in "The Spy," by Hughes in "Tom Brown," and by Thackeray in "The Newcomers."

Dr. Tardieu may be right, but let him prove it. And if he is wrong he has at least brought once more to the forum of the world a great question. Before the origin of the cocktail vanishes in the "twilight of fable, let the truth be captured."

4. *What'll You Have*, compiled and edited by Julien J. Roskauer, A. L. Burt Company, Chicago, 1933; more on Betsy Flanagan's Inn; "How the Cocktail Got Its Name!:"

In revolutionary days there was a famous roadhouse in what is now known as Westchester County, called "Betsy's Tavern," which later became known as "The Bracer Tavern." Here the American and French officers came for their liquor, ale, lager and rum, not to mention fine fowl.

One day the American officers raided a British Commissary and stole several male birds. Then as now, this fowl was known as a "cock." At the wild boisterous party which followed, Betsy poured many kinds of liquor into wine glasses and stirred it with the tail of a cock pheasant. The drinks were delicious.

A toast to Betsy and the new mixed drink was: "Here's to the divine liquor which is as delicious to the palate, as the cock's tails are beautiful to the eye."

Hardly had this toast ended, when one of the French officers cried out: "Vive le cocktail!"

And that's how "cocktail" came into the world's vocabulary."

5. *The Mexican Story.*

A visiting sailor drank local punches at Campeche, Gulf of Mexico, stirring them with wooden spoons. One bartender substituted a local root known as "Cola de gallo"—translated, "Cocktail."

6. *The English Stories.*

From John Doxat, Mixologist and Author (who found the word "mocktail," a non-alcoholic drink).

A. English Story Number I: An Englishman, Dr. Johnson, introduced to a wine from a friend named Boswell, told that this wine was mixed with gin replied "to add spirits to wine smacks of our alcoholic hyperbole. It would be a veritable cocktail of a drink."

"What is a Cocktail?" asked Boswell.

"In parts of the country, it is a custom to dock the tails of certain horses of mint, yet which one not of entirely pure stock. Such animals of mixed province are known as cocktails."

B. English Story Number II: The cocktail was named in honor of "The Officer of the Second Regiment of Royal Sussex Fusileers, in the British Army. The men of this regiment wore plumes resembling rooster feathers in their caps, were commonly called "the Cocktails" by the men of other regiments."

7. *The Mississippi Stories*

A. Winning gamblers aboard river-steamers made a drink with a selection of every liquor in the bar. They drank this drink out of glasses shaped like a cock's breast, and the stirrer had a resemblance of a tail feather. There also was an illustration to a ballad published in 1871 called An American Cocktail of this event.

B. Mississippi River men challenged one another to become "The Cock of the Walk," meaning the strongest, meanest and best wrestler on the river. The winner earns the right to wear a bright red rooster feather in his hat. He could proclaim to all he could out drink and out fight all. Cock of the Walk plus tail = Cocktail.

8. *The Horse Trainer Story. (Another horse's tale)*
   Horse trainers would give their horses a strong mixture of spirits that would make the horses "cock their tails" and run faster.

9. *The Fighting-Cocks Story.*
   More mixtures (cock-ale) but this time to fighting cocks. Plus a toast to the winner with as many different spirits as feathers on the winning bird (could these men also be Mississippi gamblers?)!

10. *New Orleans Story.*
    A French physician served a drink to his friends using double-ended, gallic-style egg cup, coquetiers. His friends called them, you guessed it, Cocktails!

11. *The H. L. Mencken Story, published in The Sunday Sun, December 13, 1908, Editor, H. L. Mencken.*
    The cocktail was invented on April 17, 1846 at 8:15am by John Welby Henderson of North Carolina at the Old Palo Alto Hotel in Bladensburg, Maryland. The first cocktail was served to John A. Hopkins of Fairfax, Virginia. The story goes on that it was served to Mr. Hopkins, to have his nerves restored after a duel.
    This could be one of H. L. Mencken's many hoaxes.

And there you have it. Eleven versions of how the word cocktail originated. Which do you believe?

This mystery will go on forever. We will never know why this word became associated with America's favorite past time.

© FOLEY PUBLISHING CORP.

NAMES & ORIGINS

—THE MARTINI—

1. By Bartender Professor Jerry Thomas of San Francisco from a stranger on his way to Martinez. Made with Gin, Vermouth, Bitters, Dash of Maraschino.

2. By a Bartender in Martinez, California, for a gold miner who struck it rich. The miner ordered champagne for the house. But there was none. The Bartender offered something better, a "Martinez Special," some (Souterne) and Gin. The rich miner spread the word ordering throughout California a "Martinez Special."

3. After the British army rifle: The Martini and Henry. The rifle was known for its kick, like the first sip of Gin and "it" ("it" being Vermouth).

4. After Martini and Rossi Vermouth, because it was first used in the drink, Gin and It, with ½ Gin and ½ Martini and Rossi Vermouth.

5. At the Knickerbocker Hotel in the Early 1900's, a Bartender named Martini di Arma Tiggia mixed a Martini using only a dry Gin and only dry Vermouth.

Bellini

Invented at Harry's Bar in Venice, Italy, around 1943.

Black Russian

By Bartender Gus Tops of the Hotel Metropoli in Brussels. Gus also dispensed scarfs with his silhouette and recipe of his cocktail.

Bloody Mary

Invented by Pete Petiot at Harry's Bar, 5 Rue Daunou, Paris, France, in 1921; he later became Captain of Bars at the St. Regis Hotel, New York, NY.

The Bronx

By Johnny Solon of the Waldorf Bar in New York's Waldorf Astoria. Johnny created it the day after a trip to the Bronx Zoo.

Cuba Libre

This drink is a political statement as well as a cocktail. It translates to "Free Cuba," a status the country enjoyed in 1898 at the end of the Spanish-American war. Cuban/American relations were friendly around the turn of the century, when a US Army lieutenant in Havana mixed some light native rum with a new-fangled American soft drink called Coca Cola and braced the libation with a lime.

Daiquiri

Connived by workers from Bethlehem Steel during a malaria epidemic in the Village of Daiquiri, near Santiago, Cuba.

French 75

If one requests this drink, you might receive a mix of gin and champagne. In the French trenches of World War I, however, gin was scarce but cognac and champagne were not. American doughboys soon discovered that a combination of the two produced an effect similar to getting zapped by an artillery piece known as a French 75.

The Gibson

Named after New York artist, Charles Dana Gibson, by his Bartender, Charles Connoly, of the Players Club in New York. Another version credits Billie Gibson, a fight promoter.

Gin Rickey

By a Bartender at Shoemaker's in Washington, DC, for his customer, "Colonel Jim" Rickey, a Lobbyist.

Harvey Wallbanger

Created by Bill Doner at Newport Beach, California. The Harvey Wallbanger started as a fad by Bill and was first served at a bar called The Office. Bill was last seen as Vice President of Marketing at Caesars Palace in Las Vegas. Before that, he ran a fleet of fishing boats in Cabo San Lucas, Mexico. Thank you Bill for a great drink and legend. . .wherever you are.

Irish Coffee

Was originated at the Buena Vista Cafe in San Francisco, where the late Chronicle columnist and travel writer Stanton Delaplane often frequented. On a trip to Ireland during the early fifties, Delaplane noted the custom of bolstering airport coffee with whiskey. Intending to elaborate on these crude airport toddies, he and his cronies at the Buena Vista settled on the perfect recipe: three sugar cubes, an ounce and a half of Irish whiskey, coffee, and a float of quickly agitated whipped cream.

Kioki Coffee

Created by George Bullington, founder of Southern California's Bully's restaurant chain. During the sixties, Kahlua-based coffee drinks were popular at his LaJolla location. Perhaps to defray costs, Bullington made a drink with one-half jigger of Kahlua, one-half jigger of the less expensive but similar-tasting dark creme de cocoa and a float of brandy and whipped cream. Bullington's Hawaiian customers started referring to the drink as a Coffee Kioki — "Kioki" meaning "George" in Hawaiian.

Kir

After the Mayor of DiJon (Major Kir) to increase sales of Cassis.

Long Island Iced Tea

Hails from Long Island, specifically the Oak Beach Inn in Hampton Bays. Spirits writer John Mariani credits Bartender Robert "Rosebud" Butt as the inventor, whose original recipe calling for an ounce each of clear liquors (vodka, gin, tequila, light rum), a half ounce of triple sec, lemon juice and a splash of cola is still popular with young drinkers. (Though not with those who have to get up early the next day).

Mai Tai

Invented by Vic Bergeron in 1944 at his Polynesian-style Oakland bar. He did not want fruit juices detracting from the two ounces of J. Wray Nephew Jamaican rum he poured as the base for his creation. He merely added a half ounce of French orgeat (an almond-flavored syrup), a half ounce of orange curacao, a quarter ounce of rock candy syrup and the juice of one lime. Customer Carrie Wright of Tahiti was the first to taste the concoction, to which she responded, "Mai tai. . . roe ae", (Tahitian for "Out of this world. . .the best"). The Mai Tai became famous, and conflicting stories about its origins aggravated Bergeron so much that he elicited a sworn statement from Mrs. Wright in 1970, testifying to his authorship of the cocktail.

The Manhattan

By John Welby Henderson, a Bartender for a John A. Hopkins of Fairfax, Virginia. Hopkins had been wounded in a duel with Baron Henri de Vrie at Challono at Bladesburg, MD, in April 1846. Hopkins was rushed to Hotel Palo Alto, where Henderson was working. Henderson filled a glass with Maryland Rye, some syrup and some bitters. The Manhattan survived, whether Hopkins did is unknown.

Moscow Mule

Unveiled at Hollywood's Cock N' Bull by owner Jack Morgan and one Jack Martin in 1946 to rid himself of an overstock of ginger beer.

Negroni

It seems that a certain Count Negroni of Florence once requested a drink that would stand apart from all the Americanos ordered at his favorite neighborhood cafe. The Bartender answered his request with a cocktail composed of equal parts gin, sweet vermouth and Campari, and he garnished the result with a tell-tale orange slice. Unfortunately for the Count, the drink became as popular as the Americano.

Old Fashioned

Originated by a Bartender at the Louisville Pendennis Club in Kentucky for Colonel James E. Pepper, a distiller of Bourbon Whiskey.

Pina Colada

Two stories, take your pick. On a plaque at 104 Forales Street, once the Barrchina Bar and now a perfumery, reads: "The house where in 1963 the Pina Colada was created by Don Ramon Portas Mingat." Across town at the Caribe Hilton, Bartender, Ramon (Monchito) Marrero, says he created the Pina Colada in 1954...

Planters Punch

To a Bartender at Planters Hotel in St. Louis; also credited to a Jamaican Planter's wife offering a drink one part sour, two parts sweet, three parts strong and four parts weak to cool off from the Jamaican sun.

Ramos Fizz

By the proprietor of the Old Stagg Saloon in New Orlean's French Quarter, called Ramos, of course. Stories say it took eight to ten waitresses to shake this drink.

Rob Roy

From Robert MacGregor, Scotland's Robin Hood, Roy being the Scottish nickname for a man with red hair.

Screwdriver

By Texas oil-rig workers who stirred vodka and orange juice with their screwdrivers.

Side Car

Harry's New York Bar in Paris, according to owner at that time, Harry MacElhone, after a motorcycle sidecar in which a customer was driving into the bar.

Silk Panties

Created by Sandra Gutierrez of Chicago, IL, and winner of BARTENDER MAGAZINE'S 1986 Schnapps Contest.

Singapore Sling

By Bartender at the Long Bar in Singapore's Raffes Hotel around 1915.

Tom Collins

By John Collins, a waiter at Lipmmer's Old House, Coduit Street, Hanover Square in England. "Tom" was used instead of John from the use of Old Tom Gin. Today a "John Collins" would use whiskey.

The Ward Eight

From Boston's Ward Eight, a dominant political subdivision of the community, known for it's bloody political elections. A Whiskey Sour with a splash of grenadine. Locke-O'Ber's in Boston is a great place to try one.

Zombie

Inventor Don Beaches was an innovator of the Polynesian-style, umbrella-bedded fufu drink. Real Polynesians never drank such things. But the tropical atmosphere at Beaches' Los Angeles restaurant, Don the Beachcomber, made Scorpions, Beachcombers and Zombies seem as island-indigenous as poy. He invented the Zombie back in the thirties as a mix of three different rums, papaya juice, orange juice, pineapple juice, lemon juice, grenadine, orgeat, Pernod and curacao. What has survived is the 151 float. That and the effect its name suggests.

PRODUCT INFORMATION & DRINK RECIPES

ABSOLUT VODKA

In America, Swedish products have always been recognized for their superior balance of form and function, born out of an exacting tradition of quality. Swedish vodka — one of the newest of these "naturalized" Americans — is no exception to the rule, and in seven short years U.S. consumers have adopted Absolut (Country of Sweden) Vodka as their favorite imported brand.

What few Americans realize, however, is that while Absolut is a relative newcomer to the U.S., vodka distillation has been an important part of Swedish tradition for centuries. It was in Sweden that the distillation process was perfected in the 19th century by L. O. Smith. With the new purification system he invented, Smith produced a spirit he called "Absolut renat Brannvin," meaning "Absolutely pure vodka." The phrase was ultimately shortened to the pure and simple Absolut.

Brannvin (the old Swedish term for unflavored spirit or vodka) was first used in the 15th century for the manufacture of gunpowder, its potability recognized only by the end of the century. By the 16th century, however, vodka was widely used to treat some 40 diseases, its importance growing accordingly. Swedish parliament described it as "the only medicament for the conservation of health in the eyes of farmers and peasants." Grain-distilled vodka soon became so popular in the late 16th century that authorities had to prohibit distillation during bad harvest years.

Soon vodka was being enjoyed in cities, villages and farms throughout Sweden. Servants were paid in vodka as a substitute for money. Vendors peddled the spirit from booths outside churches. And, in the 18th century, an estimated 180,000 pot stills were in use to satisfy "household requirements."

Through the 18th century Swedish vodka, like that of other countries, was often flavored. Housewives used herbs from their gardens to spice vodka, the most popular flavorings being caraway, aniseed, cinnamon, fennel seed and bitter orange. Aquavit (in Swedish akavit) is a general term for these popular spiced and or/sweetened spirits.

Other traditional ways of enjoying vodka have endured through the centuries. Since early times, vodka has not only been flavored but also mixed with other beverages such as water, lemonade, coffee and fruit juices. The most popular way to drink vodka today in Sweden is as "snaps" or "sup" chilled and served straight without ice in a small glass.

Food has always been a natural accompaniment to vodka in Sweden. Occasionally with beer as a chaser, vodka is most commonly served with Smorgasbord, freshwater crayfish cooked in dill, dill-cured salmon (gravlax), marinated herring, fermented Baltic herring (surstromming), caviar and various cold cuts.

Finally, for dessert there is Swedish coffee — simple, but with an added twist. Swedes prepare this beverage by first placing a silver 10-ore coin in the bottom of a coffee cup. Coffee is then poured over the coin until it disappears. Lastly, vodka is added until the coin reappears once more.

The revolution in Sweden vodka production occurred in the mid-nineteenth century, when Lars Olsson "L. O." Smith (1836 - 1913), known as the "King of Vodka," stepped into the picture. A businessman of unusual talent and international stature, Smith was a prominent Stockholm vodka wholesaler. By the end of the 1860's, the ambitious Smith had eliminated his small competitors and controlled more than half of the nation's business in vodka.

Smith's considerable interests in Sweden's vodka

trade propelled his efforts into the distillation of larger and larger quantities of vodka. The common method of distilling unspiced vodka — cold charcoal filtration — failed to remove impurities. Smith would eventually change this process.

In 1869 Smith founded Sweden's first modern distillery, Spirit Export-Aktie-Bolaget (Spirits-Export, Inc.) on Reimer's Island. This company was dissolved in 1872 and its successor, Win & Spirituosa Aktie-Bolaget (Wine & Spirits Inc.), formed.

Smith equipped his distillery at Reimer's island with state-of-the-art machinery, including two redistillation columns with mid-basins and reflux pipes for the production of pure grain alcohol. While this type of equipment had been developed in Europe during the 1860's, in Sweden it was a revolutionary innovation.

It was during the beginning of the 1870's that Smith began his crusade for the production of heat-distilled vodka with minimal impurities.

Through the teachings of French professor Angel Marvaud, who published a thesis on the subject in 1871, Smith became aware of the purifying efficiency of heat distillation.

As a result of Smith's effective marketing strategies, what is known as the "Stockholm Vodka War" broke out on October 1, 1877. On that day, the same day that the rival Stockholm Liquor Company took over the sale of vodka in the city, Smith opened a retailing outlet on Reimer's Island, which was then outside the jurisdiction of Stockholm. Smith publicized the event with enormous advertisements, offering both low-priced, charcoal-distilled vodka and a new heat-distilled type called "Purified Tenfold."

To entice further new customers, Smith offered them free boat rides to Reimer's Island. The vodka rush to Reimer's Island soon became a stampede, and Smith's "Purified Tenfold" vodka became the popular favorite.

In 1878 the Parliamentary Committee on Alcohol issued a recommendation in favor of heat-distilled vodka. Smith saw victory at last.

In 1917, four years after L. O. Smith's death, *AB Vin-& Spritcentralen*, the Swedish state liquor monopoly, was founded. AB Vin-& Spritcentralen is the country's sole distiller and importer of wines and spirits. It owns the world's largest and most modern ethanol refinery and five production units located in Stockholm, Sodertalje, Sundsvall, Ahus and Falkenberg.

In the mid-70's, Lars Lindmark, director of AB Vin-& Spritcentralen and former budget director of Sweden, sought to develop an export product which would reflect Sweden's high-quality standards. Extensive research showed that the century-old Absolut would be the perfect export product.

AB Vin-& Spritcentralen, which produces Absolut at its Ahus (Aw-hoos) plant located in the southern region of Sweden, uses the finest domestic wheat, sterilized high quality water treated to remove chlorine, and a very small amount (much less than 1 percent) of an aged component to round out the flavor. Coupled with L. O. Smith's "Purified Tenfold" method for producing vodka free of impurities, this technique has resulted in the development of a product which has a pure, clean smooth taste.

Absolut (Country of Sweden) Vodka was first made available in duty-free shops. It was introduced in the U.S. in 1979 by Carillon Importers Ltd., its sole U.S. importer.

Absolut is available in 80 and 100 proof, 1.75 litre, one-litre, 750 ml and 500 ml bottles. Miniatures are available in 80 proof only.

Since 1979 Absolut on the Rocks has been called for in Bars all over the United States. It has had a great effect on the call of the Martini (Vodka/Gin, dash of Vermouth). Below is the recipe for Absolut Vodka Martini and the many variations of this popular drink (also see Gin pg. 121).

ABSOLUT VODKA MARTINI
1½ oz. ABSOLUT VODKA
dash Martini & Rossi Extra Dry Vermouth

Stir in cocktail glass with ice. Strain and serve straight up or on the rocks with some ice in cocktail glass. Add lemon twist or olive. OR: Shake and strain and serve up or on the rocks with some ice.

Many customers and Bartenders agree that shaking will ruin a Martini because of the slight taste of the metal from the shaker. Use your own judgement!

Below are a few variations:

CORNET:	Replace Vermouth with Port Wine
DEWEY:	Add dash orange bitters
DILLATINI:	Dilly Beam (try and find one)
ELEGANT:	Add dash Grand Marnier
FASCINATOR:	Add dash Pernod and sprig mint
GIBSON:	Add onion
GIMLET:	Replace Vermouth with Rose's® Lime Juice. Garnish with lime
GYPSY:	Add cherry
HOMESTEAD:	Add orange slice muddled
ITALIAN:	Replace Vermouth with Hiram Walker Amaretto
JACKSON:	Replace Vermouth with Dubonnet and dash of bitters
LADIES' CHOICE:	Add ¼ oz. Hiram Walker Kummel
LONE TREE:	Add dash lemon juice
MICKEY FINN:	Add splash of Hiram Walker White Creme de Menthe, garnish with mint
NAKED MARTINI:	Just Absolut Vodka
NAVAL COCKTAIL:	Replace Extra Dry with Rosso Vermouth; add onion and twist
ORANGETINI:	Add splash of Hiram Walker Triple Sec and orange peel
PERFECTION:	Replace Extra Dry Vermouth with Rosso Vermouth
QUEEN ELIZABETH:	Add splash Benedictine
RICHMOND:	Replace Vermouth with Lillet, add twist of lemon
ROSA:	Add Hiram Walker Cherry Flavored Brandy
ROSALIN RUSSELL:	Replace Vermouth with Aquavit
ROSELYN:	Add Rose's® Grenadine and lemon twist
SAKITINI:	Replace Vermouth with Sake
SILVER BULLET:	Float J&B Scotch on top
SOUR KISSES:	Add egg white, SHAKE
TRINITY aka TRIO, PLAZA:	Replace Extra Dry Vermouth with half Rosso and half Extra Dry. Equal parts of Vermouth and Absolut Vodka
VELOCITY:	Add orange slice and Shake
WALLICK:	Add dash of Hiram Walker Orange Curacao
WARDEN:	Add dash of Pernod

ABSOLUT AND TONIC
1¼ oz. ABSOLUT VODKA
    Tonic

In a tall glass with ice, fill with tonic. Add squeeze of lime.

ABSOLUT COOLER
1¼ oz. ABSOLUT VODKA
½ tsp. Powdered Sugar
    Ginger Ale or
    Carbonated Water

Stir powdered sugar with 2 oz. carbonated water. Fill glass with ice and add vodka. Fill with carbonated water or ginger ale and stir again. Insert a spiral of orange or lemon peel (or both), dangle over rim.

ABSOLUT MADRAS
1½ oz. ABSOLUT VODKA
    Orange Juice
    Cranberry Juice

In a tall glass with ice, fill with half orange juice, half cranberry juice.

ABSOLUT SALTY DOG
1½ oz. ABSOLUT VODKA
¾ oz. Grapefruit Juice
¼ tsp. Salt

Coat rim of glass with salt. Mix and pour on the rocks.

ABSOLUT SEABREEZE
1¼ oz. ABSOLUT VODKA
    Cranberry Juice
    Grapefruit Juice

Serve in a tall glass with ice, fill with half cranberry juice, half grapefruit juice.

ABSOLUT TRANSFUSION
1¼ oz. ABSOLUT VODKA
    Grape Juice

In a tall glass with ice, fill with grape juice. Can top with club soda.

ABSOLUT VODKA COLLINS
1¼ oz. ABSOLUT VODKA
¾ oz. Sweetened
    Lemon Mix
    Club Soda

Shake with ice and pour in tall glass with ice. Fill with club soda.

ABSOLUTION
1 part ABSOLUT VODKA
5 parts Laurent Perrier
    Champagne

In a fluted champagne glass, cut a lemon peel in the form of a ring to represent a halo. The lemon peel can be either wrapped around the top of the glass or float on top of the champagne.

ALMOND LEMONADE
1¼ oz. ABSOLUT VODKA
¼ oz. Hiram Walker
    Creme de Almond
    Lemonade

Pour over ice in a tall glass. Garnish with lemon slice.

AQUEDUCT
¾ oz. ABSOLUT VODKA
¼ oz. Grand Marnier
¼ oz. Asbach Uralt
½ tbs. Rose's® Lime Juice

Combine with ice in a shaker. Strain into chilled cocktail glass.

BERRY LEMONADE

1 oz. ABSOLUT VODKA
¼ oz. Hiram Walker
Strawberry
Liqueur
Lemonade

*Pour over ice in a tall glass.
Garnish with fresh strawberry.*

BLIZZARD

1¼ oz. ABSOLUT VODKA
Fresca

*In a tall glass with ice. Garnish
with twist of lemon.*

BLOODY BULL

1¼ oz. ABSOLUT VODKA
V-8 Tomato
Cocktail
1½ oz. Beef Bouillon
1-2 tsp. Lemon Juice
dash Worcestershire
Sauce
dash Tabasco Sauce
Pepper

*Combine with ice in shaker.
Strain into old-fashioned glass,
pepper to taste.*

BLOODY MARY

1½ oz. ABSOLUT VODKA
V-8 Tomato
Cocktail or
Tomato Juice
1-2 tsp. Lemon Juice
dash Tabasco
dash Worcestershire
Sauce
Pepper

*Combine in shaker. Strain into
chilled old-fashioned glass,
pepper to taste.*

BLUE LAGOON

1 oz. ABSOLUT VODKA
¼ oz. Hiram Walker Blue
Curacao
½ oz. Pineapple Juice
Bitters

*Combine in shaker with ice.
Strain into chilled cocktail glass.
Twist lemon peel over drink and
add.*

BLUE MONDAY

1 oz. ABSOLUT VODKA
¼ oz. Hiram Walker
Triple Sec
dash Hiram Walker Blue
Curacao

*Combine with ice in shaker.
Strain into chilled cocktail glass.*

BROWN DERBY

1¼ oz. ABSOLUT VODKA
Cola

*In a tall glass with ice, fill with
cola.*

CAPE CODDER

1¼ oz. ABSOLUT VODKA
3 oz. Cranberry Juice
dash Rose's® Lime Juice

*Combine in a chilled cocktail
glass over ice.*

CHI CHI

1½ oz. ABSOLUT VODKA
¾ oz. Pineapple Juice
1½ oz. Creme of Coconut

*Blend with ice to slush. Add
cherry.*

CLAMDIGGER

1¼ oz. ABSOLUT VODKA
2 oz. Tomato Juice
1 oz. Clam Juice
   dash Tabasco Sauce
   dash Worcestershire
     Sauce

Combine in mixing glass, stir well. Add ice and strain into chilled old-fashioned glass. Twist lemon peel and add.

CLOUDY NIGHT

1 part ABSOLUT VODKA
1 part Tia Maria
Stir on the rocks.

COPPERHEAD

1¼ oz. ABSOLUT VODKA
   Ginger Ale
In a tall glass filled with ice, add a squeeze of lime and garnish with lime wedge.

DARK EYES

1 oz. ABSOLUT VODKA
¼ oz. Hiram Walker
   Blackberry Brandy
½ tsp. Rose's® Lime Juice
Combine with ice in shaker. Strain into brandy snifter. Garnish with lime slice or mint sprig.

DUBLIN DELIGHT

¾ oz. ABSOLUT VODKA
½ oz. Melon Liqueur
Combine with ice in shaker. Strain into old-fashioned glass half filled with crushed ice. Garnish with green maraschino cherry.

FIG NEWTON

½ oz. ABSOLUT VODKA
½ oz. Grand Marnier
¼ oz. Hiram Walker
   Creme de Almond
   Orange Juice
   Sweetened
   Lemon Juice
Pour over ice in shaker. Shake and pour into rocks glass, garnish with orange and cherries.

FIRE FLY

1¼ oz. ABSOLUT VODKA
   Grapefruit Juice
   Rose's® Grenadine
Combine vodka and grapefruit juice in tall glass over ice. Add grenadine.

GODMOTHER

1 oz. ABSOLUT VODKA
¼ oz. Hiram Walker
   Amaretto
Serve in rocks glass over ice.

GOLDEN DAY

¾ oz. ABSOLUT VODKA
½ oz. Liquore Galliano
Serve in rocks glass over ice.

GORKY PARK

1¼ oz. ABSOLUT VODKA
1 tsp. Rose's® Grenadine
   dash Orange Bitters
Combine in shaker with crushed ice, or blend. Strain into chilled cocktail glass. Garnish with ½ strawberry.

GREYHOUND

1¼ oz. ABSOLUT VODKA
     Grapefruit Juice

In a tall glass with ice, fill with grapefruit juice.

HAWAIIAN EYE

½   oz. ABSOLUT VODKA
½   oz. Kahlua
¼   oz. Wild Turkey 101
     splsh Hiram Walker
       Banana Liqueur
3   oz. Pineapple Juice
½   oz. Heavy Cream
1   Egg White

Combine in blender. Pour into chilled cocktail glass. Garnish with pineapple spear.

HOP-SKIP-AND-GO-NAKED

1   oz. ABSOLUT VODKA
1   oz. Bombay Gin
     Juice of ½ Lime

In a mug; serve over ice. Fill with Budweiser.

HORSESHOT

1¼ oz ABSOLUT VODKA
4   oz. Tomato Juice
1¼ tsp. Horseradish

Over ice in a cocktail glass. Garnish with celery stalk.

ICE PICK

1¼ oz. ABSOLUT VODKA
     Lemon-flavored
     Iced Tea

Pour over ice in a tall glass. Garnish with a slice of lemon.

IMPERIAL CZAR

¼   oz. ABSOLUT VODKA
¼   oz. Grand Marnier
¾   oz. Dry Sparkling
       Wine
     dash Rose's® Lime Juice
     dash Orange Bitters

Combine in shaker, except wine. Strain into chilled wine glass. Add wine, stir.

KAMAKAZI

1   oz. ABSOLUT VODKA
     splsh Grand Marnier
     splsh Rose's® Lime Juice

Combine and shake well with ice. Strain into shot glass or on the rocks.

KREMLIN COLONEL

1¼ oz. ABSOLUT VODKA
2   tbs. Sugar Syrup

Combine in shaker with ice. Strain into cocktail glass. Garnish with 3 to 4 mint leaves torn in half.

MIDNIGHT MARTINI aka
BLACK RUSSIAN

1   oz. ABSOLUT VODKA
¼   oz. Kahlua

Serve up with a twist of lemon peel.

PANZER

1   part ABSOLUT VODKA
1   part Bombay Gin
1   part Hiram Walker
       Triple Sec

Combine in shaker with ice. Strain into chilled cocktail glass

PINEAPPLE LEMONADE

1¼ oz. ABSOLUT VODKA
2 oz. Pineapple Juice
4 oz. Lemonade

Pour over ice in a tall glass. Garnish with pineapple spear.

PINK MINK

¾ oz. ABSOLUT VODKA
¼ oz. Bacardi Rum
¼ oz. Hiram Walker Strawberry Liqueur

Combine with ice in shaker. Strain into a cocktail glass with rim moistened with strawberry liqueur and sugar-frosted. Garnish with ½ strawberry.

PRAIRIE OYSTER

1¼ oz. ABSOLUT VODKA
2 oz. Tomato Juice
dash Worcestershire Sauce
1 Egg Yolk
Salt
Pepper
1 tsp. Lemon Juice

Drop unbroken egg yolk on bottom of chilled wine glass. In separate mixing glass, combine other ingredients, mix well. Pour over egg yolk. Salt and pepper to taste.

PURPLE PASSION

1¼ oz. ABSOLUT VODKA
2 oz. Grapefruit Juice
2 oz. Grape Juice

Chill, stir, add sugar to taste, and serve in a collins glass.

SALT LICK

1¼ oz. ABSOLUT VODKA
2 oz. Bitter Lemon Soda
2 oz. Grapefruit Juice

Pour over ice in salt-rimmed wine glass.

SCREWDRIVER

1¼ oz. ABSOLUT VODKA
Orange Juice

In a tall glass with ice, fill with orange juice.

SLALOM

1 part ABSOLUT VODKA
1 part Hiram Walker White Creme de Cacao
1 part Sambuca Romana
1 tsp. Heavy Cream

Combine in Blender with ice. Strain into chilled cocktail glass.

SLIM JIM

1¼ oz. ABSOLUT VODKA
Diet Soda

In a highball glass with ice, fill with diet soda. Garnish with lemon or lime slice.

SPOTTED DOG

¼ oz. ABSOLUT VODKA
¾ oz. Hiram Walker Amaretto
¼ oz. Hiram Walker White Creme de Cacao
Vanilla Ice Cream

Mix all ingredients in a blender until smooth. Pour into cocktail glass and serve.

SUN BURST

1¼   oz. ABSOLUT VODKA
dash Hiram Walker
    Triple Sec
    Grapefruit Juice

Serve in rocks glass over ice. Add dash of triple sec.

SWEDISH BEAR

¾   oz. ABSOLUT VODKA
½   oz. Hiram Walker
    Dark Creme de
    Cacao
1   tbs. Heavy Cream

Pour over ice in chilled old-fashioned glass, and stir.

SWEDISH COCKTAIL

¾   oz. ABSOLUT VODKA
¼   oz. Bombay Gin
¼   oz. Hiram Walker
    White Creme de
    Cacao

Combine in shaker with ice. Strain into chilled cocktail glass.

SWEDISH LADY

1   oz. ABSOLUT VODKA
¼   oz. Hiram Walker
    Strawberry
    Liqueur
1   oz. Lemon Juice
1   oz. Sugar Syrup
½   oz. Heavy Cream

Combine in shaker with ice. Strain into chilled whiskey sour glass.

THE TWIST

¾   oz. ABSOLUT VODKA
½   oz. Hiram Walker
    White Creme de
    Menthe
    Orange Sherbert

Blend. Pour into a champagne glass.

VODKA RICKEY aka
ABSOLUT AND SODA

1¼   oz. ABSOLUT VODKA
    Club Soda

In a tall glass with ice. Fill with club soda. Add squeeze of fresh lime.

WHITE ELEPHANT

1   oz. ABSOLUT VODKA
¼   oz. Hiram Walker
    Creme de Cacao
    Milk

In a tall glass with ice.

WOO WOO

¾   oz. ABSOLUT VODKA
¾   oz. Hiram Walker
    Peppermint
    Schnapps

In a tall glass with ice.

ABSOLUT PEPPAR VODKA

In July 1988 Carillon Importers Ltd. introduced Absolut Peppar, a natural jalapeno pepper and paprika flavored vodka.

In keeping with Absolut tradition, Absolut Peppar is absolutely clear; while other pepper flavored vodkas generally have a cloudy or colored appearance. The new super-premium brand offers a robust yet mellow flavor—plus the warmth and crisp note of jalapeno.

Since the introduction of Absolut to the U.S. in 1979, the product has enjoyed a steady increase in market share, largely because of discriminating drinkers' trading up to premium brands, according to Carillon. "Absolut Peppar inherits a well-established brand reputation," Mr. Roux, President/CEO of Carillon, said.

The new clear product is produced in Sweden by the state-owned AB Vin- & Spritcentalen. Like Absolut Vodka, it is made from the finest Swedish grain and water. It is sold in Absolut's familiar clear-glass bottle, with lettering in black and red.

ABSOHOT
½ shot ABSOLUT PEPPAR
1 dash Hot Sauce
Serve with Budweiser chaser.

ABSOLUT HOLY HAIL MARY
1¼ oz. ABSOLUT PEPPAR
5 dshs Tabasco Sauce
splsh Tomato Juice
Mix the tabasco, tomato and Peppar and strain into a chilled rocks or shot glass.

ABSOLUT PEPPAR BLOODY MARY
1¼ oz. ABSOLUT PEPPAR
4-6 oz. Tomato Juice
Mix with ice in a 12 or 14 oz. double old-fashion, highball or collins glass.

ABSOLUT PEPPAR BULL SHOT
1¼ oz. ABSOLUT PEPPAR
5 oz. Beef Consomme
5 dshs Worcestershire Sauce
1 tsp. Lemon Juice
pinch Celery Salt or Seed
Mix ingredients with ice in a 14 oz. double old-fashioned glass.

ABSOLUT PEPPAR SALTY DOG
1¼ oz. ABSOLUT PEPPAR
4 oz. Grapefruit Juice
Rim glass with salt. Serve on the rocks.

ABSOLUT PEPPARMINT
1¼ oz. ABSOLUT PEPPAR
¼ oz. Hiram Walker Peppermint Schnapps
In a shot glass.

AFTERBURNER
½ oz. ABSOLUT PEPPAR
½ oz. Kahlua
½ oz. Hiram Walker Cinnamon Schnapp
Serve in 2 oz. sherry glass.

BLACK PEPPER
1¼ oz. ABSOLUT PEPPAR
¼ oz. Hiram Walker Blackberry Flavored Brandy
In a shot glass.

BLOODY BURNS
1 oz. ABSOLUT PEPPAR
1 oz. Fernet Branca
4 oz. Tomato Juice
1 lg. Clove Garlic
1 dash Celery Salt
½ oz. Worcestershire Sauce
2 dshs Tabasco
Score the garlic with a knife and rim a 12-14 oz. tumbler. Fill with ice and add ingredients, top with Fernet. Garnish with cucumber slice.

CAJUN MARY
1¼ oz. ABSOLUT PEPPAR
4 oz. Tomato Juice
Juice of ½ Lemon
2 dshs Worcestershire Sauce
½ tsp. Horseradish
Salt
Celery Salt
Combine all ingredients. Fill an 8-oz. glass with ice and pour in mixture. Place celery stalk in drink as stirrer.

DOYLE'S MULLIGAN
1 oz. ABSOLUT PEPPAR
4 oz. Budweiser
Add Absolut Peppar slowly while drinking beer.

DRAGON FIRE
1 oz. ABSOLUT PEPPAR
¼ oz. Hiram Walker
      Green Creme de
      Menthe
In rocks glass over ice.

FIREBIRD
1¼ oz. ABSOLUT PEPPAR
4   oz. Cranberry Juice
Serve on the rocks.

FIREWATER
1 oz. ABSOLUT PEPPAR
⅔ cup Chilled Orange
      Juice
1 cup Chilled Buttermilk
Combine ingredients. Pour over ice in prechilled, 14-oz. tumbler. Place ½ orange slice on rim of glass.

GARBO
1¼ oz. ABSOLUT PEPPAR
5   oz. Clear Borscht
Mix over ice in 14 oz. double old-fashioned glass.

HOT LAVA
1¼ oz. ABSOLUT PEPPAR
¼   oz. Hiram Walker
      Amaretto
Serve on the rocks.

HOT PANTS
¼ oz. ABSOLUT PEPPAR
1 oz. Hiram Walker
      Peach Schnapps
Serve on the rocks.

LONG ISLAND HOT TEA
¼ oz. ABSOLUT PEPPAR
¼ oz. Sauza
      Conmemorativo
      Tequila
¼ oz. Bacardi Rum
¼ oz. Bombay Gin
      Sweet & Sour Mix
      Cola
In a tall glass with ice, shake. Top with cola.

LONG ISLAND ICE TEA
Substitute Absolut Vodka for Absolut Peppar.

PEPPAR BAYOU MARTINI
1¼ oz. ABSOLUT PEPPAR
¼   oz. Martini & Rossi
      Extra Dry
      Vermouth
1 small Pickled Jalapeno
Place four ice cubes in a small pitcher and add vodka and vermouth. Stir briskly. Serve in chilled martini glass. Add pickled jalapeno.

PEPPAR PASSION
1¼ oz. ABSOLUT PEPPAR
1   oz. La Grande Passion
In a rocks glass with ice.

PEPPAR SOMBRERO
1 oz. ABSOLUT PEPPAR
½ oz. Kahlua
1 tbs. Heavy Cream
Combine vodka and Kahlua. Pour over ice in a 4-oz. goblet. Float cream on top.

PEPPAR SOUTHSIDE

1 oz. ABSOLUT PEPPAR
2 tbs. Rose's® Lime Juice
2 tsp. Sugar
½ tsp. Fresh Mint Leaves, torn

Place all ingredients in a blender. Blend until smooth. Pour into chilled, 4-oz. glass. Place lime on rim of glass.

PEPPAR TODDY

1 oz. ABSOLUT PEPPAR
4 oz. Cranberry Juice
½ Cinnamon Stick
2 Allspice Berries
Orange Peel
1 tsp. Sugar
2 tsp. Lemon Juice

Combine all ingredients, except vodka in saucepan. Boil two minutes, add vodka.

PEPPARED ROSE

1 oz. ABSOLUT PEPPAR
3 oz. De Venoge Cremant Rose Champagne

In a champagne glass.

RAGIN' CAJUN

1¼ oz. ABSOLUT PEPPAR
4 oz. Tomato Juice
2 dshs Salt
Cayenne Pepper

In a tall glass with ice.

SCANDANAVIAN LIGHTNING

2 parts ABSOLUT PEPPAR
1 part Skane Akvavit

Mix with ice in mixing glass. Strain into chilled cocktail glass. Garnish with small red chili pepper.

SCORPION'S STING

1¼ oz. ABSOLUT PEPPAR
¼ oz. Hiram Walker White Creme de Menthe

In a rocks glass over ice.

SEA & SOL

1¼ oz. ABSOLUT PEPPAR
4-6 oz. Clamato Juice
4-6 dshs Bloody Mary Maker

Build over ice in highball or collins glass. Garnish with scallion spear, pepperoncini pepper and lime wedge.

SPARKS

1 oz. ABSOLUT PEPPAR
3 oz. Laurent Perrier Champagne

In a champagne glass.

SWEDISH BULL

1¼ oz. ABSOLUT PEPPAR
4 oz. Beef Broth (Bouillon)

Serve over rocks. Garnish with lime.

TEAR DROP

1¼ oz. ABSOLUT PEPPAR
¼ oz. Grand Marnier

In a shot glass, drop a cherry in.

THE ABSOLUT PEPPAR CAJUN MARTINI

1¼ oz. ABSOLUT PEPPAR
dash Martini & Rossi Extra Dry Vermouth (to taste)

Mix with ice in a mixing glass. Strain and pour on the rocks, or serve in a chilled cocktail glass.

THE ABSOLUT PEPPAR EXPERIENCE

1¼   oz. ABSOLUT PEPPAR

Pour over ice in a chilled glass. Serious vodka drinkers may prefer it neat in a shot glass, poured from a freezer-cold bottle.

THE FLAME

1¼   oz. ABSOLUT PEPPAR
¼   oz. Cherry Marnier
        Liqueur

Serve on the rocks.

THE SWEDISH VOWELIZER

1¼   oz. ABSOLUT PEPPAR
        Hot Tea (2 bags)

Absolut Peppar 1¼ oz.

Embelish the glass rim with a 2 in. circumference fresh lemon.

Ice, shaven, not cubed.

Only use perfectly brewed tea.

Umbrella garnish is always optional.

Yours to enjoy—sometimes!

"Because you like it".

ULTIMATE SHOOTER

A raw oyster or clam in a shot glass with ABSOLUT PEPPAR *topped with a spoonful of cocktail sauce or a dash of horseradish and a squeeze of lemon.* SHOOT IT DOWN.

VODKA STEAMER

1   oz. ABSOLUT PEPPAR
3   oz. Clam Juice
2   oz. Tomato Juice

Combine clam and tomato juice in a small saucepan. Heat only until warmed through and pour over vodka in a mug. Garnish with lemon slice.

VOLCANO

1¼   oz. ABSOLUT PEPPAR
        dash Rose's® Grenadine

In a shot glass.

© FOLEY PUBLISHING CORP.

ABSOLUT CITRON

Absolut Citron is a lime, mandarin orange, grapefruit and predominately lemon flavored super-premium vodka which became available in selected U.S. markets in the summer of 1988.

Imported from Sweden as an extension to the increasingly popular Absolut product line, the 80 proof vodka offers a totally new, cool distinctive taste.

Absolut Citron, which keeps the Absolut tradition of being absolutely clear, is packaged in a frosty bottle with bold yellow lettering to reflect the citrus taste of the product.

Helping to fuel the spirits market is the growing popularity of flavored vodkas, a long tradition in Europe. Since the early times in Sweden, where Absolut is produced using the finest grain grown in the rich fields of Southern Sweden, vodka has been flavored with lemonade and fruit juices. Traditionally enjoyed chilled, served straight-up.

Because vodka is the most nearly neutral of all spirits, it is uniquely versatile, absorbing and heightening the flavors it is mixed with. Thus creating new taste sensations which are limited only by one's imagination.

Absolut Citron is available in 750 ml and 1 litre bottles and is priced slightly higher than Absolut 100 proof Vodka.

ABSOLUT CITRON & TONIC
2   oz. ABSOLUT CITRON
    Tonic
In a tall glass with ice, fill with tonic. Add squeeze of lemon.

ABSOLUT CITRON COLLINS
1¼ oz. ABSOLUT CITRON
1   oz. Lemon Juice
½ oz. Sugar Syrup
    Club Soda
Mix ingredients in a collins glass. Stir well, add ice, garnish with fruit, top with club soda.

ABSOLUT CITRON GODMOTHER
1¼ oz. ABSOLUT CITRON
¾ oz. Hiram Walker Amaretto
Serve in rocks glass over ice.

ABSOLUT CITRON MARTINI
1½ oz. ABSOLUT CITRON
¼ oz. Martini & Rossi Extra Dry Vermouth
Serve up with a green olive.

ABSOLUT CITRON RICKEY
1¼ oz. ABSOLUT CITRON
    Club Soda
In a tall glass with ice, fill with club soda. Add squeeze of fresh lime.

ABSOLUT CITRON SOUR
1¼ oz. ABSOLUT CITRON
¼ oz. Lemon Juice
1   tsp. Sugar Syrup
Mix in a shaker. Strain into chilled glass and garnish with cherry.

ABSOLUT LEMONADE
1¼ oz. ABSOLUT CITRON
¼ oz. Grand Marnier
½ Sweet & Sour Mix
½ 7-Up
In a tall glass with ice put Absolut Citron and Grand Marnier, fill with ½ sweet & sour and ½ 7-Up. Mix, do not shake. Garnish with a lemon wheel.

ABSOLUT MONTAUK CITRON BREEZE
1¼ oz. ABSOLUT CITRON
5   oz. Grapefruit Juice
3   oz. Cranberry Juice
Mix in chilled collins glass with ice cubes. Garnish with lime slice.

B.C.
1 part ABSOLUT CITRON
1 part Kahlua
Stir on the rocks.

BEACH BALL COOLER
1¼ oz. ABSOLUT CITRON
½ oz. Hiram Walker Creme de Casis
1   tsp. Rose's® Lime Juice
    Ginger Ale
Mix in a collins glass with ice. Fill with ginger ale. Garnish with lemon and cherry.

BLUE LEMONADE
1¼ oz. ABSOLUT CITRON
    splsh The Original Blue Juice
Pour over ice in a tall glass.

CAJUN KING MARTINI

½ oz. ABSOLUT CITRON
1½ oz. Absolut Peppar
dash Martini & Rossi
Extra Dry
Vermouth
Jalapeno Pepper

Mix with ice in a small pitcher and strain into a chilled glass. Add pepper and twist of lemon.

CILVER CITRON

1¼ oz. ABSOLUT CITRON
½ oz. Laurent Perrier
Champagne

Serve up.

CITRON CELEBRATION

1¼ oz. ABSOLUT CITRON

Serve on the rocks and celebrate.

CITRON CHI CHI

1¼ oz. ABSOLUT CITRON
1¼ oz. Coco Lopez
Creme of Coconut
¾ oz. Pineapple Juice

Blend with ice to slush. Add cherry.

CITRON CODDER

1½ oz. ABSOLUT CITRON
Cranberry Juice

In a tall glass with ice, fill with cranberry juice.

CITRON COOLER

1¼ oz. ABSOLUT CITRON
½ oz. Rose's® Lime
Juice
Tonic Water

Mix with ice cubes in a chilled collins glass and fill with cold tonic water. Garnish with a lime wedge.

CITRON MADRAS

1¼ oz. ABSOLUT CITRON
Orange Juice
Cranberry Juice

In a tall glass with ice, fill with half orange and half cranberry juice.

COOL CITRON

1 oz. ABSOLUT CITRON
½ oz. Hiram Walker
White Creme de
Menthe

Stir on the rocks.

FLORIDA JOY

1¼ oz. ABSOLUT CITRON
½ oz. Grand Marnier

Mix with cracked ice in a shaker or blender and pour into a chilled highball glass. Garnish with lemon slice.

GOLFER

1 oz. ABSOLUT CITRON
½ oz. Bombay Gin
¼ oz. Martini & Rossi
Extra Dry
Vermouth

Serve on the rocks with a twist of lemon peel.

LEMONDROP

1¼ oz. ABSOLUT CITRON

Serve with a wedge of lemon coated with sugar. Shoot the Absolut Citron, then suck the lemon.

PERFECT RON

1¼   oz. ABSOLUT CITRON
dash Martini & Rossi
    Extra Dry
    Vermouth
dash Martini & Rossi
    Rosso Vermouth
dash Bitters

Serve on the rocks with a twist of lemon peel.

PILOT HOUSE FIZZ

1   oz. ABSOLUT CITRON
1   oz. Grand Marnier
dash Rose's® Lime
    Juice
dash Orange Bitters

Mix all except champagne with ice in a shaker, strain into a chilled wine goblet. Fill with champagne.

PINK BABY

1¼   oz. ABSOLUT CITRON
½   oz. Cherry Marnier
½   oz. Lemon Juice

Mix with cracked ice in a shaker or blender and strain into a chilled cocktail glass.

PINK LEMONADE

1¼   oz. ABSOLUT CITRON
splsh Rose's®
    Grenadine

Pour over ice in a tall glass.

RAINBOW

1¼   oz. ABSOLUT CITRON
    Grapefruit Juice
    Grape Juice

In a tall glass with ice, fill with half grapefruit and half grape juice.

SALTY GROG

1¼   oz. ABSOLUT CITRON
4   oz. Grapefruit Juice
pinch Salt
dash Raspberry Syrup
    or Grenadine

Mix with ice in a large, chilled wine goblet.

SUPER LEMON COOLER

1½   oz. ABSOLUT CITRON
3   oz. Tonic Water
3   oz. Bitter Lemon
    Soda

Mix with ice in a chilled collins glass and garnish with a lemon slice.

SWEDISH BLACKBERRY

1½   oz. ABSOLUT CITRON
½   oz. Hiram Walker
    Blackberry
    Flavored Brandy
½   oz. Lemon Juice or
    Rose's® Lime Juice

Mix in shaker and strain into chilled glass. Garnish with lemon slice.

THE RIGHT IDEA

1½   oz. ABSOLUT CITRON
½   oz. Grand Marnier
½   oz. Lemon Juice or
    Rose's® Lime Juice

Mix in a shaker and strain into chilled cocktail glass. Garnish with orange slice.

THE TEANECK TOT (COOLER)

1¼ oz. ABSOLUT CITRON
3 oz. Grape Juice
Ginger Ale

Mix Absolut Citron and grape juice with ice in a chilled collins glass. Fill with ginger ale. Garnish with lemon slice.

TROPICAL ORCHARD

1¼ oz. ABSOLUT CITRON
½ oz. Grand Marnier
4 oz. Orange Juice
½ oz. Rose's® Lime Juice
½ oz. Grapefruit Juice

Mix with cracked ice in a shaker and pour into chilled double old-fashioned glass.

TWISTED BULL

1 oz. ABSOLUT CITRON
4 oz. Beef Broth (Boullion)

Serve over rocks. Garnish with lime.

WHITE CITRON

1½ oz. ABSOLUT CITRON
½ oz. Kahlua
2 oz. Half & Half

Shake with ice and pour over ice.

© FOLEY PUBLISHING CORP.

ASBACH URALT

From the heart of the Rheingau: Asbach Uralt

It was in Ruedesheim, a picturesque little town, in the heart of the Rheingau vine area, where Hugo Asbach, at the end of the last century, found the ideal site for his brandy distillery. He realized that the people of Ruedesheim were already experts in the art of wine making, and he knew that it would be easier in this area to find people in wine related crafts to help him set up his brandy distillery. As a skilled distiller and businessman, Hugo Asbach had travelled extensively and had gained his experience in the bigger wine-growing areas of Europe.

Distinctively different from cognac

It was his idea to create a new kind of brandy, distinctively different from cognac, one in which perhaps less emphasis is laid upon the bouquet, and in which the taste and smoothness is of prime importance. He spent years experimenting with different distillation processes and with distillates of different wines from well known European wine growing areas until he found a superb combination, specially suitable for the German palate because of its mild and winey flavor. This result could be achieved by combining the elegant Charente wines with their fine, fruity flavor and the full bodied dry and spicy wines of other viticultural areas.

By law, cognac has to be distilled on open fire; the remaining yeast in the wine is thus exposed to direct heat, which creates a taste which is often described as "soapy." The heavy bouquet of cognac is mainly due to this fact. For Asbach Uralt, however, a special distillation process in a steam-heated, pot-still helps to avoid impurities and gives the distillate a winey flavor lacking in most competitive brands.

During the second distillation process, the so-called primary, middle and after flows appear and have to be most carefully separated. Only the middle flow, the essence, is looked upon as a pure distillate. The distillate is transferred to small "barriques," barrels made from the expensive limousine oak. They allow the distillate to oxidize and to lose harshness. At the same time valuable esters and rare essences, which the distillate absorbs from the wood during the long storage period, give Asbach Brandy its deep, golden-topaz color. It takes approximately seven litres of wine to produce one litre of Asbach Uralt.

Weinbrand

The brand name Asbach Uralt and the label were registered in 1907 with the Imperial Patent office in Berlin. Asbach Uralt was the first German brand of brandy registered.

When after the first World War, the French laid claim to the appellation "Cognac" as the "description of origin" for "eau-de-vie de Vin" from Cognac, the term "Weinbrand" was officially incorporated into the German Wine law. It is today the correct description for high quality brandy in Germany.

A connoisseur's brandy

Asbach Uralt is of course a connoisseur's brandy which is best enjoyed in a large snifter, but it is also a versatile mixer and may be consumed with equal pleasure on the rocks or in a cocktail.

Over the years, the light and smooth taste of Asbach Uralt was well accepted by the public, and the product developed into one of the most prestigious and best selling brandies in the world.

The special light character and the taste appeal of German Brandy made brandy the top selling category in the spirit market of the Federal Republic of Germany.

AMBROSIA

1 oz. ASBACH URALT
1 oz. Applejack
dash Hiram Walker
Triple Sec
dash Chilled
Champagne
Juice of 1 lemon

Shake all ingredients except champagne and pour into highball glass with ice cubes.

ASBACH BEAUTY

¾ oz. ASBACH URALT
¾ oz. Martini & Rossi
Extra Dry
Vermouth
1 dash Hiram Walker
White Creme de
Menthe
1 oz. Port
¾ oz. Orange Juice
1 dash Rose's® Grenadine

In shaker filled with ice, pour all ingredients except port. Shake vigorously. Strain into chilled cocktail glass. Pour port slowly down the side so that it floats on top.

ASBACH COLA

1 part ASBACH URALT
3 parts Cola

Pour into tall glass with ice.

ASBACH SODA

1 part ASBACH URALT
4 parts Club Soda

In a tall glass, add a lime or lemon.

ASBACH SOUR

1 part ASBACH URALT
1 part Fresh Lemon
Juice
½ part Fresh Orange
Juice
½ part Sugar Syrup

Shake well with ice, pour into a cocktail glass, garnish with slice of orange and a cocktail cherry.

BLACK FOREST SPECIAL

¼ part ASBACH URALT
½ part Kammer Black
Forest
Kirschwasser
¼ oz. Freshly Squeezed
Grapefruit Juice

Serve in cocktail glass with cherry.

BLUE BRACER

3 parts ASBACH URALT
3 parts Hiram Walker Blue
Curacao
3 parts Lemon Juice
½ part Egg White

Shake well and serve in a champagne saucer glass.

BRANDTINI

1¼ oz. ASBACH URALT
1 oz. Bombay Gin
1 tsp. Martini & Rossi
Extra Dry
Vermouth

Stir well with ice. Strain into chilled cocktail glass. Twist lemon peel over drink and drop into glass or serve with cocktail onion.

BRANDY ALEXANDER
1   oz. ASBACH URALT
1   oz. Hiram Walker
     Creme de Cacao
1   oz. Sweet Cream

Shake well with cracked ice and strain into cocktail glass.

BRANDY AND SODA
1¼ oz. ASBACH URALT
     Club Soda to
     taste

In a chilled highball glass with ice, pour brandy and add club soda. Stir gently.

BRANDY CASSIS
1¼ oz. ASBACH URALT
2   tsp. Hiram Walker
     Creme de Cassis
½   oz. Lemon Juice

Shake well with ice. Strain into chilled cocktail glass. Twist lemon peel over drink and drop into glass.

BRANDY COLLINS
1¼ oz. ASBACH URALT
2   tsp. Superfine Sugar
1   oz. Fresh Lemon
     Juice
     Club Soda

In a cocktail shaker with ice add Asbach, sugar and lemon juice. Place 2 ice cubes in a tall glass and add the mixed ingredients into it. Fill the glass with club soda and garnish with lemon slice, orange slice and maraschino cherry.

BRANDY FIZZ
1¼ oz. ASBACH URALT
1   tbs. Superfine Sugar
2   tbs. Lemon Juice
1   tbs. Rose's® Lime
     Juice
     Club Soda to
     taste

In a cocktail shaker with ice, add ingredients except club soda, shake. Strain into a tall glass with ice, add club soda. Garnish with lime slice.

BRANDY FLIP
1¼ oz. ASBACH URALT
1   Egg
1   tsp. Superfine Sugar
2   tsp. Heavy Cream
     Freshly Grated
     Nutmeg

Fill a cocktail shaker with ice. Beat egg, sugar, and cream together until pale yellow. Pour brandy into the mixture and stir slightly. Pour over ice in the shaker and shake vigorously until frothy. Garnish with nutmeg.

BRANDY FLOATER
1¼ oz. ASBACH URALT
     Mineral Water

Float Asbach on your favorite mineral water.

BRANDY HIGHBALL
1¼ oz. ASBACH URALT
     Ginger Ale or
     Mineral Water

In a highball glass with ice, add brandy and fill with ginger ale or mineral water. Twist a peel of lemon over the drink and drop it in glass.

BRANDY MANHATTAN

1¼ parts ASBACH URALT
¼ part Martini & Rossi
Rosso Vermouth
1 dash Bitters

Mix well with ice and strain into chilled cocktail glass. Add cherry and twist of lemon.

BRANDY OLD FASHIONED

1¼ oz. ASBACH URALT
1 Sugar Cube
2 dshs Bitters
1 tsp. Water

Stir sugar, bitters and water in an old-fashioned glass until sugar is dissolved. Add ice to fill. Pour Asbach over ice and stir until well mixed. Twist lemon peel over the drink and drop it in glass.

BRANDY SLING

1¼ oz. ASBACH URALT
1 tsp. Superfine Sugar
2 tbs. Fresh Lemon
Juice

Place sugar and lemon juice in bottom of cocktail mixer. Stir until sugar is dissolved. Add ice cubes to fill and pour brandy over the ice. Stir until well blended. Strain into a chilled cocktail glass.

CARROL COCKTAIL

1¼ oz. ASBACH URALT
¼ oz. Martini & Rossi
Rosso Vermouth

In a mixer with ice, stir until well blended. Garnish with cherry.

CLASSIC

1 oz. ASBACH URALT
½ oz. Hiram Walker
Orange Curacao
1 tbs. Lemon Juice
1 tsp. Superfine Sugar
1 oz. Maraschino

In a mixing glass with ice, add lemon juice and sugar and stir until sugar dissolves. Add remaining ingredients and stir vigorously. Strain into chilled glass that has been dipped in lemon juice and sugar. Twist peel over drink and drop into glass.

DUTCH TREAT

1¼ oz. ASBACH URALT
Hot Chocolate
Whipped Cream

Serve in mug. Add straw.

FRENCH 75

1½ oz. ASBACH URALT
Champagne
1½ tsp. Lemon Juice
½ tsp. Powdered Sugar

Combine everything except champagne over ice; shake well. Strain into tall glass; add ice and fill with champagne. Add a twist of lemon.

FROUPE

1¼ oz. ASBACH URALT
1¼ oz. Martini & Rossi
Rosso Vermouth
1 tsp. Benedictine

Stir well with ice. Strain into chilled cocktail glass.

HARRY LIME

1¼ oz. ASBACH URALT
3 oz. Tonic Water

Garnish with a cocktail cherry and a slice of orange.

HARVARD

1¼ oz. ASBACH URALT
½ oz. Martini & Rossi
    Rosso Vermouth
2 tbs. Lemon Juice
1 dash Bitters
1 tsp. Rose's® Grenadine

In a cocktail mixer with ice, stir vigorously until well blended. Strain into cocktail glass.

HERMAN'S SPECIAL

¼ oz. ASBACH URALT
1¼ oz. Peachtree Cream
¼ oz. Absolut Vodka
   splsh Chambord

Combine ingredients into tall glass and add Chambord last to give effect.

HUETCHEN

1 part ASBACH URALT
3 parts Cola

Pour Asbach Uralt over ice in brandy snifter, add cola, enjoy.

LADY BE GOOD

½ oz. ASBACH URALT
¼ oz. Martini & Rossi
    Rosso Vermouth
¼ oz. Hiram Walker
    White Creme de
    Menthe

In a shaker with cracked ice. Strain into a chilled glass.

LAJOLLA

1½ oz. ASBACH URALT
½ oz. Hiram Walker
    Creme de Banana
2 tsp. Lemon Juice
1 tsp. Orange Juice

Shake with ice and strain into cocktail glass.

MARIPOSA

½ oz. ASBACH URALT
1 oz. Bacardi Light Rum
1 tbs. Lemon Juice
1 tbs. Orange Juice
   dash Rose's® Grenadine

Shake with ice and strain into cocktail glass.

McBRANDY

1¼ oz. ASBACH URALT
1 oz. Apple Juice
1 tsp. Lemon Juice

Shake well with ice. Strain into chilled cocktail glass. Add lemon slice.

MIKADO

1 oz. ASBACH URALT
1 dash Hiram Walker
    Triple Sec
1 dash Hiram Walker
    Creme de Noyaux
1 dash Rose's® Grenadine
1 dash Bitters

In an old-fashioned glass with ice, stir until well blended.

MISSISSIPPI
PLANTERS PUNCH

1 oz. ASBACH URALT
½ oz. Bacardi Light Rum
½ oz. Wild Turkey 101
1 tbs. Powdered Sugar
    Juice of 1 Lemon

Shake ingredients with ice and strain into collins glass with cubed ice. Fill with carbonated water and stir.

NICKOLASKA

1¼ part ASBACH URALT

Pour Asbach Uralt in a snifter or shotglass. Cover with a slice of lemon. Cover ½ of the lemon with sugar and ½ with ground coffee. Eat the lemon center with the sugar and the coffee while you enjoy your Asbach Uralt.

OLYMPIC COCKTAIL

¾ oz. ASBACH URALT
¾ oz. Hiram Walker Triple Sec
¾ oz. Orange Juice

Shake with ice and strain into cocktail glass.

PEPPERMINT FIZZ

1¼ oz. ASBACH URALT
½ oz. Hiram Walker Peppermint Schnapps
2 oz. Sweetened Lemon Mix

Shake with ice and serve in tall glass. Top with club soda and add decorate mint leaf.

PHOEBE SNOW

1¼ oz. ASBACH URALT
1 oz. Dubonnet
¾ tsp. Pernod

In a cocktail mixer with ice. Strain into a chilled cocktail glass.

PRINCE OF WALES

2 parts ASBACH URALT
5 parts Riesling Wine
5 parts Dry Sparkling Wine
dash Bitters

Garnish with a slice of lemon. An ideal aperitif.

QUAKER

1 oz. ASBACH URALT
½ oz. Bacardi Rum
½ oz. Lemon Juice
1 tsp. Raspberry Syrup or Rose's® Grenadine

Shake well with ice. Strain into prechilled cocktail glass. Twist lemon peel and drop into glass.

RUEDESHEIM ICED COFFEE

2 oz. ASBACH URALT
2 scps. Vanilla Ice Cream Cold Sweetened Coffee

Place ice cream in Ruedesheim Coffee cup. Add double Asbach and fill up with cold sweetened coffee. Top with whipped cream and sprinkled chocolate. Serve with a straw.

RUEDESHEIMER COFFEE

1-2 parts ASBACH URALT
     Hot Coffee
3   Sugar Cubes

Place sugar in coffee cup previously warmed up. Add Asbach Uralt, set aflame, stir and allow to burn for a good minute. Fill up with good hot coffee to within an inch of the top of the cup. Stir well. Cover with a layer of whipped cream, spiced with vanilla, and sprinkle with grated chocolate.

SIDECAR

2 parts ASBACH URALT
2 parts Hiram Walker
     Triple Sec
1 part Lemon Juice

Shake well and serve in a champagne saucer glass.

SLOE BRANDY

1   oz. ASBACH URALT
½   oz. Hiram Walker Sloe
     Gin
1   tsp. Lemon Juice

Shake well with ice. Strain into chilled cocktail glass. Twist lemon peel over drink and drop into glass.

SNOWBALL

1 part ASBACH URALT
1 part Hiram Walker
     Peppermint
     Schnapps
1 part Hiram Walker
     White Creme de
     Cacao

Shake with ice and strain in glass over crushed ice.

SOUTH PACIFIC

1   oz. ASBACH URALT
¼   oz. Pineapple Liqueur
¼   oz. Hiram Walker
     White Creme de
     Menthe
½   oz. Lemon Juice

Shake well with ice. Strain over rocks in chilled old-fashioned glass. Garnish with pineapple stick.

STINGER

¾   oz. ASBACH URALT
¾   oz. Hiram Walker
     White Creme de
     Menthe

Shake well with ice. Strain into chilled cocktail glass.

DRY STINGER: *Increase to 1¼ oz. Asbach Uralt and decrease to ¼ oz. Hiram Walker White Creme de Menthe.*

UNPUBLISHED HEMINGWAY

1½   oz. ASBACH URALT
¼   oz. Grand Marnier

Mix in a brandy snifter.

BACARDI RUM

How is it that Bacardi rum is the most popular spirit in the world today? Unique taste. Outstanding quality. Unequaled mixability. And a natural complement to so many great foods. It's a rum as rich in taste as in its own history.

In the 19th century, when spirits were consumed straight, rum was little more than a harsh, fiery drink favored mostly by sailors who sailed the seven seas. Neither its reputation nor its taste were suited to the elegance of 19th century drawing rooms. However, a successful wine merchant in Santiago de Cuba, named Don Facundo Bacardi, felt that with the right care, distillation, and mellowing, rum could be quite civilized. So, Don Facundo created a recipe and distillation formula around his ideas. And in 1862, Bacardi rum was born — a light dry taste and mellow smoothness that forever changed the way people thought of rum.

And because the rum bore his proud family name, to this day the quality of Bacardi rum has never been allowed to falter.

Soon, the taste of Bacardi rum began winning awards for excellence all over the world, including the title of Purveyors to the Royal Household, bestowed upon Bacardi by Queen Maria Cristina of Spain. Hence, the Spanish royal coat of arms proudly displayed on the label.

Toward the close of the 19th century, when people began experimenting with mixed drinks, Bacardi rum became a natural favorite for a whole range of exciting new concoctions.

In 1896, an American mining engineer in Cuba invented a unique way to quench his thirst by mixing lime juice, sugar and Bacardi rum. Naming his drink after the Daiquiri copper mines where he worked, he created one of the world's most requested cocktails, the famous Bacardi Daiquiri.

In 1900, Teddy Roosevelt's Rough Riders were relaxing in a Havana bar one hot August afternoon when they combined a new soda called Coca-Cola® with their Bacardi rum; they called it a Cuba Libre. Today Bacardi and Coke® is a great American favorite.

Rum, one of America's favorite drinks, is also one of the most mixable. It can be used with all mixes and juices and a great product to use when creating your own special drink.

® Registered Trademark

ACAPULCO

1¼   oz. BACARDI LIGHT RUM
¼   oz. Hiram Walker Triple Sec
½   oz. Rose's® Lime Juice
½   Egg White
½ tsp. Sugar

Mix in shaker or blender with ice and strain into a cocktail glass.

APPLE COOLER

1¼   oz. BACARDI LIGHT RUM
3   oz. Apple Juice

Pour into a highball glass and fill with ice.

APPLE PIE COCKTAIL

¾   oz. BACARDI LIGHT RUM
¼   oz. Martini & Rossi Rosso Vermouth
¼   oz. Apple Brandy
½   oz. Lemon Juice
    dash Rose's® Grenadine

Stir in a mixing glass with ice and strain into a chilled cocktail glass. Garnish with twist of a lemon peel.

APPLE RUM RICKEY

¾   oz. BACARDI LIGHT or DARK RUM
½   oz. Apple Brandy
    Soda

Pour rum in a highball glass filled with ice. Add apple brandy and fill with soda. Squeeze a wedge of lime and add.

APPLE RUM SWIZZLE

¾   oz. BACARDI LIGHT or DARK RUM
½   oz. Apple Brandy
1   oz. Rose's® Lime Juice
1 tsp. Sugar
    Bitters

Place sugar in bottom of a highball glass and add several dashes of bitters. Add rum, lime juice and apple brandy and fill glass with shaved or crushed ice. Stir until frosty.

BACARDI & COLA

1¼   oz. BACARDI LIGHT or DARK RUM
    Cola

Pour rum into tall glass filled with ice. Fill with your favorite cola and garnish with a squeeze of a lemon or lime wedge. Aka CUBA LIBRE, adding lime wedge.

BACARDI & TONIC

1¼   oz. BACARDI LIGHT RUM
    Tonic

Pour rum into a tall glass filled with ice. Fill with tonic and garnish with a slice of lime or lemon.

BACARDI ALEXANDER

¾ oz. BACARDI DARK RUM
½ oz. Hiram Walker Dark Creme de Cacao
½ oz. Cream Nutmeg (optional)

Mix in a shaker or blender with ice and strain into a cocktail glass. Sprinkle nutmeg on top, if desired.

BACARDI ANCIENT MARINER

1 part BACARDI GOLD RESERVE RUM
1 part Grand Marnier

Pour over ice in a rocks glass and stir.

BACARDI BLACK RUSSIAN

1 oz. BACARDI LIGHT or DARK RUM
¼ oz. Kahlua

Pour over ice in an old-fashioned glass. Stir and serve.

BACARDI BLOODY MARY

1¼ oz. BACARDI LIGHT or DARK RUM
4 oz. Tomato Juice
dash Worcestershire Sauce
Salt
Pepper

Pour rum and tomato juice into a tall glass filled with ice. Add worcestershire sauce, salt and pepper to taste. Garnish with squeeze of lemon or lime.

BACARDI BLOSSOM

1¼ oz. BACARDI LIGHT RUM
1 oz. Orange Juice
½ oz. Lemon Juice
½ tsp. Sugar

Mix in a shaker or blender with ice and strain into a cocktail glass.

BACARDI BUCK

1¼ oz. BACARDI LIGHT or DARK RUM
Ginger Ale

Pour rum in highball glass filled with ice. Add ginger ale and garnish with twist of a lemon peel.

BACARDI CHAMPAGNE COCKTAIL

1 oz. BACARDI SILVER RUM
Champagne
1 tsp. Sugar
dash Bitters

In tall glass, mix rum, sugar and bitters. Fill with champagne.

BACARDI COCKTAIL*

1¼ oz. BACARDI LIGHT RUM
1 oz. Rose's® Lime Juice
½ tsp. Sugar
½ oz. Rose's® Grenadine

*Mix in shaker or blender with ice and strain into a chilled cocktail glass or serve on the rocks. *The NY Supreme Court ruled in 1936 that a BACARDI COCKTAIL is not a BACARDI COCKTAIL unless it's made with BACARDI RUM.*

BACARDI COLLINS

1¼   oz. BACARDI LIGHT RUM
1¼   oz. Lemon or Rose's® Lime Juice
1   tsp. Sugar
    Club Soda

Mix rum, juice and sugar in shaker or blender with ice and pour into a tall glass. Fill with soda and garnish with a cherry and fruit slice.

BACARDI DAIQUIRI*

1¼   oz. BACARDI LIGHT RUM
½   oz. Lemon Juice
½   tsp. Sugar

*Mix in shaker or blender with ice and strain into a chilled cocktail glass or serve on the rocks. *The original Daiquiri was made with BACARDI RUM in 1896.*

BACARDI EGGNOG

1¼   oz. BACARDI LIGHT or DARK RUM
1   Egg
1   tsp. Sugar
    Milk

Mix in a shaker and strain into a tall glass. Sprinkle with nutmeg.

BACARDI FIRESIDE

1¼   oz. BACARDI LIGHT or DARK RUM
1   tsp. Sugar
    Hot Tea

In a mug place sugar and rum. Fill with very hot tea and one cinnamon stick. Stir well, top with a slice of lemon.

BACARDI FIZZ

1¼   oz. BACARDI LIGHT RUM
¼   oz. Lemon Juice
¼   oz. Rose's® Grenadine Soda

Pour rum and lemon juice in a highball glass filled with ice. Add the grenadine and fill with soda.

BACARDI FROZEN DAIQUIRI

1¼   oz. Bacardi Light Rum
¼   oz. Lemon or Rose's® Lime Juice
½   tsp. Sugar

Mix in shaker or blender with ice and strain into a chilled cocktail glass.

BACARDI BANANA DAIQUIRI
Add one banana.
BACARDI ORANGE DAIQUIRI
Add 1 oz. orange juice.
BACARDI PEACH DAIQUIRI
Add peeled fresh peach half.
BACARDI PINEAPPLE DAIQUIRI
Add ½ slice canned pineapple.
BACARDI STRAWBERRY DAIQUIRI - *Add 1 cup of strawberries.*

Substitute your favorite fruit or two or more fruits for your own special Daiquiri.

BACARDI GIMLET

1¼ oz. BACARDI LIGHT RUM
½ oz. Rose's® Lime Juice

Stir in a mixing glass with ice and strain into a chilled cocktail glass or serve on the rocks.

BACARDI GRASSHOPPER

1 oz. BACARDI LIGHT RUM
¼ oz. Hiram Walker Green Creme de Menthe
½ oz. Cream

Mix in shaker or blender with ice and strain into a cocktail glass.

BACARDI HOT BUTTERED RUM

1¼ oz. BACARDI SILVER RUM
1 tsp. Sugar
½ tsp. Butter
4 Whole Cloves

In a mug, mix sugar, butter, rum and cloves. Fill with boiling water and stir.

BACARDI IRISH COFFEE

1¼ oz. BACARDI GOLD RESERVE RUM
Hot Black Coffee

In a mug, pour rum and hot coffee. Top with whipped cream.

BACARDI NIGHTCAP

1¼ oz. BACARDI SILVER, AMBER or GOLD RESERVE RUM

Pour into glass filled with cracked ice. Garnish with twist of lemon.

BACARDI OLD FASHIONED

1¼ oz. BACARDI DARK RUM or BACARDI GOLD RESERVE
2 dshs Bitters
splsh Club Soda
1 tsp Sugar

In old fashioned glass dissolve sugar in bitters and club soda. Add 2 ice cubes and fill with rum. Garnish with fruit.

BACARDI ON-THE-ROCKS OR MIST

1¼ oz. BACARDI LIGHT or DARK RUM

Pour rum over ice or crushed ice and garnish with a twist of lemon peel.

BACARDI PINA COLADA

1¼ oz. BACARDI LIGHT or DARK RUM
2 oz. Unsweetened Pineapple Juice
1 oz. Cream of Coconut

Mix in a shaker or blender with crushed ice, or stir and serve on the rocks. Garnish with a pineapple spear, if desired. For best results, blend.

BACARDI RICKEY

1¼	oz. BACARDI LIGHT RUM
½	Lemon or Lime
	Club Soda

Squeeze lemon or lime into a tall glass filled with ice. Add rum and fill with club soda.

BACARDI RUM PUNCH

1	oz. BACARDI LIGHT RUM
¼	oz. Hiram Walker White Creme de Menthe
	Milk or Cream

Pour rum and white creme de menthe into a tall glass half filled with ice. Fill with milk or cream.

BACARDI SOUR

1¼	oz. BACARDI DARK RUM
1	oz. Lemon Juice
½	tsp. Sugar

Mix in a shaker with ice and strain into a sour glass. Garnish with a red cherry and half an orange slice.

BACARDI TOM & JERRY

1	oz. BACARDI LIGHT or DARK RUM
¼	oz. BACARDI GOLD RESERVE
1	Egg
1	tsp. Sugar

Separate yolk from white of egg and beat each separately. When white is fairly stiff, add sugar and beat to a stiff froth, combine white and yolk. Put rums in mug, add boiling water, 1 tbs. of egg mixture and sprinkle with nutmeg.

BALI HAI

1¼	oz. BACARDI LIGHT RUM
	Champagne
2	oz. Lemon Juice or Rose's® Lime Juice
½	oz. Rose's® Grenadine
¼	oz. Orgeat Syrup

Pour rum, lemon or lime juice and grenadine into a tall glass filled with crushed or shaved ice. Add the orgeat syrup and fill with champagne.

BANANA MAN

1	oz. BACARDI LIGHT RUM
¼	oz. Hiram Walker Banana Liqueur
½	oz. Lemon or Rose's® Lime Juice

Mix in a blender with ice and blend until smooth. Pour into a cocktail glass.

BARRACUDA

1¼	oz. BACARDI DARK RUM
	Champagne
1	oz. Pineapple Juice
½	oz. Rose's® Lime Juice
¼	tsp. Sugar

Pour rum and juices into a tall glass with ice. Add the sugar and fill with champagne. Garnish with a lime wheel.

BAT BITE

1¼ oz. BACARDI SILVER RUM
¾ cup Cranberry Juice

In 10 oz. glass filled with ice. Squeeze and drop in 1 lime or lemon wedge. Stir and serve.

BEACH PARTY

1¼ oz. BACARDI LIGHT or DARK RUM
1 oz. Pineapple Juice
1 oz. Orange Juice
1 oz. Rose's® Grenadine

Mix in a shaker or blender with ice and pour into a tall glass.

BEACHCOMBER

1 oz. BACARDI LIGHT or DARK RUM
¼ oz. Hiram Walker Cherry Liqueur
1 oz. Lemon or Rose's® Lime Juice

Mix in a shaker or blender with ice and strain into a cocktail glass.

BEACHCOMBER'S SPECIAL

1 oz. BACARDI LIGHT RUM
¼ oz. Hiram Walker Orange Curacao
¾ oz. Lemon or Rose's® Lime Juice
¼ tsp. Sugar (optional)

Mix in a shaker or blender with ice and strain into a cocktail glass or serve on the rocks.

BISHOP COCKTAIL

1 oz. BACARDI LIGHT or DARK RUM
¼ oz. Red Wine
¼ oz. Lemon or Rose's® Lime Juice
¼ tsp. Sugar (optional)

Mix in a shaker or blender with ice and strain into a cocktail glass.

BOLERO COCKTAIL

¾ oz. BACARDI LIGHT or DARK RUM
¼ oz. Apple Flavored Brandy
¼ oz. Martini & Rossi Rosso Vermouth

Stir in a mixing glass with ice and strain into a chilled cocktail glass. Garnish with a twist of lemon peel.

BONBINI

1 oz. BACARDI LIGHT or DARK RUM
¼ oz. Hiram Walker Orange Curacao Bitters

Stir in a mixing glass with ice and strain into a chilled cocktail glass.

BONGO DRUM

1 oz. BACARDI LIGHT RUM
¼ oz. Hiram Walker Blackberry Flavored Brandy Pineapple Juice

Pour rum into a tall glass half filled with ice. Fill with pineapple juice and float the blackberry flavored brandy on top.

BROADWAY COOLER

1 oz. BACARDI LIGHT or DARK RUM
¼ oz. Hiram Walker Green Creme de Menthe
½ oz. Lemon or Rose's® Lime Juice
Soda

Pour rum, creme de menthe and juice into a tall glass filled with ice. Fill with soda and garnish with a sprig of mint.

BUCK-A-ROO

1¼ oz. BACARDI LIGHT or DARK RUM
Root Beer

Pour rum into a highball glass filled with ice. Fill with root beer and garnish with lemon or lime wedge.

CALIFORNIA COOL-AID

1¼ oz. BACARDI LIGHT or DARK RUM
Orange Juice
Milk

Pour rum into a tall glass half filled with ice. Add half orange juice and half milk. Stir.

CALIFORNIA LEMONADE

1¼ oz. BACARDI LIGHT RUM
3 oz. Lemon Juice
1½ tsp. Sugar
Bitters
Club Soda

Pour rum, lemon juice, sugar and bitters into a tall glass half filled with ice. Fill with club soda and stir.

CALYPSO COOL-AID

1¼ oz. BACARDI LIGHT RUM
1 oz. Pineapple Juice
½ oz. Lemon or Rose's® Lime Juice
½ tsp. Sugar
Soda

Mix rum, juices and sugar in a shaker or blender with ice and pour into a tall glass. Fill with soda and garnish with pineapple spear and lime wheel.

CARIBBEAN COCKTAIL

1¼ oz. BACARDI LIGHT RUM
1 oz. Orange Juice
1 oz. Lemon or Rose's® Lime Juice
Soda

Pour rum and juice into a tall glass filled with crushed or shaved ice. Fill with soda and garnish with an orange slice and red cherry.

CARIBBEAN JOY

1¼ oz. BACARDI LIGHT RUM
1 oz. Pineapple Juice
¾ oz. Lemon Juice

Mix in shaker or blender with ice and strain into a cocktail glass.

CASA BLANCA

¾ oz. BACARDI LIGHT RUM
¼ oz. Hiram Walker Cherry Liqueur
¼ oz. Hiram Walker Orange Curacao
dash Bitters

Stir in a mixing glass with ice and strain into a chilled cocktail glass.

CHICAGO STYLE

¾ oz. BACARDI LIGHT RUM
¼ oz. Hiram Walker Triple Sec
¼ oz. Hiram Walker Anisette
½ oz. Lemon or Rose's® Lime Juice

Mix in a shaker or blender with ice and strain into a cocktail glass.

CHOCOLATE CREAM

¾ oz. BACARDI DARK RUM
¼ oz. Hiram Walker Dark Creme de Cacao
¼ oz. Hiram Walker White Creme de Menthe
1 oz. Cream

Mix in a shaker or blender with ice and strain into a cocktail glass.

CIDERIFIC

3 cups BACARDI AMBER RUM
7½ cups Apple Cider

In saucepan, bring apple cider to a boil. Remove from heat, add rum. Ladle into 8 oz. mugs. Add 1 tsp. butter to each mug or substitute 1 slice lemon or lime. Then add 1 cinnamon stick and 1 whole clove. Serves 10-12.

CLAM VOYAGE

1 oz. BACARDI LIGHT or DARK RUM
¼ oz. Apple Flavored Brandy
1 oz. Orange Juice
dash Orange Bitters

Mix in a shaker or blender with ice and strain into a cocktail glass.

COCONUT PUNCH

1¼ oz. BACARDI LIGHT or DARK RUM
2 oz. Cream of Coconut
½ oz. Lemon Juice
3-4 tbs. Vanilla Ice Cream

Mix all ingredients in a shaker or blender with crushed ice and pour into a tall glass.

COFFEE CREAM COOLER

1¼ oz. BACARDI LIGHT or DARK RUM
Cold Coffee
Cream

Pour rum into a tall glass half filled with ice. Fill with cold coffee and cream to desired proportions.

CONTINENTAL

1 oz. BACARDI LIGHT RUM
¼ oz. Hiram Walker Green Creme de Menthe
¾ oz. Rose's® Lime Juice
¼ tsp. Sugar (optional)

Mix in a shaker or blender with ice and strain into a cocktail glass.

CORKSCREW

¾ oz. BACARDI LIGHT RUM
¼ oz. Asbach Uralt
¼ oz. Port Wine
½ oz. Lemon or Rose's® Lime Juice

Stir in a mixing glass with ice and strain into a cocktail glass.

COW PUNCHER

1 oz. BACARDI LIGHT or DARK RUM
1 oz. Hiram Walker White Creme de Cacao
  Milk

Pour rum and creme de cacao into a tall glass half filled with ice. Fill with milk.

CRICKET

¾ oz. BACARDI LIGHT RUM
¼ oz. Hiram Walker White Creme de Cacao
¼ oz. Hiram Walker Green Creme de Menthe
1 oz. Cream

Mix in a shaker or blender with ice and strain into a cocktail glass.

DERBY DAIQUIRI

1¼ oz. BACARDI LIGHT RUM
½ oz. Lemon or Rose's® Lime Juice
½ oz. Orange Juice
  dash Bitters
¼ tsp. Sugar (optional)

Mix in a shaker or blender with ice and strain into a cocktail glass.

DUNLOP COCKTAIL

1 oz. BACARDI LIGHT or DARK RUM
1 oz. Sherry
  dash Bitters

Stir in a mixing glass with ice and strain into a cocktail glass.

EYE OPENER

½ oz. BACARDI LIGHT RUM
¼ oz. Hiram Walker Anisette
¼ oz. Hiram Walker Orange Curacao
¼ oz. Hiram Walker White Creme de Cacao
1 Egg Yolk

Mix in a shaker or blender with ice and strain into a cocktail glass.

FLORIDA SUNRISE

1¼ oz. BACARDI LIGHT RUM
½ oz. Rose's® Grenadine Orange Juice

Pour grenadine into the bottom of a tall glass. Fill with crushed ice. Pour in rum and fill with orange juice.

FRENCH DAIQUIRI

1 oz. BACARDI LIGHT RUM
¼ oz. Grand Marnier
½ oz. Lemon Juice or Rose's® Lime Juice

Mix in a shaker or blender with ice and strain into a cocktail glass.

GARTER BELT

1¼ oz. BACARDI AMBER RUM

Serve in shot glass.

GRAPE PUNCH

1¼ oz. BACARDI LIGHT RUM
Grape Juice
Lime or Lemon Wedge

Pour rum into a tall glass filled with ice. Fill with grape juice and garnish with a squeeze of lime or lemon.

HARD HAT

1¼ oz. BACARDI SILVER RUM
1¼ oz. Fresh Lime Juice
1 tsp. Sugar
¼ oz. Rose's® Grenadine Club Soda

In a shaker with ice, all but club soda. Strain into 10 oz. glass. Fill with club soda. Garnish with red cherry.

HAWAIIAN NIGHT

1 oz. BACARDI LIGHT RUM
¼ oz. Hiram Walker Cherry Flavored Brandy Pineapple Juice

Pour rum into a tall glass half filled with ice. Fill with pineapple juice and float cherry flavored brandy on top.

HEAT WAVE

1¼ oz. BACARDI SILVER or AMBER RUM
4 oz. Orange Juice

In a blender with ½ cup ice, blend until smooth. Pour into a 10 oz. glass. Serve immediately.

LUCKY LADY

¾ oz. BACARDI LIGHT RUM
¼ oz. Hiram Walker Anisette
¼ oz. Hiram Walker White Creme de Cacao
¾ oz. Cream

Mix in a shaker or blender with ice and strain into a cocktail glass.

MAI-TAI

¾ oz. BACARDI LIGHT RUM
¼ oz. BACARDI 151 RUM
½ oz. Hiram Walker Orange Curacao
½ oz. Rose's® Lime Juice
½ oz. Orgeat Syrup
½ oz. Simple Syrup

In an old-fashioned or stem glass half filled with cracked ice, put juice, syrups and orange curacao (or use Mai-Tai mix). Add rums and stir gently. Garnish with mint sprigs, pineapple spear and red cherry.

MIAMI SPECIAL

1 oz. BACARDI LIGHT RUM
¼ oz. Hiram Walker White Creme de Menthe
¾ oz. Lemon or Rose's® Lime Juice

Mix in a shaker or blender with ice and strain into a cocktail glass.

OLD SAN JUAN COCKTAIL

1¼ oz. BACARDI DARK RUM
¼ oz. Pineapple Juice
¼ oz. Rose's® Grenadine
½ oz. Lemon Juice or Rose's® Lime Juice

Stir in a mixing glass with ice and strain into a cocktail glass.

OLD SAN JUAN SIPPER

1 oz. BACARDI DARK RUM
¼ oz. Hiram Walker White Creme de Menthe
1 oz. Lemon Juice or Rose's® Lime Juice
¼ oz. Rose's® Grenadine

Mix in a shaker or blender with ice and strain into a cocktail glass.

PINA VERDE

1 oz. BACARDI LIGHT RUM
¼ oz. Hiram Walker Green Creme de Menthe
Pineapple Juice

Pour rum into a tall glass half filled with ice. Fill with pineapple juice and float the green creme de menthe on top.

PINK PANTHER

1¼ oz. BACARDI LIGHT RUM
¾ oz. Lemon Juice
¾ oz. Cream
½ oz. Rose's® Grenadine

Mix in a shaker or blender with ice and strain into a cocktail glass.

PLANTER'S PUNCH

1¼ oz. BACARDI LIGHT RUM
splsh BACARDI DARK RUM
2 tsp. Sugar
2 oz. Orange Juice
dash Rose's® Grenadine

Place sugar in shaker or blender and dissolve with fruit juice. Add rum, cracked ice and mix well or blend until frothy. Strain into an 8-ounce glass with cracked ice. Float dark rum on top. Garnish with orange and cherry.

RACER'S EDGE

1 oz. BACARDI LIGHT RUM
¼ oz. Hiram Walker Green Creme de Menthe
Grapefruit Juice

Pour rum into a tall glass half filled with ice. Fill with grapefruit juice and float the green creme de menthe on top.

RED HOT MAMA

1¼ oz. BACARDI SILVER RUM
4 oz. Cranberry Juice
2 oz. Chilled Club Soda

In a 10 oz. glass. Garnish with lime wedge.

RUDOLPH'S NOSE

1¼ oz. BACARDI SILVER OR AMBER RUM
Cranberry Juice
1½ oz. Lemon Juice
½ oz. Rose's® Grenadine

Mix in a tall glass. Add ice and garnish with lemon wedge.

RUM-TA-TUM

1½ cups BACARDI SILVER RUM
2 cups Pineapple Juice
½ cup Fresh Lemon Juice
½ oz. Rose's® Grenadine
1 liter Chilled Club Soda

In 2 ½ qt. pitcher, add ice cubes. Pour into 8 oz. glasses with ice. Garnish with half orange slices. Serves 8.

SAN JUAN COCKTAIL

1 oz. BACARDI LIGHT RUM
¼ oz. BACARDI 151 RUM
1 oz. Grapefruit Juice
½ oz. Lemon or Rose's® Lime Juice
¼ oz. Cream of Coconut

Mix light rum, juices and cream of coconut in a shaker or blender with ice. Strain into a cocktail glass and float the Bacardi 151 Rum on top.

SAN JUAN COLLINS

1 oz. BACARDI LIGHT RUM
¼ oz. Hiram Walker White Creme de Menthe
Lemon Juice
Sugar

Pour rum into a tall glass half filled with ice. Fill with lemon juice and sugar to taste. Float white creme de menthe on top and garnish with lemon slice and a red cherry.

SAN JUAN SUNSET

1 oz. BACARDI LIGHT RUM
¼ oz. Hiram Walker Cherry Flavored Brandy
Orange Juice

Pour rum into a tall glass half filled with ice. Fill with orange juice and float the cherry flavored brandy on top. Serve with straws.

SCORPION

10 oz. BACARDI SILVER RUM
½ oz. Bombay Gin
½ oz. Asbach Uralt
3 oz. White Wine

In glass pitcher, add Scorpion Mix according to directions or 2 oz. orgeat, 2 oz. orange juice, 4 oz. lemon juice and 1 mint sprig. Stir well. Add ice cubes. Refrigerate at least one hour. Pour into 6 oz. champagne glasses. Serves 4.

SLOE SUNSET

1 oz. BACARDI LIGHT RUM
¼ oz. Hiram Walker Sloe Gin
Orange Juice

Pour rum into a tall glass half filled with ice. Fill with orange juice and float the sloe gin on top.

TAILGATE

1¼ oz. BACARDI SILVER RUM
1 tsp. Sugar
3 oz. Hot Water

In 8 oz. mug or tankard. Fill with hot water and stir well. Add 1 twist lemon or orange peel.

TEXAS SUNDOWNER

1 oz. BACARDI LIGHT RUM
½ oz. Hiram Walker Anisette
½ oz. Rose's® Grenadine

Pour into an old-fashioned glass filled with ice.

TROPICAL STORM

1 oz. BACARDI LIGHT
RUM
¼ oz. Hiram Walker
Blackberry
Flavored Brandy
Grapefruit Juice

Pour rum into a tall glass half filled with ice. Fill with grapefruit juice and float the blackberry flavored brandy on top.

YELLOW BIRD

¾ oz. BACARDI RUM
¼ oz. Liquore Galliano
¼ oz. Hiram Walker
Creme de Banana
2 oz. Pineapple Juice
2 oz. Orange Juice

Shake well. Pour into a tall glass with ice cubes and decorate with a pineapple ring, cherry and orange slice.

ZOMBIE

¾ oz. BACARDI LIGHT
RUM
¼ oz. BACARDI DARK
RUM
¼ oz. BACARDI 151 RUM
1 oz. Pineapple Juice
1 oz. Orange Juice
1 oz. Lemon or
Rose's® Lime
Juice
1 tsp. Powdered Sugar
(optional)

Mix rums and juices with ice in a shaker or blender and pour into a tall glass. Garnish with a pineapple spear and red cherry. If desired, float ¼ tsp. Bacardi 151 Rum on top with 1 tsp. powdered sugar.

BAILEYS ORIGINAL IRISH CREAM LIQUEUR

The success of Baileys Original Irish Cream Liqueur is more than just the luck of the Irish. It is the creation of a mixture with the richness of cream, the tastes of vanilla, chocolate and other natural flavorings, and the spirit of fine Irish Whiskey.

Baileys is made from fresh dairy cream (not more than two hours old), Irish Whiskey, and natural flavorings. The mixture is then homogenized to ensure uniformity in every bottle, pasteurized to preserve freshness, and then cooled and bottled. The Irish Whiskey acts as a preservative for the cream, which is why Baileys does not have to be refrigerated, though it should be stored between 40 - 80 degrees Fahrenheit.

Baileys was introduced to the U.S. in 1979 after five years of painstaking research in dairy product technology. It is the first liqueur to successfully create a blend of *real* cream and spirits that is shelf-stable. Baileys has spawned a slew of imitators, but none of them have succeeded in capturing America's imagination — and taste buds — as has Baileys Original Irish Cream Liqueur.

Baileys now has annual sales of one million cases in the U.S. Studies show that it is largely word-of-mouth recommendations that have helped create Baileys' faithful following. One recent survey showed that 60% of the people who try Baileys will buy a bottle.

Most people consume Baileys straight up or on-the-rocks, though it is increasingly being used for a variety of mixed drinks. In winter it is often mixed with coffee or hot chocolate. Summer time consumption is moving to Baileys being blended with cream and crushed ice. Also it is being blended with a scoop of ice cream into a cool thick malt. The following recipes show the surprising versatility of Baileys.

Baileys is imported into the U.S. by The Paddington Corporation, Fort Lee, NJ. Paddington is a subsidiary of Grand Metropolitan, a British conglomerate, which is one of the largest wine and spirit companies in the world.

"B" ORIGINAL

The traditional way to enjoy BAILEYS ORIGINAL IRISH CREAM is to serve a double measure in its own glass at room temperature.

BAILEYS COFFEE

Add a generous pour of BAILEYS ORIGINAL IRISH CREAM to create the perfect blend of coffee. Top with fresh whipped cream and sprinkle with shaved chocolate.

50-50 BAR

1 oz. BAILEYS ORIGINAL
   IRISH CREAM
1 oz. Kahlua
   splsh Bacardi 151 Rum

Float rum; serve as a shooter.

AFTER 5

½ oz. BAILEYS ORIGINAL
   IRISH CREAM
½ oz. Hiram Walker
   Peppermint
   Schnapps
½ oz. Kahlua

Layer first Kahlua, schnapps, then Baileys as a shot or on the rocks.

AFTER 8

1 part BAILEYS ORIGINAL
   IRISH CREAM
1 part Hiram Walker
   Coffee Flavored
   Brandy
1 part Hiram Walker
   Green Creme de
   Menthe

Shake. Serve straight in shot glass.

AFTER SIX SHOOTER

   BAILEYS ORIGINAL
   IRISH CREAM
1 shot Kahlua
1 shot Hiram Walker
   White Creme de
   Menthe

In a pony/cordial glass, top with Baileys.

B-52

1 part BAILEYS ORIGINAL
   IRISH CREAM
1 part Kahlua
1 part Hiram Walker
   Orange Curacao

Layer into a small snifter or large shot glass.

BAIL-OUT aka IRISH BULLDOG

1 oz. BAILEYS ORIGINAL
   IRISH CREAM
1 oz. Absolut Vodka

Serve over ice in rocks glass.

BAILEYS ALEXANDER

1 oz. BAILEYS ORIGINAL
   IRISH CREAM
1 oz. Hiram Walker
   White Creme de
   Cacao
1 oz. Cream

Blend with ice until smooth, serve straight up.

BAILEYS BLIZZARD

1 oz. BAILEYS ORIGINAL
   IRISH CREAM
1 oz. Hiram Walker
   Peppermint
   Schnapps
½ oz. Asbach Uralt
   scp. Vanilla Ice Cream

Blend until smooth. Serve straight up.

BAILEYS CHOCOLATE COVERED CHERRY

1 oz. BAILEYS ORIGINAL
   IRISH CREAM
¼ oz. Kahlua
¼ oz. Rose's® Grenadine

Layer, first grenadine, Kahlua, then Baileys. As a shot or on the rocks.

BAILEYS COCONUT FRAPPE

¾ oz. BAILEYS ORIGINAL IRISH CREAM
½ oz. Malibu Rum Liqueur
¾ oz. Milk

Shake or blend until frothy, then pour over ice and garnish with toasted coconut.

BAILEYS COMET

1 oz. BAILEYS ORIGINAL IRISH CREAM
1 oz. Kahlua
Cream

Fill with cream, serve over ice.

BAILEYS CREAM DREAM

1¼ oz. BAILEYS ORIGINAL IRISH CREAM
3 oz. Half & Half

Blend with ½ cup crushed ice for 60 seconds.

BAILEYS CUDDLER

1 oz. BAILEYS ORIGINAL IRISH CREAM
½ oz. Hiram Walker Amaretto

Combine ingredients for a truly spirited pleasure.

BAILEYS DREAM SHAKE

1¼ oz. BAILEYS ORIGINAL IRISH CREAM
2 scps. Vanilla Ice Cream

Blend for 60 seconds.

BAILEYS EGGNOG

1 oz. BAILEYS ORIGINAL IRISH CREAM
¼ oz. Jameson Irish Whiskey
1 Egg
2 cups Milk
Nutmeg

Mix with cracked ice in a shaker, strain and serve in tall glasses. Sprinkle nutmeg.

BAILEYS FIZZ

1¼ oz. BAILEYS ORIGINAL IRISH CREAM
Club Soda

Combine ingredients and pour over crushed ice.

BAILEYS FLOAT

1¼ oz. BAILEYS ORIGINAL IRISH CREAM
2 scps. Softened Ice Cream

Blend ingredients until frothy. Top with one more scoop of ice cream.

BAILEYS HOT MILK PUNCH

1 oz. BAILEYS ORIGINAL IRISH CREAM
¼ oz. Cognac
1½ tsp. Sugar
Hot Milk
dash Freshly Ground Nutmeg

Combine liquors to dissolve sugar. Add hot milk and stir. Sprinkle with nutmeg.

BAILEYS IRISH COFFEE

1 oz. BAILEYS ORIGINAL
IRISH CREAM
¼ oz. Jameson Irish
Whiskey
Fresh Coffee
Whipped
Sweetened Cream

After brewing coffee, combine with Baileys and whiskey. Top with cream.

BAILEYS ITALIAN DREAM

1¼ oz. BAILEYS ORIGINAL
IRISH CREAM
½ oz. Hiram Walker
Amaretto
3 oz. Half & Half

Blend with ½ cup crushed ice for 60 seconds.

BAILEYS MINT KISS

¾ oz. BAILEYS ORIGINAL
IRISH CREAM
¼ oz. Hiram Walker
Peppermint
Schnapps

Top with fresh whipped cream.

BAILEYS MIST

2 oz. BAILEYS ORIGINAL
IRISH CREAM

Pour in a glass filled with crushed ice.

BAILEYS MOCHA CREAM

2 oz. BAILEYS ORIGINAL
IRISH CREAM
2 tbs. Chocolate Syrup
5 oz. Hot Coffee

Fill with coffee, top with whipped cream.

BAILEYS PRALINE SUPREME

1 oz. BAILEYS ORIGINAL
IRISH CREAM
½ oz. Hiram Walker
Amaretto
5 oz. Coffee

Fill with coffee. Top with whipped cream and cinnamon.

BAILEYS ROMA

1 part BAILEYS ORIGINAL
IRISH CREAM
1 part Sambuca Romana

Serve over ice.

BAILEYS SHILLELAGH

1 oz. BAILEYS ORIGINAL
IRISH CREAM
¼ oz. Jameson Irish
Whiskey
4 oz. Strong Coffee
1 tbs. Heavy Cream

Moisten rim of glass with drop of Irish Whiskey, and sugar-frost rim. Pour Baileys, whiskey, and coffee into prepared glass, stir well. Top with whipped cream and green cherry.

BARNUM & BAILEY

1 oz. BAILEYS ORIGINAL
IRISH CREAM
¼ oz. Hiram Walker
Apricot Flavored
Brandy
1 tsp. Bombay Gin

Combine in a shaker, strain into chilled cocktail glass. Garnish drink with clown face by floating cherry in center (nose) and one miniature marshmallow on each side (eyes).

BARNUMENTHE & BAILEYS

1 oz. BAILEYS ORIGINAL IRISH CREAM
¼ oz. Hiram Walker White Creme de Menthe

In a rocks glass over cracked ice.

BERRY BAILEYS

1¼ oz. BAILEYS ORIGINAL IRISH CREAM
2-3 oz. Strawberries

Blend with ice until smooth and frothy.

BIT O'HONEY

1 oz. BAILEYS ORIGINAL IRISH CREAM
1 oz. Hiram Walker Green Creme de Menthe
scp. Vanilla Ice Cream

Blend until smooth and frothy.

BUSHWACKER

1 oz. BAILEYS ORIGINAL IRISH CREAM
1 oz. Jameson Irish Whiskey

Serve over ice in rocks glass.

CAFE ROMA

½ oz. BAILEYS ORIGINAL IRISH CREAM
½ oz. Malibu Rum Liqueur
½ oz. Hiram Walker Amaretto
Hot Coffee

Serve with coffee and topped with cream.

CALIFORNIA SHOT

½ oz. BAILEYS ORIGINAL IRISH CREAM
½ oz. Sauza Conmemorativo Tequila
splsh Coffee

Serve in shot glass.

COFFEE BEANS

½ oz. BAILEYS ORIGINAL IRISH CREAM
½ oz. Kahlua
½ oz. Hiram Walker Amaretto
Coffee

Fill with coffee. Top with whipped cream and cinnamon.

DUBLIN HANDSHAKE

¾ oz. BAILEYS ORIGINAL IRISH CREAM
¼ oz. Jameson Irish Whiskey
¼ oz. Hiram Walker Sloe Gin

Shake with crushed ice. Strain into cocktail glass.

EMERALD ISLE

1 oz. BAILEYS ORIGINAL IRISH CREAM
1 oz. Asbach Uralt
splsh Cream

Serve over ice.

EYES R SMILIN

½ oz. BAILEYS ORIGINAL IRISH CREAM
¼ oz. Absolut Vodka
¼ oz. Bombay Gin
¼ oz. Hiram Walker Triple Sec

Build over ice, stir and serve.

FIFTH AVENUE

¾ oz. BAILEYS ORIGINAL IRISH CREAM
¼ oz. Hiram Walker Apricot Flavored Brandy
¼ oz. Hiram Walker White Creme de Cacao

Shake with ice. Strain into cocktail glass.

HOT MINT KISS

1 oz. BAILEYS ORIGINAL IRISH CREAM
½ oz. Hiram Walker Peppermint Schnapps
5 oz. Coffee

Fill with hot coffee, top with whipped cream.

IRISH COCONUT

1 part BAILEYS ORIGINAL IRISH CREAM
1 part Malibu Rum Liqueur

Shake with ice and serve on the rocks.

IRISH DREAM

¾ oz. BAILEYS ORIGINAL IRISH CREAM
¼ oz. Jameson Irish Whiskey
¼ oz. Hiram Walker White Creme de Cacao

Shake well with ice and serve on the rocks.

IRISH RULE

1 part BAILEYS ORIGINAL IRISH CREAM
1 part Irish Mist

Stir on the rocks.

NUTCRACKER SWEET

1 oz. BAILEYS ORIGINAL IRISH CREAM
1 oz. Hiram Walker Amaretto
½ oz. Caramel Liqueur

Mix and serve over ice.

O'CASEY SCOTCH TERRIER

1 part BAILEYS ORIGINAL IRISH CREAM
1 part J&B Scotch

Stir well on the rocks.

ORGASM NO. 1

¾ oz. BAILEYS ORIGINAL IRISH CREAM
¾ oz. Hiram Walker Amaretto

Combine in a shaker with 3 to 4 ice cubes and strain into glass.

ORGASM NO. 2

1 part BAILEYS ORIGINAL IRISH CREAM
1 part Kahlua
1 part Absolut Vodka

Blend ingredients with ice. Strain into a chilled cocktail or stemmed glass. No garnish.

PAINT THINNER

1 shot BAILEYS ORIGINAL
   IRISH CREAM
1 part Bacardi Dark Rum
   Hot Coffee

In a collins glass, fill with hot coffee.

PEACHES N' CREAM

1¼ oz. BAILEYS ORIGINAL
   IRISH CREAM
1 oz. Hiram Walker
   Peach Schnapps
   splsh Cream
   splsh Soda

Serve over ice with a splash of cream and soda.

POND SCUM

½ oz. BAILEYS ORIGINAL
   IRISH CREAM
¾ oz. Absolut Vodka
3 oz. Club Soda

Float Baileys on top.

RUSSIAN QUAALUDE

1 oz. BAILEYS ORIGINAL
   IRISH CREAM
1 oz. Absolut Vodka

Serve over ice in rocks glass.

SCHNAPPY SHILLELAGH

¾ oz. BAILEYS ORIGINAL
   IRISH CREAM
½ oz. Hiram Walker
   Peppermint
   Schnapps

Stir well on the rocks.

SCREAMING ORGASM

1 part BAILEYS ORIGINAL
   IRISH CREAM
1 part Absolut Vodka
1 part Kahlua
1 part Hiram Walker
   Amaretto

Blend ingredients with ice and pour into a chilled rocks glass.

SLIPPERY NIPPLE

1 oz. BAILEYS ORIGINAL
   IRISH CREAM
1 oz. Sambuca Romana

Serve in shot glass or on the rocks. Add coffee to make **Hot Slippery Nipple.**

SUPER BOWL COCKTAIL/ REFEREE'S REVENGE

¾ oz. BAILEYS ORIGINAL
   IRISH CREAM
¾ oz. Frangelico
3 oz. Vanilla Ice Cream
1 oz. Orange Juice
1 Oreo cookie

Combine in blender. Pour unstrained into chilled old-fashioned glass. Accompany with cookie.

THE IRISH ITALIAN CONNECTION

1 oz. BAILEYS ORIGINAL
   IRISH CREAM
1 oz. Hiram Walker
   Amaretto
3 oz. Cream

Serve over ice in rocks glass.

THE NUTTY IRISHMAN

1 part BAILEYS ORIGINAL
  IRISH CREAM
1 part Hiram Walker
  Hazelnut Liqueur

Shake well and pour over ice.

THREE LEAF CLOVER

1 oz. BAILEY'S ORIGINAL
  IRISH CREAM
¼ oz. Jameson Irish
  Whiskey
¼ oz. Irish Mist

Shake with ice and serve on the rocks.

TIDY BOWL

1/8 oz. BAILEYS ORIGINAL
  IRISH CREAM
1/8 oz. Hiram Walker
  Spearmint
  Schnapps
1 oz. Hiram Walker Blue
  Curacao

Served in a cordial glass.

TINKER'S TEA

1¼ oz. BAILEYS ORIGINAL
  IRISH CREAM
  Hot Tea

Pour Baileys in mug or cup. Fill with hot tea.

TOOTSIE ROLL

½ oz. BAILEYS ORIGINAL
  IRISH CREAM
1 oz. Hiram Walker
  Root Beer
  Schnapps

Topped with Baileys (not too much, just a dash).

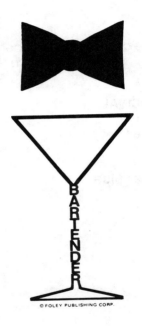

© FOLEY PUBLISHING CORP.

BOMBAY DRY GIN

It all started with a Dutch professor of medicine. Franciscus de la Boe is credited with being the originator of the botanical flavoured spirit known as gin. He called it "Essence de Genievre" because of its strong juniper aroma. This later became known as "Geneva."

Originally used as a medicine for Dutch Travellers to the East Indies, gin was popularized in the 16th century by English soldiers returning from the wars in the Low Countries. They used the spirit for other than medicinal purposes. English distillers soon began to make it for themselves by a distillation in pot stills.

In 1743, new legislation was drawn up and reinforced in 1751 which increased the duty on spirits and controlled the sale of gin. This measure led to higher quality gins and brought respect to the distillers at the same time.

In 1830, Aeneas Coffey introduced his continuous still which provided a means of obtaining rectified spirit for re-distillation with botanicals. This new still produced a lighter, cleaner spirit which became the basis of the subtly flavoured unsweetened gin which we know today as London Dry Gin. Of which Bombay is one of the most sophisticated.

An 86 proof, extraordinarily dry and distinctive British gin produced by International Distillers and Vintners, Ltd., Bombay is the fastest growing imported gin in America.

The recipe for Bombay Gin dates back to 1761, and the botanicals — including coriander, lemon peel, angelica, licorice, anise, juniper, almonds and cassia bark— are imported from around the world. The spirit used in Bombay's production comes from a distillery in Ayrshire, Scotland and the soft, pure water is drawn from the Welsh hills.

Bombay owes its growing success to a unique distillation process. Ordinary gins are distilled by heating the spirit and botanicals together in specially designed stills. To produce Bombay, the botanicals are placed inside individual compartments in a rack or basket. By positioning this basket at the end of the swan neck near the condenser, the spirit vapour passing through the rack acquires the flavour of the selected natural ingredients. It's this unique process that gives Bombay its soft, light, distinctive flavour. Finally, the slow, unhurried process of the distillation ensures the consistently high standard of Bombay Gin.

BOMBAY GIN MARTINI
1½ oz. BOMBAY GIN
dash Martini & Rossi Extra Dry Vermouth

Stir in cocktail glass with ice. Strain and serve straight up or on the rocks with some ice in cocktail glass. Add lemon twist or olive. OR: Shake and strain and serve up or on the rocks with some ice.

Many customers and Bartenders agree that shaking will ruin a Martini because of the slight taste of the metal from the shaker. Use your own judgement!

Below are a few variations:

CORNET:	Replace Vermouth with Port Wine
DEWEY:	Add dash orange bitters
DILLATINI:	Dilly Beam (try and find one)
ELEGANT:	Add dash Grand Marnier
FASCINATOR:	Add dash Pernod and sprig mint
GIBSON:	Add onion
GIMLET:	Replace Vermouth with Rose's® Lime Juice. Garnish with lime
GYPSY:	Add cherry
HOMESTEAD:	Add orange slice muddled
ITALIAN:	Replace Vermouth with Hiram Walker Amaretto
JACKSON:	Replace Vermouth with Dubonnet and dash of bitters
LADIES' CHOICE:	Add ¼ oz. Hiram Walker Kummel
LONE TREE:	Add dash lemon juice
MICKEY FINN:	Add splash of Hiram Walker White Creme de Menthe, garnish with mint
NAKED MARTINI:	Just Bombay Gin
NAVAL COCKTAIL:	Replace Extra Dry with Rosso Vermouth, add onion and twist
ORANGETINI:	Add splash of Hiram Walker Triple Sec and orange peel
PERFECTION:	Replace Extra Dry Vermouth with Rosso Vermouth
QUEEN ELIZABETH:	Add splash Benedictine
RICHMOND:	Replace Vermouth with Lillet, add twist of lemon
ROSA:	Add Hiram Walker Cherry Flavored Brandy
ROSALIN RUSSELL:	Replace Vermouth with Aquavit
ROSELYN:	Add Rose's® Grenadine and lemon twist
SAKITINI:	Replace Vermouth with Sake
SILVER BULLET:	Float J&B Scotch on top
SOUR KISSES:	Add egg white, SHAKE
TRINITY aka TRIO, PLAZA:	Replace Extra Dry Vermouth with half Rosso and half Extra Dry. Equal parts of Vermouth and Bombay Gin
VELOCITY:	Add orange slice and SHAKE
WALLICK:	Add dash of Hiram Walker Orange Curacao
WARDEN:	Add dash of Pernod

APPARENT

¾ oz. BOMBAY GIN
¾ oz. Hiram Walker
White Creme de
Cacao
dash Pernod

Shake. Serve over rocks.

BERMUDA ROSE

1 oz. BOMBAY GIN
¼ oz. Hiram Walker
Apricot Flavored
Brandy
½ oz. Rose's® Lime
Juice
dash Rose's® Grenadine

Shake. Strain into cocktail glass.

BLUE LADY

1 oz. BOMBAY GIN
¼ oz. The Original Blue
Juice
1 oz. Lemon Mix

Shake, serve over ice.

BOMBAY GRAND

1 oz. BOMBAY GIN
¼ oz. Grand Marnier
1 oz. Lemon Juice

Shake. Serve over ice. Garnish with orange slice.

BRONX COCKTAIL

½ oz. BOMBAY GIN
2 tsp. Martini & Rossi
Extra Dry
Vermouth
2 tsp. Martini & Rossi
Rosso Vermouth
2 oz. Orange Juice

Shake with ice. Serve over the rocks.

CLARIDGE

½ oz. BOMBAY GIN
¼ oz. Martini & Rossi
Extra Dry
Vermouth
¼ oz. Hiram Walker
Triple Sec
¼ oz. Hiram Walker
Apricot Flavored
Brandy

Stir. Serve on the rocks.

CREST OF THE WAVE

1¼ oz. BOMBAY GIN
Grapefruit Juice
Cranberry Juice

In a tall glass with ice, fill with half grapefruit juice and half cranberry juice.

CROSS BOW

¾ oz. BOMBAY GIN
¼ oz. Hiram Walker
Triple Sec
¼ oz. Hiram Walker
White Creme de
Cacao

Shake. Serve on the rocks.

EVERYTHING

1 oz. BOMBAY GIN
½ oz. Martini & Rossi
Extra Dry
Vermouth
½ oz. Martini & Rossi
Rosso Vermouth
dash Hiram Walker
White Creme de
Menthe
2 dshs Bitters

Stir on the rocks.

FALLEN ANGEL

½ oz. BOMBAY GIN
½ oz. Hiram Walker
  Apricot Flavored
  Brandy
¼ oz. Asbach Uralt

Shake, serve up.

GIN ALEXANDER

1 part BOMBAY GIN
1 part Hiram Walker
  White Creme de
  Cacao
3 parts Half & Half

Shake with ice and serve up or on the rocks. Dust with nutmeg.

GIN AND CRAN

1¼ oz. BOMBAY GIN
2½ oz. Cranberry Juice

Serve over the rocks.

GIN AND SIN

1¼ oz. BOMBAY GIN
¼ oz. Orange Juice
¼ oz. Lemon Juice
2 dshs Rose's® Grenadine

Shake gin, orange juice, lemon juice and grenadine with ice. Strain into a chilled cocktail glass.

GIN AND TONIC

1¼ oz. BOMBAY GIN
  Tonic

In a tall glass filled with ice, add gin and fill with tonic. Add squeeze of lime.

GIN CASSIS

3 parts BOMBAY GIN
1 part Hiram Walker
  Creme de Cassis

Stir on the rocks.

GIN COCKTAIL
aka DUBONNET COCKTAIL

1 part BOMBAY GIN
2 parts Dubonnet

Stir on the rocks. Add lemon twist.

GIN DRIVER

1¼ oz. BOMBAY GIN
4 oz. Orange Juice
  Tonic Water

In a tall glass filled with ice, add gin and orange juice. Fill with tonic water.

GIN JULEP

1¼ oz. BOMBAY GIN
4 sprgs Mint
I tsp. Sugar

In a highball glass filled with shaved ice, stir until glass is frosted. Garnish with fresh mint.

GIN OLD FASHIONED

1¼ oz. BOMBAY GIN
2 dshs Bitters
¼ tsp. Sugar
  Club Soda

Crush (muddle) orange slice and cherry on bottom of rock glass. Add ingredients, fill with ice and club soda.

GIN RICKEY

1¼ oz. BOMBAY GIN
  Club Soda

In a tall glass filled with ice, add gin and fill with club soda. Add squeeze of lime.

GIN SCREWDRIVER

1¼ oz. BOMBAY GIN
  Orange Juice

In a tall glass filled with ice, add gin and fill with orange juice.

GIN SIDECAR

1	oz. BOMBAY GIN
1/4	oz. Hiram Walker Triple Sec
1/4	oz. Lemon Juice

Shake with ice and serve on the rocks or up in a sugar rimmed glass.

GIN SOUR

1 1/4	oz. BOMBAY GIN
1	oz. Sweetened Lemon Mix
1	oz. Orange Juice

Shake with ice. Serve up or on the rocks. Garnish with orange slice and cherry.

GIN SOUTHERN

1	oz. BOMBAY GIN
1/4	oz. Southern Comfort
1 1/4	oz. Grapefruit Juice

Stir on the rocks.

GIN SPIDER

1 1/4	oz. BOMBAY GIN
	dash Bitters
	Ginger Ale

In a tall glass filled with ice, add gin and bitters and fill with ginger ale.

GIN STINGER

| 1 | oz. BOMBAY GIN |
| 1/4 | oz. Hiram Walker White Creme de Menthe |

Stir well on the rocks.

GOLDEN BILL

2	parts BOMBAY GIN
1	part Hiram Walker Apricot Flavored Brandy
2	parts Orange Juice

Stir on the rocks.

GOLDEN GIRL

1	oz. BOMBAY GIN
1/4	oz. Sherry
	dash Bitters

Stir well on the rocks.

GREEN DRAGON

1	oz. BOMBAY GIN
1/4	oz. Hiram Walker Green Creme de Menthe
1/4	oz. Hiram Walker Kummel
1/4	oz. Lemon Juice

Shake well with ice cubes and strain into cocktail glass.

JOHN BULL

1 1/4	oz. BOMBAY GIN
3	oz. Beef Boullion
	Juice of 1/2 Lemon
	dash Worcestershire Sauce
	dash Pepper

Stir over ice cubes.

MINT COOLER

1	oz. BOMBAY GIN
1/4	oz. Hiram Walker Peppermint Schnapps
	Club Soda

Pour in tall glass with ice and fill with club soda.

MOONSHOT
1¼ oz. BOMBAY GIN
3   oz. Clam Juice
     dash Red Pepper Sauce
Stir over ice cubes.

ORANGE BLOSSOM
1¼ oz. BOMBAY GIN
1   oz. Sweetened
     Lemon Mix
2   oz. Orange Juice
Shake with ice and pour on the rocks.

ORANGE SUNSET
1   oz. BOMBAY GIN
¼   oz. Hiram Walker
     Banana Flavored
     Liqueur
1   oz. Sweetened
     Lemon Mix
1   oz. Orange Juice
Shake well with ice and serve on the rocks.

PINK LADY
1¼ oz. BOMBAY GIN
2   tsp. Rose's® Grenadine
3   oz. Half & Half
Shake with ice and strain into cocktail glass or serve on the rocks.

POLO
1¼ oz. BOMBAY GIN
     Grapefruit Juice
     Orange Juice
In a tall glass with ice, fill with half grapefruit juice and half orange juice.

SALTY DOG
1¼ oz. BOMBAY GIN
     Grapefruit Juice
     Salt
Wet rim of tall glass with juice or water and dip into salt to coat (optional). Pour gin over ice, fill with grapefruit juice and stir.

SEE-THRU
1¼ oz. BOMBAY GIN
Pour over lots of ice.

SINGAPORE SLING
1¼ oz. BOMBAY GIN
½   oz. Hiram Walker
     Cherry Flavored
     Brandy
3   dshs Benedictine
     dash Rose's® Grenadine
     Sweetened
     Lemon Mix
     Club Soda

Shake all ingredients with ice (except club soda and Benedictine). Fill tall glass, top with club soda and float Benedictine.

SLIM GIN
1¼ oz. BOMBAY GIN
Your favorite diet soda in a tall glass filled with ice.

THE GUIDO
1¼ oz. BOMBAY GIN
     dash Campari
2   oz. Grapefruit Juice
Shake. Pour over ice.

THE SURE GIN FIZZ
¾   oz. BOMBAY GIN
¾   oz. Hiram Walker Sloe
      Gin
2   oz. Sweetened
      Lemon Mix
      Club Soda

Shake with ice. Serve in a tall glass filled with ice. Top with club soda.

THE YELLOW FELLOW
1   oz. BOMBAY GIN
¼   oz. Yellow Chartreuse

Shake, strain into cocktail glass.

TOM COLLINS
1¼   oz. BOMBAY GIN
      Sweetened
      Lemon Mix
      Club Soda

Shake gin and lemon mix with ice, fill tall glass. Add club soda. Garnish with cherry and orange slice.

TROPICAL GIN
1¼   oz. BOMBAY GIN
½   cup Melon Cubes,
      Fresh or Frozen
1   tsp. Rose's® Lime
      Juice

In a blender with ⅓ cup crushed ice, blend until smooth. Pour over ice in chilled goblet. Garnish with a slice of lime.

VELVET CROWN
1¼   oz. BOMBAY GIN
3   oz. Grape Juice
      Juice of ½ Lemon

Pour over ice in a highball glass. Splash with soda.

WHITE LADY
2 parts BOMBAY GIN
1 part Hiram Walker
      Triple Sec
1 part Sweetened
      Lemon Mix

Shake well with ice and serve on the rocks.

B&B/BENEDICTINE LIQUEURS

People have been sharing Benedictine since 1510 when it was created by Dom Bernardo Vincelli at an Abbey in Fecamp, France. Dom Bernardo's elixir was believed to have magical healing properties and was offered to travelers and guests at the Abbey. One particular guest, King Francois I, gave his approval to Benedictine, exclaiming, "Upon my soul, I never tasted better!", recognizing another of Benedictine's attributes — its unique taste. Dom Bernardo dedicated his elixir, "D.O.M.," or "Deo Optimo Maximo," Latin for "To God, Most Good, Most Great." Dom Bernardo's secret was guarded by the monks and handed down through the generations. Unfortunately, it was lost when the Abbey was destroyed in 1789 during the French Revolution.

The recipe was rediscovered 75 years later by Alexandre Le Grand, a local wine merchant and collector of religious artifacts. Le Grand was fascinated by the recipe's list of exotic ingredients. So he made a small quantity in a miniature still and arrived at a recipe that called for 27 ingredients including hyssop, myrrh, lemon rind, aloe and angelica seeds. He steeped these various herbs and spices in brandies and distilled them to create four distinct spirits. After aging them separately, he blended the four to create the final liqueur, which returned to the casks until the flavors were properly "married." The result was miraculous — a deep, honeyed liqueur with a rich, aromatic bouquet. The ingredients and process are so essential to this character that Benedictine continues to be made the same today as it was in Alexandre Le Grand's day.

In the 1930's, Benedictine inspired the creation of a new liqueur. It happened at the 21 Club in New York

City when the Bartender mixed Benedictine with brandy and called it B&B. B&B quickly became the rage. So much so, the House of Benedictine began making it themselves. But with a difference. They allowed their blend of Benedictine and fine Cognac Brandy to age in oaken casks until the two flavors "married" and achieved the proper balance. The Americans agreed and B&B soon began outselling the popular Benedictine.

B&B ALEXANDER
1¼   oz. B&B
¾   oz. Cream
Shake with ice. Strain into cocktail glass.

B&B AMERICANO
1   oz. B&B
¼   oz. Wild Turkey 101
Serve in an old-fashioned glass.

B&B AND TEA
1¼   oz. B&B
     Hot Tea
Serve in a mug or cup.

B&B AND TONIC
1¼   oz. B&B
     Tonic
In a tall glass with ice, fill with tonic. Add squeeze of lemon.

B&B CAFE
1¼   oz. B&B
4   oz. Hot Coffee
¼   cup Unsweetened
     Whipped Cream
Pour B&B and hot coffee into a coffee cup. Top with whipped cream and serve immediately.

B&B COLLINS
¼   oz. B&B
1   oz. Cognac
1   tsp. Sugar Syrup
1   tsp. Lemon Juice
     Club Soda
Combine cognac, juice and sugar syrup with ice. Shake and strain, add ice and club soda. Float B&B on top. Garnish with lemon slice.

B&B FLOAT
1¼   oz. B&B
     Cream
Pour B&B into cordial glass, pour cream very slowly down side of glass or over back of teaspoon, just touching B&B.

B&B MANHATTAN
1   oz. B&B
¼   oz. Martini & Rossi
     Extra Dry
     Vermouth
Stir. Serve straight up or on the rocks.

B&B MIST
1¼   oz. B&B
Serve in an old-fashioned glass over crushed ice. If preferred, add twist of lemon or lime.

B&B STINGER
1   oz. B&B
¼   oz. Hiram Walker
     White Creme de
     Menthe
Blend with ice and strain over the rocks in an old-fashioned glass.

BEWITCHED
1   part B&B
1   part Absolut Vodka
1   part Cream
Pour ingredients in order listed in cocktail glass. Stir.

BRIGHTON PUNCH

¾ oz. B&B
½ oz. Wild Turkey 101
2 tsp. Lemon Juice
 Club Soda

Combine all but club soda in shaker with ice. Strain, add ice and fill with club soda. Garnish with orange and lemon slice.

CHAMPAGNE CUPID

1 oz. B&B
 Champagne

In a large chilled champagne glass, pour B&B and fill with champagne.

EROS

1 part B&B
1 part Bombay Gin

Stir gently, chill and serve in a cocktail glass. Garnish with twist of lemon.

FRENCH GOLD

1 part B&B
1 part Hiram Walker
 White Creme de
 Cacao
½ part Orange Juice

Mix over ice in an old-fashioned glass.

JE TAIME

¾ oz. B&B
¾ oz. Absolut Vodka

Serve straight up or on the rocks.

MIDNIGHT ENCOUNTER

1¼ oz. B&B
 Orange Juice

In a tall glass with ice, fill with orange juice.

THE FRENCH SPRING

1¼ oz. B&B
 Sparkling Water

In a wine glass filled with ice, add B&B. Fill with sparkling water and garnish with slice of lemon.

WIDOW'S KISS

1¼ oz. B&B
¼ oz. Yellow Chartreuse
 dash Bitters

Combine in shaker with ice. Strain into cocktail glass, garnish with a strawberry.

B AND TEA

1¼ oz. BENEDICTINE
 Hot Tea

Serve in mug or cup.

BENEDICT

1 part BENEDICTINE
1 part J&B Scotch
1 part Ginger Ale

Pour over ice. Fill with ginger ale.

BENEDICTINE COCKTAIL

1¼ oz. BENEDICTINE
1 dash Bitters
 Powdered Sugar
½ Lemon

Combine Benedictine with bitters, shake. Rub lemon around rim of glass, press in powdered sugar. Drop a cherry in glass, add ingredients with ice.

BENEDICTINE MIST

1¼   oz. BENEDICTINE

Serve in an old-fashioned glass over crushed ice. If preferred, add twist of lemon or lime.

BONBON

¼   oz. BENEDICTINE
½   oz. J&B Scotch
½   oz. Martini & Rossi Rosso Vermouth

Stir with cracked ice and strain into cocktail glass. Add twist of lemon.

CHINCHILLA

1   part BENEDICTINE
1   part Hiram Walker Triple Sec
1   part Cream

Combine in shaker with cracked ice. Strain into cocktail glass.

CREOLE

¼   oz. BENEDICTINE
½   oz. Seagram's V.O.
½   oz. Martini & Rossi Rosso Vermouth
1   dash Amer Picon

Combine with ice in shaker and strain. Add ice and twist of lemon.

CUCUMBER COOL

1   oz. BENEDICTINE
3   oz. Champagne
2   tsp. Lemon Juice
1   Cucumber Peel

Pour Benedictine and lemon juice over peel. Add champagne and stir gently.

FRISCO SOUR

¼   oz. BENEDICTINE
1   oz. Wild Turkey 101
¼   oz. Lemon Juice
¼   oz. Rose's® Lime Juice

Shake. Strain into cocktail glass. Garnish with slice of lemon and lime.

FRISCO TROLLEY

1   oz. BENEDICTINE
¼   oz. Seagram's V.O.
2   tsp. Lemon Juice

Combine in shaker with ice. Strain into cocktail glass.

GIN BENEDICTINE SANGAREE

¼   oz. BENEDICTINE
1   oz. Bombay Gin
2   tsp. Grapefruit Juice

Combine with ice, shake well. Strain, add ice. Garnish with a slice of lemon and nutmeg.

GYPSY MOTH

½   oz. BENEDICTINE
¾   oz. Absolut Vodka
1   tsp. Lemon Juice
1   tsp. Orange Juice

Combine in shaker with ice. Strain into cocktail glass, garnish with orange slice.

HONEYMOON COCKTAIL

½   oz. BENEDICTINE
½   oz. Apple Brandy
¼   oz. Hiram Walker Triple Sec
   Juice of ½ Lemon

Shake well with cracked ice and strain into cocktail glass.

HONOLULU COCKTAIL
1 part BENEDICTINE
1 part Bombay Gin
1 part Cherry Juice
Stir well with cracked ice and strain into cocktail glass.

KENTUCKY COLONEL
1/4 oz. BENEDICTINE
1 oz. Wild Turkey 101
Combine in shaker with ice. Strain into cocktail glass.

MAR DEL PLATA
1/4 oz. BENEDICTINE
1/2 oz. Bombay Gin
1/2 oz. Martini & Rossi
Extra Dry
Vermouth
1 dash Grand Marnier
Stir. Add twist of lemon.

MONA LISA
1 part BENEDICTINE
1 part Hiram Walker
Orange Curacao
1 part Amer Picon
1 tbs. Double Cream
Shake. Sprinkle cinnamon on top.

RAFFLES BAR SLING
1/4 oz. BENEDICTINE
3/4 oz. Bombay Gin
1/4 oz. Hiram Walker
Cherry Flavored
Brandy
2 dshs Bitters
1/2 tsp. Rose's® Lime
Juice
Ginger Beer
Combine spirits, bitters, lime juice with ice in highball glass. Stir in ginger beer. Float Benedictine on top. Garnish with mint.

ROYALIST
1/2 oz. BENEDICTINE
1/2 oz. Martini & Rossi
Extra Dry
Vermouth
1/4 oz. Wild Turkey 101
1 dash Peach Bitters
Stir.

SAVOY HOTEL
(Pousse Cafe)
1 part BENEDICTINE
1 part Hiram Walker
White Creme de
Cacao
1 part Asbach Uralt
Float one liqueur over another in order of ingredients listed.

STRAITS SLING
1/4 oz. BENEDICTINE
3/4 oz. Bombay Gin
1/4 oz. Hiram Walker
Cherry Flavored
Brandy
Juice of 1 Lemon
2 dshs Bitters
2 dshs Orange Bitters
Soda Water
Shake all but soda water together. Strain into highball glass with ice. Stir in soda water. Garnish with lemon slice.

WIDOW'S DREAM COCKTAIL
1 1/4 oz. BENEDICTINE
1 Egg
1 tsp. Cream
Shake well with cracked ice and strain into cocktail glass. Float cream on top.

DER LACHS GOLDWASSER

"Der Lachs" the original Danziger Goldwasser is a mysterious blend of 25 herbs, spices and real 22 karat gold flakes. Since 1958 the unparalleled liqueur of choice . . . A dazzling experience for palate and eye. The original Danziger Goldwasser has been exclusively produced by the house of "Der Lachs" since 1958. Acquire a taste for gold — try Der Lachs Goldwasser straight up, on the rocks or in one of the intriguing mixed drinks.

BERRY GOLDWATER
(Very conservative and mellow)
1 part DER LACHS GOLDWASSER
1½ parts Echte Kroatzbeere Blackberry Liqueur
Pour over rocks.

DER LACHS ON THE ROCKS
1½ oz. DER LACHS GOLDWASSER
Shake bottle, pour over rocks and enjoy the dazzling experience for palate and eye.

GO FOR THE GOLD
1½ oz. DER LACHS GOLDWASSER
Serve chilled; 25 herbs, spices and 22 karat gold flakes, the most exquisite liqueur in the world!

GOLDEN KIR
½ part DER LACHS GOLDWASSER
1 dash Hiram Walker Creme de Cassis Dry Champagne
Pour into fluted champagne glass.

GOLDMINERS DREAM
1 oz. DER LACHS GOLDWASSER
Shake bottle before using. Pour over a generous helping of chocolate ice cream. Serve with a shovel!

LIQUORE GALLIANO

Liquore Galliano traces its origin and name back to the year 1897, when Arturo Vaccari of Leghorn created a golden liqueur, distilled from the rays of the sun, to commemorate the heroic victory of Major Giuseppe Galliano over the Abyssinian forces of Emperor Menelik of Ethiopia.

The production of Liquore Galliano begins with a group of valley inhabitants who in the balsamic seasons pick herbs, small plants, roots, berries and flowers of 30 alpine and exotic varieties: some of them are cultivated and others are wild, all giving Liquore Galliano its delicate aroma and fine taste.

These botanical ingredients are ground and then put into a hyrdro-alcoholic infusion which, after separation of the liquid part, is distilled to obtain the extract. This extract is then added to a syrup made from sugar and water. Then the alcohol is added to obtain Liquore Galliano.

This secret formula is almost 100 years old. It is very well balanced, allowing the product to be mixed in cocktails and even in foods. Unlike most liqueurs, Galliano has no over-powering flavor base, but serves to deepen and give character to an astonishing range of other ingredients, both ordinary and exotic. Galliano also adds a special taste to flaming crepes, fruit salads, and ice-creams, especially lemon or vanilla flavored.

GALLIANO & TONIC

1¼   oz. LIQUORE GALLIANO
     Tonic

Pour over ice in a tall glass. Fill with tonic. Drop in lime wedge and stir.

COMFORT WALLBANGER

¼   oz. LIQUORE GALLIANO
1   oz. Southern Comfort
     Orange Juice

In a tall glass with ice cubes, stir. Float Liquore Galliano on top.

CRANBERRY DELIGHT

1   part LIQUORE
         GALLIANO
1   part Absolut Vodka
1   part Cranberry Juice

Mix with ice in a shaker. Serve in a cocktail glass.

CREAMSICLE

1   oz. LIQUORE GALLIANO
1   oz. Half & Half or
     Heavy Cream
     Orange Juice

In a tall glass with ice fill with orange juice. Stir.

FREDDIE FUDPUCKER

¼   oz. LIQUORE GALLIANO
1   oz. Sauza
     Conmemorativo
     Tequila
     Orange Juice

In a tall glass with ice, add tequila, ¾ orange juice and stir. Float Liquore Galliano on top.

GALLIANO & SODA

1¼   oz. LIQUORE GALLIANO
     Club Soda

Pour over ice. fill with club soda. Drop in a lime wedge and stir.

GALLIANO AND COFFEE

1   oz. LIQUORE GALLIANO
     Hot, Strong
     Coffee

In a mug or cup; stir.

GALLIANO AND GRAPEFRUIT JUICE

1¼   oz. LIQUORE GALLIANO
     Grapefruit Juice

In a tall glass with ice, fill with grapefruit juice and stir.

GALLIANO AND ORANGE JUICE

1¼   oz. LIQUORE GALLIANO
     Orange Juice

In a tall glass with ice, fill with orange juice. Stir.

GALLIANO CHI CHI

¾   oz. LIQUORE GALLIANO
¾   oz. Absolut Vodka
1   oz. Cream of Coconut
2   oz. Unsweetened
     Pineapple Juice

Mix ingredients in blender with crushed ice, or shake and serve on the rocks. Serve with a pineapple spear.

GALLIANO COLADA

¾ oz. LIQUORE GALLIANO
¾ oz. Bacardi Rum
1 oz. Cream of Coconut
2 oz. Unsweetened
Pineapple Juice

Mix all ingredients in blender with crushed ice or shake and serve on the rocks. Serve with a pineapple spear.

GALLIANO COLLINS

¾ oz. LIQUORE GALLIANO
¾ oz. Bombay Gin
Juice of 1 Lemon
1 tsp. Sugar

Shake well and pour into tall glass with ice cubes. Fill with club soda.

GALLIANO DAIQUIRI

¾ oz. LIQUORE GALLIANO
¾ oz. Bacardi Rum
1 tsp. Powdered Sugar
Juice of ½ Lime

Add one cup of crushed ice and mix in blender for 45 seconds.

GALLIANO KIR

¼ oz. LIQUORE GALLIANO
4 oz. Chilled White
Wine

Serve in wine glass or in tumbler with ice cubes.

GALLIANO MAI TAI

½ oz. LIQUORE GALLIANO
½ oz. Bacardi Rum
¼ oz. Hiram Walker
Orange Curacao
¼ oz. Fresh Lime Juice
¼ oz. Sugar Syrup

In double size old-fashioned glass, half filled with cracked ice. Stir gently. Garnish with mint sprigs. Serve with straws (Frozen or powdered Mai Tai Mix may be substituted for Lime Juice, sugar syrup and curacao.)

GALLIANO MANHATTAN

¼ oz. LIQUORE GALLIANO
1 oz. Seagram's V.O.

Stir with ice.

GALLIANO MARGARITA

¼ oz. LIQUORE GALLIANO
1 oz. Sauza
Conmemorativo
Tequila
1½ oz. Sweet and Sour
Mix

Blend or shake with ice and pour into champagne glass. Salt rim if desired.

GALLIANO MIST

1 oz. LIQUORE GALLIANO

In an old-fashioned glass with cracked ice. Squeeze a wedge of fresh lime and drop in glass. Stir and serve.

GALLIANO SCREWDRIVER

1 oz. LIQUORE GALLIANO
3 oz. Orange Juice
½ tsp. Lemon Juice

In an old-fashioned glass filled with ice; stir.

GALLIANO SOUR

¾ oz. LIQUORE GALLIANO
¾ oz. Seagram's V.O.
1 oz. Lemon Juice
¾ tbs. Sugar
 Club Soda

Shake well with cracked ice and strain into sour glass. Add splash of club soda. Garnish with slice of orange.

GALLIANO STINGER

¾ oz. LIQUORE GALLIANO
½ oz. Hiram Walker
 White Creme de Menthe

Shake well with ice and strain into cocktail glass.

GALLIANO SUNSHINE

1¼ oz. LIQUORE GALLIANO
1 scp. Orange Sherbert

Put in a blender for a few seconds. Serve in sherbert glass.

GOLDEN CADILLAC

¼ oz. LIQUORE GALLIANO
1 oz. Hiram Walker
 White Creme de Cacao
1 oz. Cream

In a blender with a little ice; blend at low speed for a short time. Strain into champagne glass. A scoop of vanilla ice cream can be substituted for cream.

GOLDEN DREAM

1 oz. LIQUORE GALLIANO
¼ oz. Hiram Walker
 Triple Sec
½ oz. Orange Juice
½ oz. Cream

Shake with cracked ice. Strain into cocktail glass.

GOLDEN RUSSIAN

¼ oz. LIQUORE GALLIANO
1 oz. Absolut Vodka

Shake well with ice. Strain over rocks in chilled old-fashioned glass and squeeze wedge of lime into glass. Drop in lime. Stir and serve.

GOLDEN TORPEDO

¾ oz. LIQUORE GALLIANO
¾ oz. Hiram Walker
 Amaretto
2 oz. Cream (Ice Cream Optional)

Pour ingredients into blender. Blend and strain into champagne glass.

HARVEY COWPUNCHER

1¼ oz. LIQUORE GALLIANO
4 oz. Milk

In an old-fashioned glass, stir with ice.

HARVEY WALLBANGER

¼ oz. LIQUORE GALLIANO
1 oz. Absolut Vodka
 Orange Juice

In a tall glass with ice, add vodka and fill ¾ full with orange juice. Stir. Float Liquore Galliano on top.

INTERNATIONAL

¾ oz. LIQUORE GALLIANO
½ oz. Asbach Uralt

Shake well with ice and strain into cocktail glass.

ITALIAN FLOAT

1¼ oz. LIQUORE GALLIANO
Cola
1 oz. Half & Half

In a tall glass filled with ice; add cola to near top of glass. Stir. Float 1 oz. half & half on top.

ITALIAN HEATHER

¼ oz. LIQUORE GALLIANO
1 oz. J&B Scotch

Stir in ice filled mixing glass. Strain into cocktail glass. Twist lemon peel over drink and drop into glass.

JUICY LUCY

¼ oz. LIQUORE GALLIANO
1 oz. Bacardi Rum
Orange Juice

In a tall glass with ice cubes add rum and ¾ full with orange juice; stir. Float Liquore Galliano on top.

KENTUCKY WONDER

¾ oz. LIQUORE GALLIANO
¾ oz. Hiram Walker Sloe Gin
¾ oz. Rose's® Grenadine
1 tsp. Egg White

Shake well with cracked ice and strain into cocktail glass.

KINGS CUP

LIQUORE GALLIANO
Heavy Cream

Fill pony glass ⅔ full with Liquore Galliano. Top off with heavy cream.

MILANO

¾ oz. LIQUORE GALLIANO
¾ oz. Bombay Gin
¾ oz. Fresh Lime Juice

Shake with ice and strain into cocktail glass. Serve with a cherry.

PALM BEACH

¾ oz. LIQUORE GALLIANO
¾ oz. Absolut Vodka
1 Egg White

Mix with a small amount of cracked ice in blender at a low speed for 8-10 seconds. Pour unstrained over ice cubes in highball glass. Fill with sparkling water. Garnish with lime wedge.

PINEAPPLE COOLER

1 oz. LIQUORE GALLIANO
3 tbs. Sugar
Juice of ½ Lemon
Juice of ½ Orange
4 oz. Pineapple Juice

Shake with ice and serve unstrained.

PORTOFINO COCKTAIL
S.S. HOMERIE

¼ oz. LIQUORE GALLIANO
¾ oz. Bombay Gin
¼ oz. Hiram Walker Green Creme de Menthe
½ oz. Lemon Juice
½ oz. Orange Juice

Shake with ice until chilled. Strain into cocktail glass.

RECRUIT

¾ oz. LIQUORE GALLIANO
¾ oz. Kirshwasser
Dry Champagne
(chilled)

Mix in a highball glass, add crushed ice, fill with chilled dry champagne. Garnish with fresh black cherries with stems.

ROMAN COFFEE

¾ oz. LIQUORE GALLIANO
¾ oz. Kahlua
Hot, Strong
Coffee

In a large cup or mug; stir. Top with whipped cream.

ROME BEAUTY

1 oz. LIQUORE GALLIANO
¼ oz. Hiram Walker
Cherry Liqueur
¼ oz. Rose's® Lime
Juice

Serve on the rocks.

SALT LAKE SPECIAL

½ oz. LIQUORE GALLIANO
¾ oz. Bombay Gin
3 oz. Grapefruit Juice
dash Orange Bitters
7-Up

Shake and pour into 8 oz. glass, unstrained. Fill with 7-Up.

SOUTHERN GAL

1 part LIQUORE GALLIANO
1 part Southern Comfort
1 part Hiram Walker
Triple Sec

Shake with ice and serve in cocktail glass.

SPARKLING GALLIANO

½ oz. LIQUORE GALLIANO
4 oz. Champagne (iced)
½ tsp. Lemon Juice

In a prechilled champagne glass, stir. Add cucumber rind.

TROPICANA

1¼ oz. LIQUORE GALLIANO
½ oz. Coconut Milk

Mix with ice in a shaker, serve in a cocktail glass. Garnish with fresh grated coconut and thin slice of banana.

UPSTARTER

¾ oz. LIQUORE GALLIANO
½ oz. Absolut Vodka
dash Hiram Walker
Peach Flavored
Brandy

Shake well with ice and strain into cocktail glass.

VIKING

1 oz. LIQUORE GALLIANO
¼ oz. Akvavit (ice cold)

In a tapered cordial glass, float Akvavit on top (use spoon).

WHITE MINK

¾ oz. LIQUORE GALLIANO
¼ oz. Hiram Walker
Creme de Cacao
¼ oz. Asbach Uralt
1 oz. Cream
1 scp. Vanilla Ice Cream

In a blender with ice; blend until smooth.

GRAND MARNIER LIQUEUR

More than a century ago a young Frenchman named Louis Alexandre Marnier-Lapostolle, the son-in-law of a successful French distiller, blended the essence of wild, bitter oranges with his family's finest cognacs to produce a new liqueur. He named his creation Grand Marnier.

Today, Grand Marnier reigns as the world's premier French liqueur — the elixir of style, good living and hospitality. Grand Marnier is France's number one liqueur export. Still produced according to the original formula by the family owned firm of Marnier-Lapostolle. In the United States, a market that accounts for one-third of total worldwide sales, Grand Marnier is firmly established as the nation's best-selling imported French liqueur.

Grand Marnier is still produced in the town of Neauphle-le-Chateau, just outside of Paris, where the Lapostolle family established its distillery in 1827. Jean-Baptiste Lapostolle, the firm's founder, was highly respected for the fine liqueurs his family produced. His son Eugene built upon this success by expanding the business to include the production of fine cognac from the Charente region. This cognac ultimately inspired the creation of Grand Marnier by Eugene's son-in-law, Louis Alexandre Marnier-Lapostolle.

The production process for Grand Marnier remains fundamentally unchanged today. Dried peels of wild, bitter oranges from the Caribbean are macerated and distilled. The liqueur is then added to selected cognacs from the Grande and Petite Champagne regions. This cognac is aged at the Chateau de Bourg, in the heart of the cognac producing region. The house of Marnier-

Lapostolle, which still markets this outstanding spirit under the Lapostolle label, is France's fifth largest purchaser of cognac.

The carefully proportioned blend of orange liqueur and cognac is then aged in oak vats and carefully filtered in order to eliminate any impurities. The rich, amber colored liqueur then receives its final signature: the familiar, uniquely shaped bottle with the red ribbon and wax seal, that is known and loved around the world.

Grand Marnier Cordon Rouge, 80 proof, is available in 1.75 litres, 750 ml, 375 ml and minatures in the United States. Since 1946 the liqueur has been distributed in the United States exclusively by Carillon Importers Ltd. of Teaneck, NJ.

'57 T-BIRD WITH HONOLULU LICENSE PLATES
1 part GRAND MARNIER
1 part Bacardi Dark Rum
1 part Hiram Walker Sloe Gin
1 part Orange Juice

Serve as a shot.

'57 T-BIRD WITH TEXAS LICENSE PLATES
1 part GRAND MARNIER
1 part Bacardi Dark Rum
1 part Hiram Walker Sloe Gin
1 part Grapefruit juice

Serve as a shot.

ALFONSO SPECIAL
1½ oz. GRAND MARNIER
½ oz. Bombay Gin
1 tsp. Martini & Rossi Extra Dry Vermouth
2 dshs Bitters

Combine in a shaker with ice cubes, shake vigorously. Strain into chilled cocktail glass.

ALICE IN WONDERLAND
1 part GRAND MARNIER
1 part Tia Maria
1 part Sauza Conmemorativo Tequila

Serve as a shot.

ANCIENT MARINER
1 oz. GRAND MARNIER
1 oz. Bacardi Gold Reserve Rum

Blend together and pour over ice.

APRIL IN PARIS BALL
1 tsp. GRAND MARNIER
2 oz. Dry Sparkling Wine

Pour Grand Marnier into a chilled champagne glass. Tilt and turn glass to coat inside with liqueur. Add chilled sparkling wine. Float miniature rose bud.

B-52 WITH BOMBAY DOORS
1 part GRAND MARNIER
1 part Kahlua
1 part Creme de Grand Marnier
1 part Bombay Gin

Serve as a shot.

B.J. SHOOTER
⅓ oz. GRAND MARNIER
⅓ oz. Creme de Grand Marnier

Top with a dot of whipped cream. Serve as a shooter.

BANFF COCKTAIL
½ oz. GRAND MARNIER
1 oz. Seagram's V.O.
2 dshs Kirsh
1 dash Orange Bitters

Combine in shaker with ice cubes, shake vigorously. Strain into chilled cocktail glass.

BETWEEN THE SHEETS
½ oz. GRAND MARNIER
½ oz. Asbach Uralt
½ oz. Bacardi Light Rum
½ tsp. Lemon Juice

Combine with ice; shake well. Strain and add ice.

CAFE BENITEZ

½ oz. GRAND MARNIER
1 oz. Bacardi Gold
    Reserve Rum
4 oz. Hot Strong Coffee
1 Sugar Cube
1 Cinnamon Stick

In a warm mug, pour rum, all but 1 tsp. Grand Marnier; add cinnamon stick and slowly add hot coffee while stirring. Place sugar cube in spoon with reserved Grand Marnier. Hold spoon over drink and ignite sugar cube. Allow sugar to flame for 2 or 3 seconds and slide it into drink.

CAFE GATES

½ oz. GRAND MARNIER
½ oz. Tia Maria
½ oz. Hiram Walker
    Dark Creme de
    Cacao

Shake and serve over ice.

CAFE GRANDE

1½ oz. GRAND MARNIER
3-4 oz. Hot Strong Coffee
1 Sugar Cube

Pour coffee into warm cup. Place sugar cube in spoon over coffee cup. Wet cube with a few drops of Grand Marnier and ignite. Lower flaming cube into hot coffee. Add remaining Grand Marnier and stir gently.

CAFE MARNIER

2 tbs. GRAND MARNIER
1 cup Strong Brewed
    Coffee
1 tsp. Powdered Sugar
    Whipped Cream

Stir Grand Marnier and sugar in glass, add coffee. Top with lightly whipped cream. Be careful not to mix while serving.

CAPTAIN COOK

⅓ oz. GRAND MARNIER
⅔ oz. Bacardi Light Rum
    Pineapple Juice

In a collins glass; fill with pineapple juice.

DALLAS ALICE

1 part GRAND MARNIER
1 part Sauza
    Conmemorativo
    Tequila
1 part Hiram Walker
    Amaretto

Serve as a shot.

DIRTY HARRY

1 oz. GRAND MARNIER
1 oz. Tia Maria

Shake and strain. Serve as a shooter.

FRENCH CONNECTION

¾ oz. GRAND MARNIER
¾ oz. Marnier-Lapostolle
    Cognac X.O.

Serve in snifter.

FRENCH MAID COFFEE

½ oz. GRAND MARNIER
½ oz. Kahlua
½ oz. Asbach Uralt
    Coffee

In a mug; top with whipped cream.

FRONT-PAGE DYNAMITE

½ oz. GRAND MARNIER
1 oz. Absolut Vodka
¼ oz. Hiram Walker
   Peppermint
   Schnapps

Combine in a shaker with ice cubes; shake vigorously. Strain into chilled old-fashioned glass. Garnish with mint sprig.

FULL MOON

¾ oz. GRAND MARNIER
¾ oz. Hiram Walker
   Amaretto

Pour in a snifter.

GALLICE

½ oz. GRAND MARNIER
½ oz. Liquore Galliano

Build in rock glass with cubed ice.

GLOOM CHASER

½ oz. GRAND MARNIER
½ oz. Hiram Walker
   Orange Curacao
2 tsp. Lemon Juice
2 tsp. Rose's® Grenadine

Combine with ice; shake well. Strain and add ice.

GRAND APPLE

½ oz. GRAND MARNIER
1 oz. Apple Brandy
½ oz. Cognac

Pour in a mixing glass with several ice cubes; stir well and pour into chilled old-fashioned glass. Twist lemon and orange peels over drink and drop into glass.

GRAND DE CACAO

½ oz. GRAND MARNIER
¾ oz. Hiram Walker
   White Creme de
   Cacao
1½ oz. Heavy Cream

Blend with crushed ice. Pour into wine glass.

GRAND MARGUERITA

½ oz. GRAND MARNIER
1 oz. Sauza
   Conmemorativo
   Tequila
1 oz. Rose's® Lime
   Juice

Combine with ice; shake well. Rub ½ a lime around the rim of glass and press in salt. Strain straight up.

GRAND MARNIER TODDY

1 oz. GRAND MARNIER
4 oz. Red Wine
   pinch Cinnamon
   Sugar

Heat red wine, adding a pinch of cinnamon. Pour hot wine in a toddy mug. Light Grand Marnier on a large spoon and pour flaming over the wine. Sweeten to taste.

GRAND MARNIER TONIC

1 oz. GRAND MARNIER
3-4 oz. Tonic

In a tall glass with ice, fill with tonic. Add lemon slice.

GRAND MIMOSA

1	oz. GRAND MARNIER
6	oz. Laurent Perrier Brut Champagne
3	oz. Orange Juice

All ingredients should be very cold. Combine in a pitcher, mix gently using a long handled spoon. Pour in glass and serve at once.

GRAND MOMENT

¼	oz. GRAND MARNIER
1	oz. Bombay Gin
¼	oz. Rose's® Lime Juice
1	Egg White

Mix with cracked ice in a shaker or blender. Pour into a chilled brandy snifter.

GRAND ORANGE BLOSSOM

¼	oz. GRAND MARNIER
1	oz. Bombay Gin
½	oz. Orange Juice
1	tsp. Sugar Syrup

Combine with ice; shake well. Strain and add ice.

GRAND SIDE CAR

2	tsp. GRAND MARNIER
1¼	oz. Asbach Uralt
2	tsp. Lemon Juice

Combine with ice; shake well. Strain into an old-fashioned glass with ice.

GRAND SLAM

¼	oz. GRAND MARNIER
1	oz. Bombay Gin
1	oz. Orange Juice
¾	tsp. Rose's® Grenadine

Blend with crushed ice. Pour into sour glass. Garnish with red cherry.

GRANVILLE

1	tsp. GRAND MARNIER
1¼	oz. Bombay Gin
1	tsp. Apple Brandy
1	tsp. Lemon Juice

Combine with ice; shake. Strain and add ice.

HOT GOOSE

2	oz. GRAND MARNIER
½	oz. Hot Water

Shake and strain. Serve as a shooter.

HOT SHOT

1	part GRAND MARNIER
1	part Creme de Grand Marnier Coffee

Serve in a mug.

IL PARADISO

½	oz. GRAND MARNIER
½	oz. Bombay Gin
1	oz. Asbach Uralt
1-2	oz. Orange Juice

Combine in a shaker, shake vigorously. Strain into chilled cocktail glass.

IRISH SLEEPER

½	oz. GRAND MARNIER
1	oz. Jameson Irish Whiskey
½	oz. Irish Mist

Shake and strain. Serve as a shooter.

IT DON'T MATTER

¼	oz. GRAND MARNIER
1	oz. Wild Turkey 101

Float Grand Marnier. Serve as a shot.

JELLY BEAN FIX aka CABINET COCKTAIL

½ oz. GRAND MARNIER
1 oz. Bacardi Light Rum
½ oz. Hiram Walker
White Creme de Cacao
1 tbs. Lemon Juice

Combine in a mixing glass with ice cubes; stir well. Strain into chilled old-fashioned glass with ice. Garnish with 3 jelly beans.

KING OF HEARTS

½ oz. GRAND MARNIER
½ oz. Absolut Vodka
½ oz. Liquore Galliano
1 scp. Vanilla Ice Cream

Blend with crushed ice. Pour into wine glass.

LADY GODIVA

1 part GRAND MARNIER
1 part Hiram Walker
Dark Creme de Cacao
2 parts Cream

Serve as a shooter.

MARNIER BODY WARMER

1 oz. GRAND MARNIER
6 oz. Hot Tea
Sugar

Pour Grand Marnier in a glass of hot tea. Stir and sweeten to taste.

MARNIER'S HALF N HALF

1 oz. GRAND MARNIER
1 oz. Marnier V.S.O.P. Cognac

In a snifter. If preferred cold, serve iced or on the rocks.

MARNOUCHKA

½ oz. GRAND MARNIER
1 oz. Absolut Vodka
3 oz. Orange Juice

Shake with cracked ice and strain into chilled cocktail glass. Garnish with orange slice.

MOSS LANDING

¾ oz. GRAND MARNIER
¾ oz. Hiram Walker
Creme de Banana
Coffee

Pour into coffee mug. Fill mug to ½ inch of rim with coffee. Garnish with whipped cream.

RED LION

½ oz. GRAND MARNIER
½ oz. Bombay Gin
½ oz. Orange Juice
dash Lemon Juice

Mix in cocktail shaker with crushed ice. Chill. Serve very cold in cocktail glass.

STEAMBOAT SPECIAL

¼ oz. GRAND MARNIER
1 oz. J&B Scotch

Float Grand Marnier. Serve as a shot.

SUNSTROKE

½ oz. GRAND MARNIER
1 oz. Absolut Vodka
2 oz. Grapefruit Juice

Blend with crushed ice. Pour into cocktail glass.

T-BIRD

1 part GRAND MARNIER
1 part Hiram Walker
  Amaretto
1 part Absolut Vodka
2½ oz. Pineapple Juice
1 splsh Cream (optional)

Serve as a shooter.

THE GRAND, GRAND COCKTAIL

1 oz. GRAND MARNIER
1 oz. Cherry Marnier
1 dash Bombay Gin
  (optional)
1 oz. Cream or
1 scp. Vanilla Ice Cream

Mix with cracked ice in a blender and strain into chilled cocktail glass. If ice cream is used, use generous scoop and mix in a blender for only a few seconds so mixture is slightly slushy.

TOP HAT

¾ oz. GRAND MARNIER
¾ oz. Cherry Marnier

Build in rock glass with cubed ice.

UPSIDE DOWN MARGARITA
aka HEADREST

⅔ oz. GRAND MARNIER
1 oz. Sauza
  Conmemorativo
  Tequila
1 splsh Sour Mix
½ splsh Rose's® Lime
  Juice

Poured into mouth while leaning head over bar.

VELVET HAMMER

1 part GRAND MARNIER
1 part Hiram Walker
  White Creme de
  Cacao
1 dash Asbach Uralt
1 part Cream

Serve as a shooter.

VODKA GRAND

½ oz. GRAND MARNIER
1 oz. Absolut Vodka
½ oz. Rose's® Lime
  Juice

Stir and strain into chilled cocktail glass.

YELLOW SUNSET

½ oz. GRAND MARNIER
1 oz. Absolut Vodka
2 oz. Pineapple Juice

Blend with crushed ice. Pour into cocktail glass.

ZOOM SHOOTER

2 parts GRAND MARNIER
2 parts Absolut Vodka
1 part Hiram Walker
  Triple Sec
2 parts Orange Juice
1 dash Rose's® Grenadine

Serve as a shooter.

HIRAM WALKER LIQUEURS

Simply stated, a *liqueur* is a very flavorful distilled spirit containing at least 2½% sugar by weight. Two and one half percent by weight is a mild form of sweetening material (about one and a quarter tablespoons in a 750 ml package). Most liqueurs are heavier in sugar content.

There are three elements that make a liqueur great:

First, an outstanding flavor;

Second, long shelf life; and

Finally, stability after the bottle is opened.

Hiram Walker Liqueurs possess these three qualities in such measure that Hiram Walker can proudly claim that they are the finest liqueurs in the world.

The main basic liqueur flavors come from various fruits and/or botanicals. They are gathered from the four corners of the earth and are purchased at such times as they are considered of vintage quality, just as grapes grown in a particular year produce vintage wine.

Hiram Walker has no monopoly on these fruits and botanicals. Therefore, it is through scientific research and constant and exacting quality control that Hiram Walker is able to produce the finest cordials in the world—exquisite flavor, and with stability that maintains the flavor even after the bottle is opened.

In addition to this, Hiram Walker is one of the leading, if not the leading, distillers in the field of analytical flavor research. Hiram Walker's purpose in this regard has been to attain liqueur flavors that are identical with the fruits and botanicals at the most succulent periods in their growing cycles and also to keep these flavors intact and free from deterioration once the bottle is opened.

The three major methods used to produce or obtain the flavor for liqueurs are: 1. Infusion; 2. Percolation; 3. Distillation.

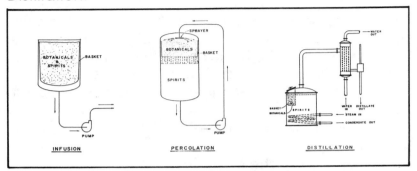

The *infusion* method, very much like making tea, is used primarily for making fruit liqueurs. By this method, the fruit is placed directly into a quantity of spirits and allowed to steep until almost all the flavor, aroma and color has been extracted.

Percolation is a method that compares exactly with the percolating of coffee and is used for making plant liqueurs.

The percolator is a large tank. Spirits are put into the bottom of the tank and the flavoring source in the form of leaves or herbs is placed in a basket-like container at the top of the tank. The spirits in the bottom of the tank are then pumped to the top where they are sprayed over the leaves or herbs and drip back to the bottom, to be repercolated over and over until all the flavor and aroma has been extracted.

Whereas with the brewing of tea or with a coffee percolator, you depend on boiling water — infusion and percolation methods of producing flavorings use room-temperature spirits. Heat resulting from hot infusion or hot percolation would be harmful to the delicate flavor source.

For most liqueurs, infusion or percolation is only the beginning. After the flavors have been extracted by these methods, the heavily flavored spirits are distilled, resulting in the delicacy of flavor desired by the maker.

The *distillation* method in some instances is used alone. The flavoring source is placed in a still, covered with spirits, and distilled. The distillate carries off the flavor of the various ingredients.

Although there are three major methods of extracting flavor from fruits and botanicals, there is no best way. Research over the years has taught Hiram Walker that the most satisfactory results are obtained only by a careful blend of flavors extracted by one or more of the methods previously mentioned.

Most liqueurs have neutral, tasteless, odorless, high-proof alcohol as their base. The flavor of the finished product comes wholly from the flavoring agents, none of it from the spirit base. Some liqueurs, however, use brandy, Scotch, Irish, bourbon, or even Canadian whisky as a base. In this case, the base will contribute significantly to the taste of the bottled liqueur. Hiram Walker Peppermint Schnapps, for example, has a special "gin-like" base spirit. It has all the delicate background flavors of gin without the dominant juniper berry or orange flavor.

Sweetening syrups are used widely in liqueur making and in many brands they have proved to be an unstable element because they crystallize when the bottle is opened; Hiram Walker's research has improved the methods of making syrups to a point where a water-clear liqueur such as Peppermint Schnapps stays water-clear. No haze or cloudiness will develop in the bottle.

Vastly important to Hiram Walker's flavor-blending of liqueurs are the special tanks and special measuring devices which are employed to measure syrup, water, flavors, spirits, etc. There cannot be any margin of error with these mechanical aids which make certain that only the right proportions of ingredients are used.

Also of extreme importance is the "marrying" or rest period. The time varies because some liqueurs require a longer aging time than others. Some producers do not take the necessary time. The Hiram Walker Liqueurs never leave the processing tanks until they have been rested, cured, matured, and found stable as to clarity, bouquet, and taste.

Hiram Walker Liqueurs offer a wide spectrum of flavors. They are served as cocktails and after-dinner drinks, and used in preparing main and side-dishes and desserts. There is something to suit every modern taste, mood and occasion. It is little wonder, therefore, that Hiram Walker is at the forefront of the liqueur business.

Proper Cordials

These Cordial flavors are the essential ingredients for drinks that have remained popular throughout the years. They are the foundation of "Margaritas," "Grasshoppers," "Brandy Alexanders," and many more. Hiram Walker built its reputation for quality and great taste with these Cordials. Try them and discover why they have endured the test of time.

Triple Sec

This product is made principally from imported orange peel—the wild Curacao orange and the sweet, aromatic Spanish Valencia.

Triple sec means "triple dry"...three distillations. The orange peel is softened in water, the spirit added, and they are distilled together. There are other complementary flavors in this product, but the exact types and amounts are closely guarded secrets. The extensive curing time, unique production techniques and exclusive flavor blending process, create the intriguing mystery of Triple Sec.

Anisette

Hiram Walker uses only the finest imported anise. Hiram Walker Anisette mixes beautifully with Hiram Walker Blackberry Flavored Brandy to make a "Jelly Bean."

Sloe Gin

Sloe Gin tends to mislead consumers with its name. Although it *is* made from sloeberries, it is *not* made from gin. The sloeberry is actually a wild plum, and belongs to the same family as the plum and cherry. It is small, cherry size, with a large seed, thin fruit, and very sour. It is primarily used as a flavoring agent. Hiram Walker uses other fruits and supporting flavors to enhance the sloeberry flavor.

Creme de Menthe

Hiram Walker is the standard for true mint flavor. The color is rich, classic mint-green; the flavor balance is pleasant, satisfying, fresh; it is not super-sugary, cloyingly sweet.

Mint is one of the most delicate flavors in Cordials. Since the flavor starts evaporating as soon as the mint is picked, the harvesting is quite interesting. A still is moved right into the mint field. The mint is picked and loaded immediately into the still. The oil of mint is collected just like a regular still run. To the oil and other complementary flavors, spearmint is added to give our product a softer, more subtle and delicate flavor.

There is no flavor/aroma difference in the Green and White Menthes.

Creme de Cacao

We have used a special blend of cacao nibs — Brazilian, Venezuelan, African, Guatemalen. Each is roasted to a different color/flavor level to lend its distinctive quality to our cacao. True Madagascan vanilla adds an appetizing difference – a rich, heady aroma, a smooth velvet taste.

Supporting flavors are married to the vanilla/cacao

combination. The final blend is aged to bring out all the distinctive characteristics.

Creme de Banana
Real banana flavor and aroma, with the natural sweetness and color of the fruit. Hiram Walker Creme de Banana makes the best tasting "Banana Daiquiri" you'll ever have.

Creme de Strawberry
Vine-ripened strawberries provide the magnificent taste and aroma. The fresh flavor will stand up in all your favorite mixed drinks.

Creme de Cassis
Imported black currants from France and other selected fruits and berries create this rare pleasure. Add Creme de Cassis to champagne to make a "Royal Kir."

Creme de Noyaux
A distinctive flavor and aroma from the combination of sweet and bitter almonds. Try the recipe for a "Pink Squirrel."

Orange Curacao
The flavor of wild Curacao oranges tamed by the sweet taste of Valencia oranges – the secret ingredient in many Polynesian drinks.

Blue Curacao
Blue Curacao has the same delightful orange flavor as Orange Curacao, with an interesting blue shade to make fun and colorful drinks. Combine Blue Curacao with vodka and pineapple juice for a "Blue Lagoon."

Rock & Rye
An old-time American favorite made with a special blend of aged rye whiskies and fresh fruit juices. A "Rock & Rye Sour" is a flavorful alternative to the common "Whiskey Sour."

Kirschwasser
A unique cherry liqueur made from Oregon and

Washington cherries, and crushed cherry pits to add a hint of nut flavor. Tremendous poured over fresh fruit.

Amaretto

All natural flavors make this Amaretto rich in body and outstanding in quality. The combination of sweet and bitter almonds is blended with extracts of selected fruits and aromatic herbs, and enhanced with natural vanilla.

Amaretto & Cognac

Only Hiram Walker has the expertise to combine their Amaretto with fine French cognac to create a perfectly balanced liqueur that brings out the best of both — the sweetness of Amaretto smoothed and sophisticated with the robust character of Cognac.

Chocolate

These Liqueurs are the ultimate in indulgence. Exclusively from Hiram Walker, the taste says it all.

Chocolate Cherry

The combination of imported cacao and vintage crop cherries makes a wonderful after-dinner treat.

Chocolate Mint

This product is made from imported cacao and field-fresh mint. Experience the perfect after-dinner mint.

Hazelnut Liqueur

A distinctive blend of rich, aromatic imported hazelnuts, complemented by the robust character of wild hazelnuts. Other imported natural flavors are skillfully blended to develop this unique flavor.

Schnapps

Schnapps are light, refreshing and full flavored fun! Hiram Walker's exclusive use of a "gin-like" base allows the fullest flavors and freshest taste of any Schnapps you'll ever know.

Schnapps can be enjoyed anytime, anywhere, in any way— as a shot, on the rocks, or in a mixed drink.

Peppermint Schnapps

One secret is the clean oil of peppermint. Hiram Walker uses three distillation processes—heat, vacuum, freeze-dry— to develop our unique flavor.

The spirit base is gin-like...a special distillation of low flavor gin.

Peach Schnapps

This represents a technical breakthrough in flavor development by Hiram Walker craftsmen.

Peach is skillfully blended from twenty-five different peach nectars—some for flavor, some for aroma, some for an incredibly delicate balance of flavor and aroma that has never before been achieved in the industry.

The peach aroma and flavor of this outstanding product are truly memorable — and a Hiram Walker exclusive.

Apple Schnapps

A distinctive blend of several apples — tartness and sweetness — aroma and true cider taste makes Cider Mill Unique.

Sampling Cider Mill recreates the memories and magic — the cidermill experience.

Every sip tastes like cider.

Root Beer Schnapps

This is the Schnapps that is closest to one of America's favorite sodas, with the authentic flavor of old-time root beer. Try the recipe for a ''Root Beer Float'' found on the bottle for a nostalgic treat.

Cinnamon Schnapps

Here is a unique and crisp Schnapps flavor. Cinnamon Schnapps is great as a spicy addition to any hot drink, or with Cider Mill Apple Schnapps.

Spearmint Schnapps

An outstanding example of a true, clean, uncluttered Spearmint flavor. There is a richness unrivaled by any other producer.

Apricot Schnapps

Several varieties of tree-ripened apricots contribute to this delicious taste and aroma. These flavors are rounded and complemented by apricot and peach pits.

The lower spirits level and reduced fruit sugar ensure a true, natural apricot flavor unrivaled in the market.

Flavored Brandies

Our Flavored Brandies reflect the tradition of quality and expertise that has made Hiram Walker the finest Cordial producers over the last fifty years.

Flavored Brandies are usually enjoyed straight, as an after-dinner drink. However, their full body and flavor provide a richer taste in many mixed drinks.

Blackberry Flavored Brandy

Here is one of the finest examples of our Cordial makers' art. Why? Blackberries have a very low flavor and aroma level. To create a rich, distinctive taste requires complementary and supporting ingredients.

Cherries, strawberries, red raspberries and twelve additional flavors support and complement our Blackberry flavor. But, appreciate the balance . . . you taste only blackberry . . . the aroma is blackberry.

Apricot Flavored Brandy

Hiram Walker Apricot Flavored Brandy has a unique flavor, unequaled by any other Apricot product on the market. Developing this celebrated flavor is a Hiram Walker exclusive. We use several varieties of tree-ripened apricots. Each variety is used for its special characteristic . . . robust flavor, body, aroma, sweetness.

Peach Flavored Brandy

A variety of peaches are used for body, aroma and sweetness.

Coffee Flavored Brandy

The aroma and flavor is FRESH ROASTED. Hiram Walker Coffee Brandy is made from a unique blend of international coffees and other imported flavors.

Cherry Flavored Brandy

Only the finest "one-crop-a-year" cherries are used as they provide the richest of cherry flavors.

Ginger Flavored Brandy

The exclusive use of imported ginger from Jamaica, and other natural ingredients bring out the wonderful taste of pure ginger.

ALABAMA SLAMMER

1 part HIRAM WALKER
AMARETTO
1 part HIRAM WALKER
SLOE GIN
1 part Southern Comfort
splsh Lemon Juice

Stir in highball glass over ice or serve straight.

ALEXANDER SWISS

1 oz. HIRAM WALKER
SWISS CHOCOLATE
ALMOND
½ oz. Asbach Uralt
1 oz. Cream

Combine in blender with 3 ice cubes. Spin until blended. Serve in on-the-rocks glass.

APPLE PIE

1½ oz. HIRAM WALKER
CIDER MILL APPLE
SCHNAPPS
¼ oz. HIRAM WALKER
CINNAMON
SCHNAPPS
1 scp. Vanilla Ice Cream

Combine in blender with 3 cracked ice cubes. Serve in on-the-rocks glass packed with ice.

APPLE TURNOVER

2 oz. HIRAM WALKER
CIDER MILL APPLE
SCHNAPPS
½ oz. HIRAM WALKER
TRIPLE SEC
1 scp. Vanilla Ice Cream

Combine in blender with 3 cracked ice cubes. Splash with soda. Serve in a tall glass.

APRICOT ALEXANDER

1 oz. HIRAM WALKER
APRICOT FLAVORED
BRANDY
1 oz. HIRAM WALKER
WHITE CREME DE
CACAO
4 oz. Vanilla Ice Cream

Mix in blender until smooth. Pour into on-the-rocks glass.

APRICOT SOURBALL

1½ oz. HIRAM WALKER
APRICOT FLAVORED
BRANDY
Juice of ½ Lemon
Juice of ½ Orange

In an on-the-rocks glass with ice, top with lemon and orange juices.

BANANA SPLIT

1½ oz. HIRAM WALKER
SWISS CHOCOLATE
ALMOND
½ oz. HIRAM WALKER
CREME DE
BANANA
3 oz. Cream

Blend with cracked ice and pour into on-the-rocks glass.

BARBERRY COAST

1¼ oz. HIRAM WALKER
RASPBERRY
SCHNAPPS
1½ oz. Cranberry Juice
½ oz. Grapefruit Juice

Serve over ice in tall glass.

BEANBERRY

1¼ oz. HIRAM WALKER
RASPBERRY
SCHNAPPS
Hot Coffee

In a mug filled with hot coffee.

BELLINI

1 oz. HIRAM WALKER
PEACH SCHNAPPS
3 oz. Champagne

Serve in champagne glass.

BERRY BERRY

1¼ oz. HIRAM WALKER
RASPBERRY
SCHNAPPS
3 oz. Cranberry Juice

Serve over ice in a tall glass.

BERRY GOOD

1¼ oz. HIRAM WALKER
RASPBERRY
SCHNAPPS
3 oz. Club Soda

Serve in a tall glass with ice.

BLACK ANGEL

1½ oz. HIRAM WALKER
BLACKBERRY
FLAVORED BRANDY
Juice of 1 Lime
Soda

In an on-the-rocks glass packed with ice, add a splash of soda. Garnish with lime wedge.

BLACK PEARL

¼ oz. HIRAM WALKER
BLACKBERRY
FLAVORED BRANDY
1 oz. HIRAM WALKER
PEACH SCHNAPPS

Serve on the rocks.

BLACKBERRY BRANDY

¾ oz. HIRAM WALKER
BLACKBERRY
FLAVORED BRANDY
½ oz. HIRAM WALKER
WHITE CREME DE
CACAO
⅔ oz. Cream

Frappe with shaved ice and strain into chilled saucer-type champagne glass. Sprinkle with nutmeg.

BURRBERRY

1¼ oz. HIRAM WALKER
RASPBERRY
SCHNAPPS
Hot Chocolate

In a mug filled with hot chocolate.

CALYPSO CIDER

1 oz. HIRAM WALKER
CIDER MILL APPLE
SCHNAPPS
1 oz. Bacardi Rum
1 oz. Orange Juice
1 oz. Pineapple Juice

Combine in blender with 3 cracked ice cubes. Serve in on-the-rocks glass packed with ice.

CHOCOLATE MINT CREAM

1½ oz. HIRAM WALKER
CHOCOLATE MINT
2 oz. Milk
Soda

Combine in tall glass filled with ice cubes. Top with soda. Garnish with mint sprig.

CHOCOLATE MINT FREEZE

1 oz. HIRAM WALKER
      CHOCOLATE MINT
4 oz. Vanilla Ice Cream

Combine in blender until smooth. Serve in champagne saucer and garnish with chocolate swirls.

CINNAMON COLA

1½ oz. HIRAM WALKER
       CINNAMON
       SCHNAPPS
     Cola

In an on-the-rocks glass packed with ice, top with cola. Garnish with lime wedge.

CINNAMON STICK

1 oz. HIRAM WALKER
      CINNAMON
      SCHNAPPS
1 oz. HIRAM WALKER
      AMARETTO
3 oz. Vanilla Ice Cream

Combine in blender with 2 cracked ice cubes. Pour into on-the-rocks glass.

COCOMINT

1¼ oz. HIRAM WALKER
       PEPPERMINT
       SCHNAPPS
     Hot Chocolate

Serve in a mug. Garnish with a sprig of mint.

CONTINENTAL STINGER

1½ oz. HIRAM WALKER
       AMARETTO &
       COGNAC
¾   oz. HIRAM WALKER
       PEPPERMINT
       SCHNAPPS

Combine in blender with cracked ice. Pour unstrained into on-the-rocks glass. Add mint leaf.

COOL ON THE ROCKS

2 oz. HIRAM WALKER
      PEPPERMINT
      SCHNAPPS

Pour over ice and stir.

CRAN MINT

1¼ oz. HIRAM WALKER
       PEPPERMINT
       SCHNAPPS
     Cranberry Juice

In a tall glass filled with ice and fill with cranberry juice.

CRANBERRY KIR

1 oz. HIRAM WALKER
      CRANBERRY
      LIQUEUR
4 oz. Chablis

Combine in on-the-rocks glass packed with ice.

CRANBERRY SNOWBLOWER

1 oz. HIRAM WALKER
      CRANBERRY
      LIQUEUR
1 oz. Bacardi Light Rum
1 oz. Orange Juice

Combine over ice in on-the-rocks glass.

FROZEN AMARETTO & APPLE

1½   oz. HIRAM WALKER
      CIDER MILL APPLE
      SCHNAPPS
½   oz. HIRAM WALKER
      AMARETTO

Combine in blender with 3 cracked ice cubes. Serve in on-the-rocks glass packed with ice.

FUZZ-BUSTER

¾   oz. HIRAM WALKER
      PEACH SCHNAPPS
¼   oz. HIRAM WALKER
      RASPBERRY
      SCHNAPPS
¼   oz. Absolut Vodka
      Orange Juice

Add ice and orange juice. Blend until frothy. Serve in a grande glass (16 oz.). Garnish with orange slice.

FUZZY NAVEL

1¼   oz. HIRAM WALKER
      PEACH SCHNAPPS
      Orange Juice

Pour over ice in on-the-rocks glass, fill with orange juice, stir well.

GIRL SCOUT COOKIE

¾   oz. HIRAM WALKER
      PEPPERMINT
      SCHNAPPS
½   oz. Kahlua
3   oz. Half & Half

Shake with ice and serve on the rocks.

GOLDEN PEACH

¾   oz. HIRAM WALKER
      PEACH SCHNAPPS
1   oz. Bombay Gin
      Orange Juice

In a tall glass with ice, fill with orange juice, stir well.

GRASSHOPPER

½   oz. HIRAM WALKER
      GREEN CREME DE
      MENTHE
½   oz. HIRAM WALKER
      WHITE CREME DE
      CACAO
½   oz. Cream

Combine in blender with ice until smooth. Strain into cocktail glass.

GRETEL

1½   oz. HIRAM WALKER
      SWISS CHOCOLATE
      ALMOND
½   oz. HIRAM WALKER
      SLOE GIN
3   oz. Vanilla Ice Cream

Combine in blender until smooth. Serve in cocktail glass. Dust with shaved chocolate.

HEAD

¾   oz. HIRAM WALKER
      ROOT BEER
      SCHNAPPS
¾   oz. Half & Half or
      Heavy Cream

Shake with ice, serve on the rocks or in a shot glass.

ITALIAN SPEAR

1 part HIRAM WALKER PEPPERMINT SCHNAPPS
1 part HIRAM WALKER AMARETTO

Stir on the rocks.

JELLY BEAN

1 part HIRAM WALKER ANISETTE
1 part HIRAM WALKER BLACKBERRY FLAVORED BRANDY

Serve in rocks glass over ice.

JOLLY RANCHER

¾ oz. HIRAM WALKER PEACH SCHNAPPS
¾ oz. HIRAM WALKER APPLE SCHNAPPS
Cranberry Juice

In a tall glass with ice.
TURBO: add Absolut Vodka.

MAD MOGUL

1¼ oz. HIRAM WALKER PEACH SCHNAPPS
Hot Apple Cider

Serve in mug.

MAI BERRY

1 oz. HIRAM WALKER RASPBERRY SCHNAPPS
¼ oz. HIRAM WALKER TRIPLE SEC
2 tbs. Rose's® Lime Juice

In a shaker, combine with ice and shake vigorously. Strain into a highball glass. Garnish with a pineapple spear and mint sprig.

MEXICAN CRANBERRY

1 oz. HIRAM WALKER CRANBERRY LIQUEUR
1 oz. Sauza Conmemorativo Tequila
1 oz. Sweet & Sour Mix

Combine in blender with ice, serve in on-the-rocks glass.

MULLBERRY

1¼ oz. HIRAM WALKER RASPBERRY SCHNAPPS
Hot Apple Cider

In a mug filled with cider. Garnish with a cinnamon stick.

NANTUCKET NIGHTCAP

1 oz. HIRAM WALKER CRANBERRY LIQUEUR
1 oz. Absolut Vodka
2 oz. Grapefruit Juice

Combine over ice in on-the-rocks glass.

PEACH BLOSSOM

1 oz. HIRAM WALKER PEACH SCHNAPPS
½ oz. HIRAM WALKER AMARETTO
1 scp. Vanilla Ice Cream

Mix in a blender until smooth.

PEACH CREAMY

¾ oz. HIRAM WALKER PEACH SCHNAPPS
½ oz. HIRAM WALKER WHITE CREME DE CACAO
¾ oz. Cream

Shake well with ice and strain into cocktail glass.

PEACH ON THE BEACH

¾ oz. HIRAM WALKER PEACH SCHNAPPS
½ oz. Absolut Vodka
Orange Juice
Cranberry Juice

In a tall glass filled with ice, equal parts of orange juice and cranberry juice.

PEACH PIRATE

¾ oz. HIRAM WALKER PEACH SCHNAPPS
½ oz. Bacardi Rum

In a shot glass.

PEACH ROYAL

1¼ oz. HIRAM WALKER PEACH SCHNAPPS
3 oz. Champagne

Add schnapps to champagne glass. Fill to top with champagne.

PEACHY

1½ oz. HIRAM WALKER PEACH FLAVORED BRANDY
Juice of ½ Lemon

Blend with cracked ice and pour into on-the-rocks glass.

PEACH SOUR

1¼ oz. HIRAM WALKER PEACH SCHNAPPS
3 oz. Sweetened Lemon Mix

Shake with ice. Serve straight up or on the rocks. Garnish with peach slice.

PEPPERMINT PATTI

¾ oz. HIRAM WALKER PEPPERMINT SCHNAPPS
½ oz. HIRAM WALKER GREEN CREME DE MENTHE

Serve over ice in a rocks glass.

PEPPERMINTINI

1 oz. HIRAM WALKER PEPPERMINT SCHNAPPS
¼ oz. Martini & Rossi Extra Dry Vermouth

Stir on the rocks.

PINK SQUIRREL

1 oz. HIRAM WALKER WHITE CREME DE CACAO
1 oz. HIRAM WALKER CREME DE NOYAUX
4 oz. Strawberry Ice Cream

Combine in blender until smooth. Pour into on-the-rocks glass. Garnish with fresh strawberry.

PINK VELVET

1 oz. HIRAM WALKER CHOCOLATE CHERRY
1 oz. HIRAM WALKER CREME DE CASSIS
3 oz. Vanilla Ice Cream

Combine in blender until smooth. Garnish with cherry.

PRALINE N CREAM

1½ oz. HIRAM WALKER
     PRALINE LIQUEUR
     Cream or Milk

In an on-the-rocks glass with ice, top with cream or milk.

PRALINE CAJUN COOLER

1½ oz. HIRAM WALKER
     PRALINE LIQUEUR
1½ oz. HIRAM WALKER
     CREME DE CACAO
1   scp. Vanilla Ice Cream

Combine in blender with 3 cracked ice cubes until smooth. Serve in on-the-rocks glass.

ROOT BEER RUSSIAN

1   part HIRAM WALKER
    ROOT BEER
    SCHNAPPS
1   part Kahlua
1   part Absolut Vodka

Shake, serve on the rocks.

ROOT BEER SUNRISE

1¼ oz. HIRAM WALKER
     ROOT BEER
     SCHNAPPS
3   oz. Orange Juice
    Rose's® Grenadine

Shake, top with a dash of grenadine.

ROOTY-TOOTY

1¼ oz. HIRAM WALKER
     ROOT BEER
     SCHNAPPS
3   oz. Orange Juice

Mix with ice in a blender, serve over ice in an on-the-rocks glass.

ROYAL KIR

splsh HIRAM WALKER
     CREME DE CASSIS
     Champagne

In a champagne glass; add splash of cassis, fill with champagne.

SCHNAPP HAPPY

1   oz. HIRAM WALKER
    RASPBERRY
    SCHNAPPS
¼   oz. Champagne

In a chilled fluted champagne glass, garnish with a cherry or strawberry.

SNOWFLAKE

1   part HIRAM WALKER
    PEPPERMINT
    SCHNAPPS
1   part Bombay Gin

Stir in wine glass filled with crushed ice.

SON OF A PEACH

1½ oz. HIRAM WALKER
     PEACH SCHNAPPS
2   oz. Pineapple Juice
3   oz. Orange Juice
1   oz. Sweet N' Sour Mix

Blend with crushed ice. Strain into stemmed cocktail glass.

SPARK PLUG

1½ oz. HIRAM WALKER
AMARETTO &
COGNAC
Cola

In an on-the-rocks glass with ice, fill with cola and add lime wedge.

SPEARMINT TROPICAL

1½ oz. HIRAM WALKER
SPEARMINT
SCHNAPPS
Orange Juice

In a tall glass with ice, top with orange juice.

ST. MORITZ

1 oz. HIRAM WALKER
SWISS CHOCOLATE
ALMOND
½ oz. HIRAM WALKER
CHERRY FLAVORED
BRANDY
1 oz. Cream

Combine in blender with 3 cracked ice cubes until smooth. Serve in cocktail glass.

SWEET SUNSHINE

1 oz. HIRAM WALKER
COFFEE FLAVORED
BRANDY
1 oz. HIRAM WALKER
TRIPLE SEC
3 oz. Orange Juice

Combine in blender with cracked ice, pour in on-the-rocks glass.

SWISS CHOCOLATE TROPICANA

1½ oz. HIRAM WALKER
SWISS CHOCOLATE
ALMOND
½ oz. HIRAM WALKER
CREME DE
BANANA
1 oz. Cream

Combine in blender with cracked ice. Serve in on-the-rocks glass.

SWISS PEACH

1½ oz. HIRAM WALKER
SWISS CHOCOLATE
ALMOND
½ oz. HIRAM WALKER
PEACH FLAVORED
BRANDY
3 oz. Vanilla Ice Cream

Combine in blender with 2 cracked ice cubes, serve in on-the-rocks glass.

THE BOTCH-A-ME

1 oz. HIRAM WALKER
AMARETTO
2 oz. Orange Juice
dash Soda

Pour over ice in on-the-rocks glass. Garnish with twist of lime.

THE LIFT

1 part HIRAM WALKER
PEPPERMINT
SCHNAPPS
2 parts Wild Turkey 101
1 dash Bitters

Stir on the rocks.

TRAVELING WILDBURYS

¼ oz. HIRAM WALKER RASPBERRY SCHNAPPS
¼ oz. HIRAM WALKER TRIPLE SEC
¼ oz. Absolut Vodka
¼ oz. Bacardi Rum
¼ oz. Bombay Gin
Sweet N' Sour
Cola

Shake, pour into a tall glass, top with cola.

TRIPLE ORANGE

1½ oz. HIRAM WALKER TRIPLE SEC
Orange Juice

In a tall glass with ice, fill with orange juice. Garnish with orange slice and cherry.

WHIPPER SCHNAPPER

1¼ oz. HIRAM WALKER RASPBERRY SCHNAPPS
2 oz. Half & Half or Heavy Cream

Blend with crushed ice. Serve in cordial glass topped with a cherry.

WILD IRISH BERRY

¾ oz. HIRAM WALKER RASPBERRY SCHNAPPS
¾ oz. Baileys Original Irish Cream

Shake, serve up or on the rocks.

THIS JUST IN!
NEW FROM HIRAM WALKER, KOKOMO
A TROPICAL DELIGHT

BLACK BAT

1 oz. KOKOMO
1 oz. Bacardi Premium Black Rum
Soda

Splash with soda. Serve over ice.

KAHUNA

1 oz. KOKOMO
1 oz. Kahlua
Soda

Splash of soda. Pour over ice.

KOKO CODDLER

1 oz. KOKOMO
Cranberry Juice.

Fill with cranberry juice. Serve over ice.

KOKO SUNSET

1 oz. KOKOMO
1 oz. Bacardi Premium Black Rum
Orange Juice

Fill with orange juice. Add splash of fresh lime. Stir.

© FOLEY PUBLISHING CORP.

JAMESON PREMIUM IRISH WHISKEY

In seeking the origin of whiskey, look no further than sixth century Ireland where, most historians agree, Irish monks were the first to distill spirits. It was not until much later that these same monks carried their secret to Scotland.

Jameson Premium Irish Whiskey bears all the greatness of a whiskey distilled in the land where whiskey was invented. The marriage of its natural ingredients — rich malted and unmalted barleys and the pure waters of Ireland's crystal clear streams — yields Jameson's uniquely balanced taste.

John Jameson accepted nothing less when he opened his distillery in 1780 when Dublin was the second city of the British Empire and the seventh largest city in the world, and that same quality standard holds true today. John Jameson was one of several Scotchmen who had come to Dublin to learn the art of making whiskey but unlike others such as Haig and Dewar who returned to Scotland, Jameson stayed on. He was a man of great pioneering spirit who sponsored and encouraged Irish farmers to grow the type of barley best suited to the making of whiskey and by the end of the 19th century, Jameson's Whiskey was known the civilized world over.

Jameson's gentle taste results from allowing the barley to dry naturally in kilns. No heat or smoke is used. Unlike most other premium whiskies, Jameson is tripled distilled for extra smoothness. It is no wonder that the pleasant character achieved by this process, so favored by Sir Walter Raleigh, Queen Elizabeth I, Peter the Great, and James Joyce, continues to impress today's connoisseurs of fine whiskey.

Clearly, Jameson is a perfect ingredient for Irish Coffee. While Jameson has been around for hundreds of years, Irish Coffee is more recent in origination. When trans-atlantic air travel commenced after the Second World War, the flying boats that operated the service all stopped for refueling at Shannon Airport on the West Coast of Ireland. Passengers had to be disembarked by launch and were ready for a brief refueling themselves when they reached dry land. Joe Sheridan, the Chef in Shannon at that time, took a traditional Irish drink of tea with whiskey and sugar and substituted coffee and dressed up the drink by presenting it in a stemmed glass crowned with a collar of freshly whipped cream. Because Shannon was a gateway between East and West, Joe Sheridan's recipe soon achieved worldwide renown.

But in fact, Jameson's smooth mellow taste is why regular drinkers of premium Scotch, Bourbon, or Canadian Whiskey find that Jameson is a satisfying alternative to their regular brand, to be consumed on the rocks, or with a splash of water or soda.

B.A.S.I.L.
½ oz. JAMESON IRISH WHISKEY
¼ oz. Grand Marnier
¼ oz. Tia Maria
Cream

Stir all but cream. Float the cream on top. Add zest of orange.

BLACK AND TAN
1 oz. JAMESON IRISH WHISKEY
¼ oz. Bacardi Rum
½ oz. Rose's® Lime Juice
½ oz. Orange Juice
½ tsp. Superfine Sugar
Ginger Ale

In a cocktail shaker with ice, shake hard. Strain into collins glass with ice and top with ginger ale.

BLACKTHORN
¾ oz. JAMESON IRISH WHISKEY
¾ oz. Martini & Rossi Extra Dry Vermouth
4 drps Pernod
4 dshs Bitters

Combine with ice, shake well. Strain into an old-fashioned glass and add ice.

BOG
¾ oz. JAMESON IRISH WHISKEY
¾ oz. Baileys Original Irish Cream
4 oz. Cold Coffee

Stir well with ice and strain into old-fashioned glass. Top with whipped cream.

BRAINSTORM
1¼ oz. JAMESON IRISH WHISKEY
1 tsp. Benedictine
1 tsp. Martini & Rossi Extra Dry Vermouth

In an old-fashioned or rocks glass with ice, stir. Squeeze a strip of lemon peel above drink and add.

COMMANDO FIX
1 oz. JAMESON IRISH WHISKEY
¼ oz. Hiram Walker Triple Sec
2 dshs Hiram Walker Raspberry Schnapps
½ oz. Rose's® Lime Juice

In a sour glass with crushed ice, stir.

DANCING LEPRECHAUN
1¼ oz. JAMESON IRISH WHISKEY
1¼ oz. Lemon Juice
Club Soda
Ginger Ale

Combine the whiskey and the juice, shake with ice. Strain into a tall glass and add ice. Fill with equal parts soda and ginger ale, stir gently. Add twist of lemon.

EVERYBODY'S RUSH

1¼ oz. JAMESON IRISH WHISKEY
1 tsp. Green Chartreuse
3 dshs Hiram Walker Green Creme de Menthe

Combine with ice; shake well. Strain into an old-fashioned glass and add ice.

HUDSON'S STING

1 oz. JAMESON IRISH WHISKEY
¼ oz. Irish Mist
¼ oz. Hiram Walker Peppermint Schnapps

In a shaker, shake well. Strain into cocktail glass.

IRISH BROGUE

1 oz. JAMESON IRISH WHISKEY
¼ oz. Irish Mist

In a rocks glass with ice, stir.

IRISH COLLINS

1¼ oz. JAMESON IRISH WHISKEY
Juice of 1 Lemon
1 tsp. Sugar Syrup
Club Soda

Shake with ice. Top with club soda.

IRISH COW

1¼ oz. JAMESON IRISH WHISKEY
1 tsp. Superfine Sugar
1 cup Hot Milk

Pour hot milk into highball glass, stir in the sugar until dissolved and add the whiskey. Stir gently.

IRISH CRESTA

¾ oz. JAMESON IRISH WHISKEY
¾ oz. Irish Mist
½ oz. Orange Juice
Egg White

Combine in a cocktail shaker with ice. Strain into a cocktail glass.

IRISH HIGHBALL

1¼ oz. JAMESON IRISH WHISKEY
Ginger Ale

Pour Irish whiskey in highball glass with ice. Squeeze lemon peel over drink and drop in. Fill with ginger ale.

IRISH ROVER

¾ oz. JAMESON IRISH WHISKEY
¾ oz. Campari
2 oz. Orange Juice
dash Rose's® Grenadine

Serve on the rocks.

IRISH SHILLELAGH

1 oz. JAMESON IRISH WHISKEY
¼ oz. Hiram Walker Sloe Gin
¼ oz. Bacardi Light Rum
2 tbs. Lemon Juice
1 tsp. Superfine Sugar
2 slices Fresh Peach, coarsely chopped

Combine in shaker. Strain into a cocktail glass and garnish with 2 raspberries, 1 strawberry, and a cherry.

IRISH SPRING

1 oz. JAMESON IRISH WHISKEY
¼ oz. Hiram Walker Peach Flavored Brandy
1 oz. Orange Juice
1 oz. Sweet & Sour

In a collins glass with ice, stir well. Garnish with orange slice and cherry.

JAMESON HOT TODDY

1¼ oz. JAMESON IRISH WHISKEY
½ slice Fresh Lemon
4 Cloves
2 tsp. Brown Sugar
pinch Cinnamon

Stud lemon slice with cloves. Put lemon, sugar and cinnamon into warm cup or glass. Add boiling water and whiskey.

JAMESON IRISH COFFEE

1¼ oz. JAMESON IRISH WHISKEY
Hot Coffee

Pour into warm, stemmed glass. Sugar to taste. Stir well. Float fresh cream.

JAMESON MANHATTAN

1 oz. JAMESON IRISH WHISKEY
¼ oz. Martin & Rossi Rosso Vermouth
1 dash Bitters

Serve straight-up or over ice. Garnish with a cherry.

KERRY COOLER

1 oz. JAMESON IRISH WHISKEY
¼ oz. Sherry
1¼ tbs. Almond Extract
1¼ tbs. Lemon Juice
Club Soda

Combine (except soda) with ice; shake well. Strain into a tall glass, add ice and fill with soda. Garnish with lemon slice.

LEPRECHAUN

1¼ oz. JAMESON IRISH WHISKEY
Tonic Water

In an old-fashioned glass with ice, fill with tonic water. Twist lemon peel over drink and add.

MINGLING OF THE CLANS

1 oz. JAMESON IRISH WHISKEY
¼ oz. J&B Scotch
2 tsp. Lemon Juice
3 dshs Orange Bitters

Stir in mixing glass with ice. Strain into cocktail glass.

ONE IRELAND

1 oz. JAMESON IRISH WHISKEY
1 tbs. Hiram Walker Green Creme de Menthe
2 oz. Vanilla Ice Cream

Combine in a blender at high speed until smooth. Serve straight up.

PADDY COCKTAIL

¾ oz. JAMESON IRISH
WHISKEY
¾ oz. Martini & Rossi
Rosso Vermouth
2 dshs Bitters

Combine with ice, shake. Strain into an old-fashioned glass with ice.

RED DEVIL

1¼ oz. JAMESON IRISH
WHISKEY
1¼ oz. Clam Juice
1¼ oz. Tomato Juice
Worcestershire
Sauce
pinch Pepper

Combine with ice; shake gently. Strain straight up into a cocktail glass.

SERPENT'S TOOTH

½ oz. JAMESON IRISH
WHISKEY
1 oz. Martini & Rossi
Rosso Vermouth
½ oz. Hiram Walker
Kummel
1 dash Bitters

In a cocktail shaker with ice, shake well. Strain into cocktail glass.

SHAMROCK

1½ oz. JAMESON IRISH
WHISKEY
½ oz. Martini & Rossi
Extra Dry
Vermouth
3 dshs Green Chartreuse
3 dshs Hiram Walker
Green Creme de
Menthe

Stir well with ice and strain into glass. Serve with a green olive.

TIPPERARY

¾ oz. JAMESON IRISH
WHISKEY
¾ oz. Martini & Rossi
Rosso Vermouth
1 tbs. Green Chartreuse

Combine with ice; shake well. Strain into an old-fashioned glass with ice.

J&B SCOTCH
JUSTERINI & BROOKS LTD.

The J&B story is rather special.

In 1749, Giacomo Justerini, an Italian from Bologna, went to London and set himself up as a wine merchant. He had an English partner — George Johnson. Their business was both fashionable and successful. In 1760, the new King, George III, honoured the Company with the first of its eight Royal Warrants.

Even in 1779, Johnson and Justerini were selling Whisky. On 17 June of that year, in the Morning Post, they advertised their fine stocks of wines and spirits — amongst them, "Usque Beatha": Scotch Whisky.

In 1831, Alfred Brooks bought the Company. Since then, they have been known as Justerini and Brooks. Today their wine business continues to flourish at 61 St. James Street, London SW1 and at George Street, Edinburgh.

In 1933, Prohibition ended in the USA. Justerini and Brooks were eager to exploit this vast new market and, in 1936, appointed The Paddington Corporation as their American distributors.

J&B
RARE BLENDED SCOTCH WHISKY

A high-quality Blend like J&B RARE has been designed with several factors in mind.

Style of Blend

Its original style was planned to fill a particular demand for a Blend with a delicate but fragrant aroma and flavour. It had to be distinctive and, therefore, easily recognized. Once designed, its style remained absolutely consistent.

High Proportion of Speyside Malts. To maintain the traditional taste of the Scotch Whisky Blend, J&B RARE contains a high proportion of Malt Whiskies. Quantity alone, however, is not everything and to establish quality these Malt Whiskies are of a greater age than normal–probably around 7 years old.

The age at which the Malt Whiskies are used ensures they make their optimum contribution. The Blend has a high proportion of Speyside Malt Whiskies. This forms a base of delicately-flavored Whiskies to which they add Highland, Lowland and Islay Malt Whiskies in order to provide substance and an appropriate balance of aroma and flavour.

In the J&B RARE Blend, they use some 30 different Malt Whiskies and half a dozen different Grain Whiskies. Top Class Malt Whiskies from their own Speyside Distilleries form the heart of the Blend. This guarantees that J&B RARE will remain a brand of consistent high quality and elegance throughout the years to come.

Natural Color. There is a mistaken belief that a highly-coloured Whisky denotes much age and high alcoholic strength. New spirit is colourless but acquires a degree of colour from the oak wood cask in which it matures. The colour can be strengthened by the use of Sherry casks in aging. If too much of one's stock is held in this type of wood, the Whisky can gain a sweet and rather nutty flavour which is uncharacteristic of Scotch. Colour in Scotch Whisky, therefore, is derived in part from the containing wood but chiefly by the addition of caramel colour at the bottling stage. Too much caramel is believed to affect the taste of the blend. J&B considers that no more should be added than is necessary to bring their Blends to a consistent tint. This policy explains why J&B RARE tends to be paler in colour than its competitors.

Distilleries

Justerini and Brooks have four distilleries in the

Speyside region of the Scottish Highlands. They are: Knockando, Strathmill, Glen Spey and Auchroisk.

Knockando (pronounced to rhyme with commando) Distillery was built by Ian Thomson in the year 1898. The distillery is located in a lonely part of the Highlands on a steep bank overlooking the River Spey. The name Knockando is derived from Cnoc-an-dhu which in the Gaelic means "little black hill." The water at Knockando is drawn from Cardnach Spring. These water rights were acquired in 1890.

Strathmill Distillery was established in 1823 as an oatmeal Mill. In 1891, it was rebuilt as a distillery. Strathmill lies on the fringe of Keith beside the River Isla.

Glen Spey Distillery was built and put into production by James Stuart in the year 1885. Prior to this, it was known as the Mills of Rothes and, like Strathmill, appears to have been operated for milling cereals. James Stuart, in early legal documents, is described both as Corn Merchant and Distiller, so it is more than likely that the plant exercised two functions. Glen Spey lies in the village of Rothes in the valley of the River Spey.

Auchroisk Distillery was built to meet the growing demand for Scotch Whisky in general and J&B RARE in particular. Production began in January 1974. The distillery's name is taken from the nearby farm on whose land it is situated and means "the ford of the red stream."

BAIRN

1 oz. J&B SCOTCH
¼ oz. Grand Marnier
1-2 dshs Orange Bitters

Combine in a shaker with 3 to 4 ice cubes and shake vigorously. Strain into a 4 oz. chilled cocktail glass.

BALMORAL

¾ oz. J&B SCOTCH
¾ oz. Bombay Gin
¼ oz. Hiram Walker Anisette

In a cocktail shaker with ice, shake hard. Strain into cocktail glass.

BAGPIPE

1 part J&B SCOTCH
1 part Bombay Gin
1 part Bacardi Light Rum
1 part Hiram Walker White Creme de Cacao

In a cocktail shaker with ice, shake hard. Strain into rocks glass half filled with ice.

BEADLESTONE

1 oz. J&B SCOTCH
¼ oz. Martini & Rossi Rosso Vermouth
2 dshs Bitters

Combine with ice cubes in a shaker and shake vigorously. Strain into a 4 oz. chilled cocktail glass.

BLACK JACK

1 oz. J&B SCOTCH
¼ oz. Hiram Walker Coffee Flavored Brandy

Stir and serve on the rocks with a twist of lemon.

BLOODY JOSEPH

1¼ oz. J&B SCOTCH Bloody Mary Mix

In a tall glass with ice.

BLOODY MARY, QUEEN OF SCOTS

1¼ oz. J&B SCOTCH
4 oz. V-8 Tomato Cocktail or Tomato Juice
1-2 tsp. Lemon Juice
dash Tabasco
dash Worcestershire Sauce

Shake with ice. Serve in bucket glass with celery garnish, pepper to taste.

BLUEBLAZER

1¼ oz. J&B SCOTCH
1½ oz. Boiling Water Powdered Sugar

Pour scotch into one mug, the boiling water in another. Ignite the scotch, toss the burning liquor and the water from mug to mug. When mixed, it looks like a stream of fire. Pour it all into one of the mugs; add a teaspoon of sugar and a twist of lemon. Stir and wait until it cools enough to drink.

BOBBY BURNS

1 oz. J&B SCOTCH
¼ oz. Martini & Rossi
     Rosso Vermouth
3 dshs Benedictine

Build in cocktail glass over ice. Stir and serve.

BUTTERSCOTCH COLLINS

1 oz. J&B SCOTCH
¼ oz. Drambuie
     Juice of ½ Lemon
1 tsp. Sugar

Dissolve sugar in a little water and pour over ice in collins glass. Add other ingredients and top with soda, stir lightly. Garnish with orange slice and cherry.

CHURCHILL

1 oz. J&B SCOTCH
¼ oz. Hiram Walker
     Triple Sec
¼ oz. Martini & Rossi
     Rosso Vermouth
2 tsp. Rose's® Lime
     Juice

Combine with ice; shake well. Strain into an old-fashioned glass with ice.

DRY ROB ROY

1 oz. J&B SCOTCH
¼ oz. Martini & Rossi
     Extra Dry
     Vermouth
2 dshs Bitters

Shake well with cracked ice and strain into cocktail glass. Garnish with lemon peel.

DUNDEE

2 tbs. J&B SCOTCH
1 oz. Bombay Gin
2 tsp. Drambuie
1 tsp. Lemon Juice

Combine with ice; shake well. Strain into an old-fashioned glass with ice. Garnish with cherry and twist of lemon.

GENTLE JOHN

1¼ oz. J&B SCOTCH
3 drps Martini & Rossi
     Extra Dry
     Vermouth
3 drps Hiram Walker
     Triple Sec
1-2 dshs Orange Bitters

Combine with ice; shake well. Strain into old-fashioned glass.

GIBRALTAR

¾ oz. J&B SCOTCH
¾ oz. Dry Sherry
2 tsp. Lemon Juice
2 tsp. Passion Fruit
     Syrup

Combine in a shaker with ice cubes and shake vigorously. Strain into a 4 oz. chilled cocktail glass.

GODFATHER

2 parts J&B SCOTCH
2 parts Hiram Walker
     Amaretto

Stir on the rocks.

HEATHER COFFEE

1 oz. J&B SCOTCH
¼ oz. Drambuie
Coffee

Fill mug with coffee, top with whipped cream.

HIGHLAND COFFEE

1 oz. J&B SCOTCH
¼ oz. B&B
Coffee

Fill mug with coffee, top with whipped cream.

HIGHLAND FLING

1½ oz. J&B SCOTCH
3 oz. Milk
1 tsp. Powdered Sugar

Combine with ice; shake well. Strain into an old-fashioned glass with ice. Dust with nutmeg.

HOPSCOTCH

1¼ oz. J&B SCOTCH
4-5 oz. Perrier or Evian
Water

Serve over ice in bucket glass.

IRON LADY

1 oz. J&B SCOTCH
½ oz. Martini & Rossi
Extra Dry
Vermouth
½ oz. Martini & Rossi
Rosso Vermouth
1 dash Benedictine

Stir in a mixing glass with ice. Strain into cocktail glass.

J&B INTERNATIONAL STINGER

1 oz. J&B SCOTCH
¼ oz. Hiram Walker
Peppermint
Schnapps

Serve chilled in a Manhattan glass.

J&B ROB ROY

1 oz. J&B SCOTCH
¼ oz. Martini & Rossi
Rosso Vermouth

Serve chilled in Manhattan glass or over ice in rocks glass.

J&B SCOTCH BOUNTY

½ oz. J&B SCOTCH
½ oz. Malibu Rum
Liqueur
½ oz. Hiram Walker
Creme de Cacao
3 oz. Orange Juice
dash Rose's® Grenadine

Serve over ice in tall hurricane glass.

J&B ULTIMATE SOUR

1 oz. J&B SCOTCH
4 oz. Sweet & Sour Mix
splsh Orange Juice

Combine with ice; shake well. Strain into an old-fashioned glass with ice.

J&BEACH

1 oz. J&B SCOTCH
3 oz. Pineapple Juice
2 oz. Cranberry Juice

Serve over ice in bucket glass.

KERRY BLUE

1 oz. J&B SCOTCH
1 dash Martini & Rossi
    Extra Dry
    Vermouth
½ oz. Hiram Walker Blue
    Curacao

In a cocktail shaker with ice, shake hard. Strain into cocktail glass.

L.S.D.

½ oz. J&B SCOTCH
½ oz. Drambuie
½ oz. Lemonade

In a rocks glass with ice, combine and serve.

LOCH LOMOND

1¼ oz. J&B SCOTCH
1¼ tsp. Sugar Syrup
3 dshs Bitters

Combine with ice; shake well. Strain into an old-fashioned glass with ice.

MARLON BRANDO

1 oz. J&B SCOTCH
¼ oz. Hiram Walker
    Amaretto
    Heavy Cream

In a rocks glass with ice, float heavy cream on top.

NORTH SEA

¾ oz. J&B SCOTCH
¼ oz. Grand Marnier
2 dshs Orange Juice
2 dshs Lemon Juice

Build in a cocktail glass over ice. Stir and serve.

OLD-FASHIONED J&B

1¼ oz. J&B SCOTCH
3 dshs Bitters

In an old-fashioned glass, muddle 1 cube of sugar with ½ jigger of water, add remaining ingredients and ice cubes. Stir. Garnish with slice of orange and cocktail cherry. Add twist of lemon.

PLANTATION SCOTCH PUNCH

1¼ oz. J&B SCOTCH
2 oz. Pineapple Juice
1 oz. Rose's® Grenadine
1 oz. Sweet and Sour
    dash Bitters

In a cocktail shaker, shake hard. Pour into highball glass filled with ice. Garnish with slice of orange or pineapple.

RED FIZZ

¾ oz. J&B SCOTCH
¾ oz. Dry Red Wine
2 tsp. Lemon Juice
1 tsp. Sugar Syrup
    Club Soda

In a cocktail shaker with ice, shake hard. Pour, without straining, into rocks glass and add soda. Garnish with slice of pineapple.

ROYAL MILE

¾ oz. J&B SCOTCH
¼ oz. Hiram Walker Blue
Curacao
¼ oz. Hiram Walker
Amaretto
3 oz. Orange Juice

In a tall glass with ice.

RUSTY NAIL
aka NAIL DRIVER

1 oz. J&B SCOTCH
1 oz. Drambuie

Combine in an old-fashioned glass, add ice and stir.

SCOTCH BRU

1 oz. J&B SCOTCH
¼ oz. Hiram Walker
White Creme de
Menthe
1 dash Drambuie

Shake well and pour over ice into rocks glass.

SCOTCH COBBLER

1 oz. J&B SCOTCH
½ tsp. Hiram Walker
Orange Curacao
¼ oz. Asbach Uralt

Combine over ice in a tall glass. Garnish with a slice of lemon and/or mint.

SCOTCH COLLINS

1¼ oz. J&B SCOTCH
2 tsp. Rose's Lime Juice
1 tsp. Powdered Sugar
Club Soda

Combine all except soda with ice; shake well. Strain into a sour glass straight up; add a spritz of soda and garnish with a slice of orange and a cherry.

SCOTCH MIST

1¼ oz. J&B SCOTCH

In rocks glass with crushed ice, squeeze strip of lemon peel over drink and drop it in.

SCOTCH SIDECAR

1 oz. J&B SCOTCH
¼ oz. Hiram Walker
Triple Sec
¾ oz. Sweetened
Lemon Juice

Shake and serve in cocktail class with sugar rim.

SCOTCH SMASH

1¼ oz. J&B SCOTCH
1 tsp. Sugar Syrup
Club Soda
3 Mint Sprigs

Muddle the mint with the sugar syrup; pour scotch into a tall glass. Add ice; fill with soda and stir. Garnish with slices of fruit.

SCOTCH SOLACE

3 oz. J&B SCOTCH
½ oz. Hiram Walker
Triple Sec
½ oz. Honey
4 oz. Milk
1 oz. Heavy Cream
¼ tsp. Orange Rind

Pour scotch, honey and triple sec into a 14-oz. highball glass, until honey is thoroughly blended. Add milk and cream and orange rind.

SCOTCH SOUR

1¼ oz. J&B SCOTCH
1 oz. Lemon Juice
1 tsp. Sugar

Stir in mixing glass. Strain into sour glass, or rocks glass, with ice and serve ungarnished. Can also be shaken with cracked ice.

SCOTCH SPARKLE

1¼ oz. J&B SCOTCH
Sparkling Water

In a tall glass filled with ice, fill with sparkling water.

SCOTCH STAR

1 oz. J&B SCOTCH
¼ oz. Hiram Walker Sloe Gin
1 dash Bitters
2 oz. Sweetened Lemon Mix

Shake with ice and serve on the rocks.

SCOTCH TODDY

1¼ oz. J&B SCOTCH
Hot Water
Sugar

Heaped teaspoon of sugar in warm glass, add a little boiling water and dissove sugar. Add 1 oz. scotch and stir with silver spoon. Pour in more boiling water and top with ¼ more scotch.

SCOTIA'S SECRET

¾ oz. J&B SCOTCH
¾ oz. Hiram Walker Amaretto
2 oz. Orange Juice
2 oz. Mai Tai Mix

Blend. Serve in a highball glass.

SCOTTISH COFFEE

1 oz. J&B SCOTCH
½ oz. Hiram Walker Anisette
Expresso

Serve in expresso coffee, garnish with lemon twist.

SCOTTISH SHORTBREAD COFFEE

¾ oz. J&B SCOTCH
¾ oz. Butterscotch Schnapps
Coffee

Fill mug with coffee, top with whipped cream.

SCOTTY DOG

1¼ oz. J&B SCOTCH
1½ oz. Rose's® Lime Juice

Shake with ice and strain into a glass. Garnish with a slice of lime.

SIRROCO COCKTAIL

½ oz. J&B SCOTCH
¼ oz. Yellow Chartreuse
¼ oz. Hiram Walker Triple Sec

Combine and serve.

SOUR NAIL

1 oz. J&B SCOTCH
¼ oz. Drambuie
3 oz. Orange Juice
1 dash Rose's® Grenadine
Sugar

Blend. Pour into tall glass with ice. Garnish with orange slice and cherry.

SWEET PEAT

½ oz. J&B SCOTCH
½ oz. Cherry Marnier
¼ oz. Martini & Rossi
Rosso Vermouth
½ oz. Orange Juice

Stir in a mixing glass with ice. Strain into cocktail glass.

WALKMAN

¾ oz. J&B SCOTCH
½ oz. Cherry Marnier
¾ oz. Martini & Rossi
Rosso Vermouth
½ oz. Orange Juice

Combine in a mixing glass with ice cubes and stir well. Strain into a chilled 4 oz. cocktail glass.

WHIZZ BANG

⅔ J&B SCOTCH
⅓ Martini & Rossi
Extra Dry
Vermouth
2 dshs Pernod
2 dshs Orange Bitters
2 dshs Rose's® Grenadine

Stir well with ice and strain into glass.

WOODWARD

1 oz. J&B SCOTCH
1 oz. Martini & Rossi
Extra Dry
Vermouth
1 oz. Grapefruit Juice

Combine with ice; shake well. Strain into an old-fashioned glass and add ice.

KAHLUA

Arabia, some say. Untold centuries ago. So starts the history of Kahlua. It is a story cloaked in mystery. Clues, more than facts. Pieces of a puzzle. The discovery, for instance, that when Kahlua first appeared labeled, it displayed a turbaned man sitting under the now-famous Morrish archway on the label. Speculation has it that the turban indicates a Turkish origin. Others maintain it is Moroccan.

The only thing known for sure is that Kahlua found its way to Spain before turning up, at the start of this century, in Mexico. At some point, the turban gave way to a sombrero: creating the very figure that appears today on the Kahlua bottle.

It really shouldn't be surprising that Kahlua would have such a mystique surrounding it. Its very taste is intriguing, fascinating. Think about it. To do so is to realize it's like nothing else. Try though imitators may, Kahlua liqueur remains unique.

While its main ingredient is, of course, coffee, people also discern chocolate, vanilla. Interestingly, the recipe contains no chocolate. But when a coffee bean is rich and dark and hearty enough — something Turkish coffee would undoubtedly have been — and which the Mexican coffee bean used today most certainly is — it suggests a cocoa-like quality.

The other main ingredient is alcohol distilled from cane sugar. Which is another reason the taste of Kahlua needs no getting used to. From the very first, it's sweet and delicious — a bit like adult candy.

Understandably, the actual recipe is a closely-guarded secret, a treasure unchanged through the years. Similarly, the same distinctive label that originated so long ago, in some distant land, remains in place. It's just one of the features that makes Kahlua so easily identifiable on a bar shelf, in a liquor cabinet, and on restaurant liqueur carts the world over.

No discussion of Kahlua would be complete without mentioning the Pre-Columbian statues that are almost as well-known as the bottle itself. Thanks to the extensive advertising Kahlua has done for over 30 years, these statues are an icon for the brand.

Their story is no less compelling than the product they've come to represent, since the "pre-" in their name indicates pre-Columbus' discovery of America. And so, Pre-Columbian, by name. The statues originated in Mexico, Central and South America; sculpted as symbols of people's occupations, or personalities, or physical traits. Precisely why they appear so human. Some so happy. Some so pensive. Some holding bowls or tools.

That they found their way into Kahlua lore is serendipity: a fortuitous fact of happenstance. In the 1950's and 60's Kahlua was owned by a Los Angeles businessman named Jules Berman. He happened also to be a celebrated collector of Pre-Columbian statues. Given the south-of-the-border connection between the liqueur and the statues he proudly owned, he named his famed collection "The Kahlua Collection." It was under this banner that it was exhibited in the most prestigious museums in the country: from the Metropolitan in New York to the Art Institute of Chicago to the Los Angeles County Museum.

As the reputation of the Collection grew, Mr. Berman made the decision to use the statues in Kahlua advertising. The idea of two ancient, folklore symbols carving out a niche of distinction proved irresistible to him. It has proved equally irresistible to the ensuing decades of consumers.

Kahlua today enjoys the honor of being the best-loved, best-remembered brand of all imported liqueurs. Remarkably, Kahlua outsells its nearest competitor nearly two-to-one. Its popularity is due to many factors; starting with its extraordinary flavor. As people delightedly discover, year after year, there is virtually no end to what Kahlua can do. Its versatility is practically boundless.

While there is no official count, reports indicate over 200 drinks currently being made with Kahlua. Imagine! Everything from classic cocktails like the Kahlua Black Russian to the pure delight of Kahlua & Cream to the tropical magic of Kahlua Colada to the after-dinner coziness of Kahlua & Coffee.

Furthermore, it's a great dessert favorite — at home and in restaurants. Inventive cooks can also attest to how delicious a touch of Kahlua tastes in anything from sauces to souffles. As its advertising proudly proclaims, "Everything it touches turns delicious."

COLORADO BULLDOG

1½ oz. KAHLUA
4   oz. Cream
    Cola

Pour over ice. Add a splash of cola. Stir briefly.

DIRE STRAITS

¼   oz. KAHLUA
1   oz. Asbach Uralt
¼   oz. Liquore Galliano
¼   oz. Half & Half

Pour over ice in a rocks glass.

EVERGLADES SPECIAL

2   tsp. KAHLUA
¾   oz. Bacardi Light Rum
¾   oz. Hiram Walker
    White Creme de
    Cacao
1   oz. Light Cream

Combine with ice; shake. Strain into cocktail glass, fill with ice.

FROZEN MONK

1   part KAHLUA
1   part Hiram Walker
    Dark Creme de
    Cacao
1   part Frangelico
1   scp. Vanilla Ice Cream

Combine in a blender until smooth. Pour into a cocktail glass.

GENTLE BULL

½   oz. KAHLUA
1   oz. Sauza
    Conmemorativo
    Tequila
1   tbs. Heavy Cream

Combine with ice; shake well. Strain into an old-fashioned glass and add ice.

GOOD AND PLENTY

¾   oz. KAHLUA
¾   oz. Hiram Walker
    Anisette

Pour over ice in a rocks glass.

HARBOR LIGHTS

1   part KAHLUA
1   part Sauza
    Conmemorativo
    Tequila
1   part Bacardi 151 Rum

Layer in a cordial or sherry glass.

JOHN ALDEN

1   part KAHLUA
1   part Bacardi Gold
    Reserve Rum
1   oz. Hiram Walker
    Orange Curacao

Combine with ice; shake well. Strain straight up into a cocktail glass.

KAHLUA & COFFEE

1½ oz. KAHLUA
    Hot Coffee
    Cream, plain or
    whipped

Add Kahlua to coffee. Stir in cream or top with whipped cream.

KAHLUA & CREAM
1½ oz. KAHLUA
4   oz. Cream or Milk

Pour over ice in an old-fashioned glass, fill with cream or milk.

KAHLUA & HOT CHOCOLATE
1½ oz. KAHLUA
    Hot Chocolate
    Whipped Cream

Prepare hot chocolate according to your favorite recipe. Add Kahlua. Stir. Top with whipped cream or marshmallows. For a minty variation, try 1 oz. Kahlua and ½ oz. peppermint schnapps.

KAHLUA & ICE COFFEE
1½ oz. KAHLUA
    Chilled Coffee
    Milk or Cream

Pour in chilled coffee over ice in a tall glass. Add cream or milk, if desired.

KAHLUA & SODA
1½ oz. KAHLUA
    Club Soda

Pour Kahlua over ice in a highball glass. Add club soda. Stir. Garnish with lime wedge.

KAHLUA AGGRAVATION
1   oz. KAHLUA
½   oz. J&B Scotch
    Cream

Pour Kahlua and Scotch over ice. Fill with cream. Stir.

KAHLUA BAVARIAN COFFEE
1   oz. KAHLUA
½   oz. Hiram Walker
    Peppermint
    Schnapps
    Hot Coffee
    Whipped Cream

Add Kahlua and schnapps to coffee. Top with whipped cream. Garnish with shaved chocolate.

KAHLUA BLACK RUSSIAN
½   oz. KAHLUA
1   oz. Absolut Vodka

Pour over ice in an old-fashioned glass, stir.

KAHLUA BRANDY ALEXANDER
1   oz. KAHLUA
1   oz. Asbach Uralt
2   scps. Vanilla Ice Cream

Combine and blend briefly.

KAHLUA BRAVE BULL
¾   oz. KAHLUA
¾   oz. Sauza
    Conmemorativo
    Tequila

Pour Kahlua and tequila over ice. Stir. Garnish with lemon twist.

KAHLUA CHI CHI

1   oz. KAHLUA
¾   oz. Absolut Vodka
2   oz. Pineapple Juice
1   oz. Coconut Milk or
      Syrup

In a blender, combine all ingredients with ½ cup finely crushed ice and blend. Pour in tall glass. Garnish with mint sprig.

KAHLUA COLADA

1   oz. KAHLUA
½   oz. Bacardi Light Rum
1   oz. Cream of Coconut
2   oz. Pineapple Juice

In a blender, combine all ingredients with 1 cup crushed ice and blend. Garnish with maraschino cherry and pineapple wedge. Pina colada mix may be substituted for cream of coconut and pineapple juice.

KAHLUA CREAM SODA

1½   oz. KAHLUA
1½   oz. Cream
4   oz. Club Soda

In a tall glass, pour Kahlua and cream or milk over ice. Add club soda.

KAHLUA GRAND COFFEE

¾   oz. KAHLUA
¾   oz. Grand Marnier
      Hot Coffee

In a coffee glass or mug, fill with hot coffee. Top with whipped cream.

KAHLUA HOT SPICED APPLE CIDER

1½   oz. KAHLUA
8   oz. Hot Cider or
      Apple Juice

Pour Kahlua into hot cider or apple juice. Stir with cinnamon stick. 1 oz. apple schnapps may be added.

KAHLUA HUMMER

1   part KAHLUA
1   part Bacardi Light Rum
2   scps. French Vanilla or
      Chocolate Ice
      Cream

Combine all ingredients and blend briefly.

KAHLUA IRISH COFFEE

1   oz. KAHLUA
1   oz. Jameson Irish
      Whiskey
      Hot Coffee
      Whipped Cream

Add Kahlua and Irish whiskey to coffee and top with whipped cream.

KAHLUA KIOKI COFFEE

1   oz. KAHLUA
½   oz. Asbach Uralt
      Hot Coffee
      Whipped Cream

Add Kahlua and brandy to coffee. Top with whipped cream.

KAHLUA MEXICAN COFFEE
1 oz. KAHLUA
½ oz. Sauza
    Conmemorativo
    Tequila
    Hot Coffee
    Whipped Cream

Add Kahlua and tequila to coffee. Top with whipped cream and dust with cocoa powder.

KAHLUA MILK SHAKE
2 oz. KAHLUA
½ cup Milk
3 scps. Vanilla or
    Chocolate Ice
    Cream

Combine and blend until smooth.

KAHLUA ON THE ROCKS
1½ oz. KAHLUA

Pour over ice. Garnish with lemon or lime wedge.

KAHLUA PARISIAN COFFEE
1 part KAHLUA
1 part Grand Marnier
2 parts Asbach Uralt
    Hot Coffee
    Whipped Cream

Pour into a mug, fill with hot coffee. Top with whipped cream. Garnish with shaved chocolate or orange peel.

KAHLUA PATTYMINT
1½ oz. KAHLUA
¾ oz. Hiram Walker
    Peppermint
    Schnapps

Pour Kahlua and schnapps over ice. Stir.

KAHLUA PEACH SCHNAPPS HUMMER
1 oz. KAHLUA
1 oz. Hiram Walker
    Peach Schnapps
2 scps. Vanilla Ice Cream

Combine and blend briefly.

KAHLUA PEPPERMINT SCHNAPPS HUMMER
Substitute peppermint for peach schnapps.

KAHLUA STRAWBERRY SCHNAPPS HUMMER
Substitute strawberry for peach schnapps.

KAHLUA PEANUT BUTTER FIZZ
1½ oz. KAHLUA
3 oz. Milk
1 scp. Vanilla Ice Cream
1 tbs. Peanut Butter
    Club Soda

In blender, put first four ingredients and blend well. Pour into tall glass. Add a splash of club soda.

KAHLUA POLAR BEAR
1 oz. KAHLUA
1 oz. Absolut Vodka
2 scps. Vanilla Ice Cream

Combine and blend briefly.

KAHLUA ROOT BEER FLOAT
1½ oz. KAHLUA
1 oz. Cola
1 scp. Vanilla Ice Cream
    Club Soda

Pour Kahlua and cola over ice cream in a tall glass. Fill with club soda.

KAHLUA, RUM & SODA
1   oz. KAHLUA
½   oz. Bacardi Rum
      Club Soda
Pour over ice, fill with club soda. Stir.

KAHLUA STRAIGHT
1½ oz. KAHLUA
Pour in cordial glass.

KAHLUA TOREADOR
½   oz. KAHLUA
1   oz. Asbach Uralt
1   Egg White
Combine with ice; shake. Strain into an old-fashioned glass, add ice.

KAHLUA WHITE RUSSIAN
¾   oz. KAHLUA
¾   oz. Absolut Vodka
      Cream or Milk
Pour over ice. Top with cream or milk.

KAHLUA, COGNAC & CREAM
1   oz. KAHLUA
½   oz. Cognac
      Cream or Milk
Pour over ice in a brandy snifter. Swirl gently.

KAHLUA, IRISH & CREAM
1   oz. KAHLUA
½   oz. Jameson Irish
      Whiskey
      Cream or Milk
Pour over ice in brandy snifter. Swirl gently. Garnish with mint sprig.

KAHLUA, PEACHES & CREAM
¾   oz. KAHLUA
¾   oz. Hiram Walker
      Peach Schnapps
4   oz. Cream
Pour over ice, stir.

KAHLUA, PEPPERMINT & CREAM
¾   oz. KAHLUA
¾   oz. Hiram Walker
      Peppermint
      Schnapps
4   oz. Cream
Pour over ice, stir.

KAHLUA, STRAWBERRIES & CREAM
¾   oz. KAHLUA
¾   oz. Hiram Walker
      Strawberry
      Schnapps
4   oz. Cream
Pour over ice, stir.

LIGHTHOUSE
1 part KAHLUA
1 part Sauza
      Conmemorativo
      Tequila
1 part Hiram Walker
      Peppermint
      Schnapps
1 part Bacardi 151 Rum
Combine in a rocks glass with ice.

MIXED MOCHA FRAPPE

¾ oz. KAHLUA
1 tsp. Hiram Walker
White Creme de
Menthe
1 tsp. Hiram Walker
White Creme de
Cacao
1 tsp. Hiram Walker
Triple Sec

Combine without ice and stir. Sugar frost the rim of an old-fashioned glass. Pour over crushed ice.

MOCHA MINT

1 part KAHLUA
1 part Hiram Walker
White Creme de
Menthe
1 part Hiram Walker
White Creme de
Cacao

Combine with ice; shake. Strain into an old-fashioned glass.

MUDSLIDE

¼ oz. KAHLUA
1 oz. Absolut Vodka
¼ oz. Baileys Original
Irish Cream
Cola

Combine in a cocktail glass with ice, fill with cola.

MUDSLIDE II

¾ oz. KAHLUA
¾ oz. Baileys Original
Irish Cream

Pour over ice in a rocks glass.

OLÉ

½ oz. KAHLUA
1 oz. Sauza
Conmemorativo
Tequila
1 tbs. Sugar Syrup
Heavy Cream

Combine everything except cream without ice; stir until well blended. Pour into a cocktail glass over crushed ice; float a little cream.

PLAYBOY COOLER

¾ oz. KAHLUA
¾ oz. Bacardi Gold
Reserve Rum
3 oz. Pineapple Juice
2 tsp. Lemon Juice
Cola

Combine everything except cola with ice; shake well. Strain; add plenty of ice and fill the glass with cola. Garnish with pineapple slice.

SEVEN TWENTY-SEVEN (727)

1 part KAHLUA
1 part Absolut Vodka
1 part Grand Marnier
1 part Baileys Original
Irish Cream

Combine in a rocks glass with ice.

SMITH & KEARNS

1½ oz. KAHLUA
4 oz. Cream
Club Soda or
Carbonated Soft
Drink

Pour over ice, add splash of soda. Stir.

SOMBRERO aka MUDDY RIVER

1½   oz. KAHLUA
½   oz. Half & Half

In a snifter or rocks glass with ice.

SPANISH MOSS

2   tbs. KAHLUA
1½   oz. Sauza
     Conmemorativo
     Tequila
4 drps. Hiram Walker
     Green Creme de
     Menthe

Combine with ice; shake well. Strain over one cube of ice in an old-fashioned glass.

TOASTED ALMOND

1   oz. KAHLUA
½   oz. Hiram Walker
     Amaretto
     Cream or Milk

Pour over ice, stir.

XAVIER

½   oz. KAHLUA
½   oz. Hiram Walker
     Creme de Noyaux
½   oz. Grand Marnier
1½   oz. Half & Half

Shake well, strain into a chilled cocktail glass.

LA GRANDE PASSION

A marriage of the earthy refinements of French Armagnac with the passion fruit, La Grande Passion is a unique and versatile addition to the small, high-end fraternity of fine French liqueurs.

The base of La Grande Passion is Armagnac, the "liquid gold of Gascony," a region of France immortalized by Alexandre Dumas in the creation of D'Artagnan, the gallant Gascon musketeer. D'Artagnan's deeds are reliably said to have been fired by Armagnac, and the brandy is the source of a variety of delightful legends, among them that the grandfather of Henry IV of France moistened the lips of the newborn child with Armagnac, and that from this taste alone, he drew "wisdom and strength his whole life."

While this may sound a jot hyperbolic, a sip of this complex and earthy brandy is enough to reinforce the opinion that it is a true flower of the distiller's art. The wines that are used to make it are produced within a strictly delimited zone: only Bas-Armagnac, Haut-Armagnac and Tenareze are entitled to the Appellation d'Origine. This strictness then continues through the distillation, which is allowed to take place with only two specific types of stills. After distillation, it is the cellar-master's turn. The brandy reposes a minimum of two years in casks of hand-hewn oak, usually selected from local forests. It is this mellowing which gives Armagnac its rich color and texture, and together with the slow, continuous process of distillation produces that "gout du terroir" – that flavor of earth and vine, for which the brandy is universally renowned and admired. Sometimes called "the velvet flame," Armagnac is one of the world's finest grape brandies.

But the magic lies in the mix, and in this case the mix is an unqualified success. To produce La Grande Passion, Armagnac is married to the passion fruit, otherwise known as *passiflora edulis*. Though a native of the torrid zones of both North and South America, this versatile little fruit has till now been most commonly used in France, tincturing the gustatory concoctions of French pâtissiers, chefs and cooks for years. In sorbets and pastries, mousses and sauces of every type, it has long been used to give ambrosial shadings and aromatic zest.

Recently, the trend towards passion fruit has begun to gain on American shores, as consumers with increasingly refined tastes search for new and alternative ways of flavoring. The juice section of the supermarket attests to it: tropical nectars are sweetening palates coast to coast. And as no less venerable an authority than the *Wall Street Journal* reported in a front page article in 1984, "A passion fruit craze is sweeping the island (Puerto Rico) and may be headed for the U.S. mainland." Four years later, it can safely be reported that they were right. A trend is most certainly in the making, and the passion fruit is squarely in the center of it. "The most fragrant of all edible fruit in the world," according to the food experts, the fruit is deep purple or yellow when ripe, filled with tiny edible seeds which are surrounded by a juicy pulp. Its name derives from the 16th century Spanish missionaries who, spurred by its complex of sweet flavors, decided to name it after the Passion of Christ. To this day the fruit has an aura of mystery and sensuality about it—qualities amply reinforced by a single taste.

The French passion fruit craze began over a decade ago, sparked by the availability of pulps and concentrates which were widely used by resourceful home cooks. Its most splendid public moment was during the 1983 Vasailles summit, when it was used by Chef Pasquet. Now accepted as an ingredient in its own right, it has taken its place among that roster of tropical stars which include the mango, the papaya and of course the kiwi.

A LITTLE SLICE OF HEAVEN
¾   oz. LA GRANDE
       PASSION
¾   oz. Absolut Vodka
In a tall glass with ice.

ACAPULCO PASSION
1   oz. LA GRANDE
       PASSION
½   oz. Sauza
       Conmemorativo
       Tequila
       Juice of ½ Lime
Mix all ingredients with cracked ice in a shaker or blender. Strain and pour into a chilled cocktail glass.

ANDY WARHOL'S ABSOLUT PASSION
1 part LA GRANDE
       PASSION
2 parts Absolut Vodka
       Tropical Fruit
       Juice
       Club Soda
Pour liquors over ice in a tall glass. Fill glass with fruit juice and a dash of club soda. Garnish with a twist of lemon.

APASSIONATA
1½ oz. LA GRANDE
       PASSION
¼   oz. Hiram Walker
       Amaretto
4   oz. Grapefruit Juice
Mix all ingredients with ice in a shaker or blender and pour into a large goblet. Garnish with a red and a green maraschino cherry.

BODY HEAT
1   oz. LA GRANDE
       PASSION
¼   oz. Kahlua
¼   oz. Absolut Vodka
1   oz. Light Cream
Mix all ingredients in a shaker with cracked ice, strain and pour into a chilled cocktail glass.

BUBBLING PASSION
1½ oz. LA GRANDE
       PASSION
       Champagne or
       Sparkling Wine
Pour La Grande Passion into a chilled champagne flute or goblet and fill with ice and cold champagne. Add lemon twist.

CAPTAINS PASSION
1 part LA GRANDE
       PASSION
1 part Bacardi Dark Rum
Shake and pour in a champagne glass.

CRAN PASSION
1   oz. LA GRANDE
       PASSION
¾   oz. Cranberry Juice
¼   oz. Orange Juice
Add crushed ice in a large hurricane glass with tropical garnish.

EVENING PASSION

1 oz. LA GRANDE PASSION
½ oz. Bombay Gin
Juice of ½ Lemon
Sugar to taste
dash Rose's® Grenadine

Mix with cracked ice in a shaker or blender, strain and pour into a chilled cocktail glass.

FALL PASSION

1 oz. LA GRANDE PASSION
1 cup Hot Tea
Milk or Cream (optional)

Add La Grande Passion to hot tea and add milk or cream if you wish.

FROZEN PINEAPPLE PASSION

4 oz. LA GRANDE PASSION
2 oz. Absolut Vodka
6 oz. Can Frozen Pineapple Juice

Add ingredients and blend until smooth. Pour into two large stemmed glasses. Garnish with fruit and serve immediately.

HEART OF PASSION

2 oz. LA GRANDE PASSION
dash Cherry Juice

Shake with ice. Strain into chilled cocktail glass. Garnish with cherry.

HEART THROB

1 oz. LA GRANDE PASSION
½ oz. Cranberry Juice
1½ oz. Apple Juice

In a tall glass over ice.

HEIGHT OF PASSION

1 oz. LA GRANDE PASSION
3 oz. Champagne
1 dash Orange Bitters
½ tsp. Superfine Sugar
Juice of ¼ Orange

Garnish with curl of orange peel.

LA GRANDE AFFAIRE

1½ oz. LA GRANDE PASSION
¼ oz. Creme de Grand Marnier

Mix briefly, but briskly with cracked ice in a shaker or blender, strain and pour into a chilled cocktail glass.

LA GRANDE PASSION COCKTAIL

1½ oz. LA GRANDE PASSION
¼ oz. Grand Marnier
Juice of ½ Lemon
Sugar to taste

Mix all ingredients with cracked ice in a shaker or blender, strain and pour into a chilled cocktail glass.

LA GRANDE PASSION COOLER

1½	oz. LA GRANDE PASSION
2	dshs Rose's® Grenadine
	7-Up

Pour over ice, add grenadine and fill with 7-Up.

LA STING

| 1 | oz. LA GRANDE PASSION |
| ¼ | oz. Hiram Walker White Creme de Menthe |

Pour over cracked ice.

LOVE PASSION #9

1	part LA GRANDE PASSION
1	part Hiram Walker Dark Creme de Cacao
1	part Cream

Add ingredients over ice, stir.

MIDNIGHT PASSION

1	oz. LA GRANDE PASSION
¼	oz. Grand Marnier
½	oz. Bombay Gin or Absolut Vodka Juice of ½ Lemon or Lime

Mix all ingredients with cracked ice in a shaker or blender. Strain and serve in a whiskey sour glass.

MORNING PASSION

1½	oz. LA GRANDE PASSION
2	oz. Grapefruit Juice
2	oz. Orange Juice

Stir with cracked ice in a collins glass.

P.O.R. AMORE

| 1½ | oz. LA GRANDE PASSION |

Pour over rocks into a chilled cocktail glass.

PARADISE PASSION

1	oz. LA GRANDE PASSION
½	oz. Bombay Gin
2	tbs. Orange Juice
2	tsp. Shredded Coconut

Combine all ingredients except coconut in a shaker. Strain into glass. Sprinkle coconut on top.

PASSION BALL

1½	oz. LA GRANDE PASSION
	Juice of 1 Lemon
	Juice of 1 Orange

Add ingredients together over ice in a cocktail glass. Garnish with a cherry and orange slice.

PASSION DAIQUIRI

| 1 | oz. LA GRANDE PASSION |
| ½ | oz. Bacardi Light Rum Juice of ½ Lime Sugar to taste |

Mix all ingredients with cracked ice in a shaker or blender, strain and pour into a chilled cocktail glass.

PASSION PRINCE

1 oz. LA GRANDE
PASSION
¼ oz. Apple Brandy
¼ oz. Bombay Gin
1 dash Lemon Juice

Combine in shaker with 3-4 ice cubes, shake well. Strain into chilled cocktail glass.

PASSION PUNCH

1 shot LA GRANDE
PASSION
2 shots Pineapple Juice
1 shot Orange Juice
dash Rose's® Grenadine

In a tall glass with ice, shake.

PASSION SHAKE

3 oz. LA GRANDE
PASSION
1 cup Whole Milk
1 ripe Banana
½ pint Vanilla Ice Cream

Mix La Grande Passion, milk and banana in a blender. Add ice cream and blend. Serve in stem glass, garnish with nutmeg. Serves two.

PASSION SOUR

1½ oz. LA GRANDE
PASSION
Juice of ½ Lemon
Sugar to taste

Mix all ingredients in a shaker or blender with cracked ice, strain and pour into a whiskey sour glass. Garnish with a maraschino cherry.

PASSION WITH A TWIST

1½ oz. LA GRANDE
PASSION

Fill old-fashioned glass with small ice cubes or cracked ice, add La Grande Passion. Twist lemon peel over drink and drop into glass.

PASSIONALADA

1½ oz. LA GRANDE
PASSION
1 oz. Bacardi Light Rum
4 oz. Pineapple Juice
1-2 oz. Coconut Cream

Mix all ingredients with cracked ice in a shaker and pour into a double old-fashioned glass. Garnish with pineapple stick and cherry.

PULSE POINT

2 oz. LA GRANDE
PASSION
dash Martini & Rossi
Extra Dry
Vermouth

Mix La Grande Passion and vermouth with cracked ice in a shaker or blender, strain and pour into a chilled cocktail glass. Twist lemon peel over drink and drop into glass.

ROMEO JULIUS

1½ oz. LA GRANDE
PASSION
1½ oz. Orange Juice
1½ oz. Cream

Build in a brandy snifter with cubed ice and blend in mixer. Serve with fresh orange slice on side of glass.

SUMMER PASSION

1½   oz. LA GRANDE
         PASSION
         Perrier

In a highball glass with ice, fill with cold Perrier. Squeeze juice from quartered lime or slice of lemon into glass and stir gently.

THE FROZEN GRANDE

½   oz. LA GRANDE
        PASSION
½   oz. Cherry Grand
        Marnier
½   oz. Grand Marnier
4   oz. Ice Cream
1½   oz. Half & Half

Mix in a blender with ice and serve.

THE GRANDE SQUEEZE

¾   oz. LA GRANDE
        PASSION
¾   oz. Absolut Vodka
        Fresh-squeezed
        Orange Juice

In a tall glass with ice. Garnish with orange slice.

WHITE PASSION

1½   oz. LA GRANDE
         PASSION
1   oz. Cream

Shake ingredients with cracked ice briskly and briefly or mix in a blender for a few seconds. Serve in a chilled cocktail glass.

© FOLEY PUBLISHING CORP.

MARTINI & ROSSI

In 1863 three partners, Alessandro Martini, Teofilo Sola and Luigi Rossi, joined together to found a company which today is the market leader in the Vermouth industry. They took over an established 18th century firm that had been producing Vermouth in Torino, Italy, and by the end of the same year, were exporting the first Martini Vermouth for sale in the United States. As the firm sought to penetrate every market in the world, the main production plant was moved from Torino to Pessione, closer to the Port of Genoa for better world-wide export. The first shipment went to Brazil in 1864, to Argentina in 1866, to Greece, Portugal, Belgium, Switzerland, Egypt and Turkey in 1868.

In 1879, Rossi bought Sola's shares and the company's name became Martini & Rossi. The new enterprise was representative of the emerging technology in the 19th century — the period of the Industrial Revolution. Ernesto Trevisani, author of the "Industrial and Commercial Review of Turin and the Provinces" in 1897 wrote:

> "The first thing one notices in the factory of Pessione is the perfect order that reigns everywhere, the technical distribution of the various departments, the types of distilleries . . . the great size of the space, the distribution of numerous pieces of machinery, the appearance of light, which all together induce a total response in every one of the demands of modern industrial technology and hygiene."

The men who founded Martini & Rossi were exceptional in many ways, yet characteristic of their times. Ernesto Trevisani described them as "men of steel quick to bring to fruition their intelligence, their practicality and their will."

Luigi Rossi's sons, Ernesto, Cesare, Enrico and Teofilo took over management of the company in the year 1900. It was their plan to further increase the exports by establishing plants abroad in addition to Europe and South America. Biographers of Teofilo Rossi consider him to have been one of the greatest mayors of Torino. He was a man of a thousand interests, a senator of the kingdom and ministry, a man of culture, a scholar of Dante and a historian.

Perhaps because of the influence of Rossi, the company has always been involved with the community and its development. An active patron of the arts, M&R sponsored both instrumental and vocal concerts, especially "Belcanto," or "beautiful song," a vocal technique developed in Italy during the 18th century, emphasizing vocal flexibility and ease of singing especially for Italian opera. Also a supporter of fine art, Martini & Rossi has sponsored exhibitions of the works of Picasso in Venice, De Chirico in New York and Caravaggio in London, among others.

The company began its well-known association with sports in 1924 with the Grand Cup of Bicycling. The company name is probably best known for its association with auto racing: Porsche in the World Championship for manufactures; Tecno, Brabham, Lotus in F1; Lancia in Endurance and Rally championships. Martini & Rossi has also sponsored the offshore and F 1 in speed boating, as well as world cup skiing, fencing, golf, sailing and polo. Finally in 1960, Martini & Rossi's greatest contribution to the preservation of culture, the wine museum of Torino was created. With the assistance of the Department of Culture, it exhibits more than 500 artifacts from winemaking activities dating from as early as the 7th century B.C.

Over the course of the years, other product lines have been developed. Martini & Rossi Asti Spumante is the largest exported sweet, sparkling wine in the world. Riserva Montelera authentic brut "Champenoise," and a Riesling are others. Liquors include Chinamartini, Fernet Martini, Bosford Gin, Vodka Eristow, Menta Sacco, just to mention a few.

Today, Martini & Rossi plants around the world are engaged in the production of Vermouth under the direction of General Beverage Corporation. The shareholders of GBC include members of the Rossi de Montelera family, the only descendents of the original founders.

Alberto Viriglio, author of "Turin and the Turinese" wrote in 1898:

". . . it is said that one cannot go to a region of the world so remote that one cannot detect the passage of a missionary, a scoundrel from Lucca, or a traveling salesman. That salesman will certainly offer something from the cosmopolitan house of Martini & Rossi."

Now, more than a century after the first export, the same is true — there is hardly a place in the world where Martini & Rossi products are not available.

An Ancient Tradition

Vermouth is a true aperitif — that is a wine incorporating aromatic substances and bitter plants. It is differentiated from other aromatized wines by the presence of bitter plants which stimulate digestive juices.

It is said that Hippocrates of ancient Greece invented Vermouth over 2,000 years ago when he made a grog by blending almonds, herbs and gray amber with wine, a concoction to become known as a "Hippocras." Whether it started with him or not, the tradition of flavoring wines arose for two very practical reasons. In ancient times, wine often tasted bad and was partly spoiled due to its primitive winemaking techniques and containers. Plants and herbs covered up and improved the flavor as well as helped to resist spoilage. Additions of seawater and pine resin were also common.

The second reason for combining herbs and spices with wine was medical and mystical. Medicines, narcotics and live potions were mostly botanical and wine was the solvent of choice for the ancient pharmacist. It served as both the vehicle to imbibe desirable herbal flavors and preserve them. Many of the botanical medicines of real value are bitter such as those containing quinine, for example. As a result, a bitter taste came to be desired and preferred. The alcohol of the wine preserved the medicine, tonic or potion while the antibacterial and preservative value of the oils extracted from herbal medicines kept the wine from spoiling.

Additives commonly used in Vermouth are put into two categories: carminatives and bitters. Bitters are the principal active agents which, through their chemical effect increase the secretion of gastric juices, stimulating the appetite and facilitating the working of the digestive system. Rhubarb root relieves congestion of the liver; ginger activates the circulation; cola beans and benzoin improve digestion; and coriander, cardamon and aloes are considered intestinal regulators. Quinquina bark and thistle reduce fever.

The Mediterranean abounds in aromatic plants. From Crete comes dittany and arthemisia absinthium (wormwood), which possess tonic and digestive properties. The Romans introduced other aromatic plants and herbs such as thyme, rosemary, myrtle and celery. During the Middle Ages, the Venetians brought aromatic plants and spices from the East such as ginger, nutmeg and cloves.

The word Vermouth comes from the German "Wermut" which means wormwood — a shrub whose flowers were often added to wine. Piedmont, the region surrounding Torino in the northwest corner of Italy, favored the production of Vermouth. Aromatic plants were plentiful in the nearby Alps and the dry and sweet wines, mostly Muscat Canelli, were suited to making aromatized wines.

From the time of the Renaisance, Torino became one of the major centers of Hippocratic wines and liqueurs. There are two classes of Vermouths recognized in the trade, the sweet or Italian-type Vermouth and the dry or French-type. Each evolved because of regional tastes and nearby vineyards. While the Muscat Canelli grapes were available to Italian winemakers, a drier Vermouth was developed by a French winemaker in 1800 using the thin semi-sweet Herault grapes of the Midi, more akin to French taste. Today, both countries produce dry and sweet vermouths.

Vermouth is principally served "straight" in European countries. In the United States, it is used most often in mixed drinks such as the Martini and Manhattan cocktails. In Argentina, the consumption of a glass of Vermouth or "copetin" is such a wide-spread custom that the time of day between 5 and 6 p.m. is known as the "Vermouth Hour" and the movie shown at that time of day is called the "Vermouth feature." Around the world, drinking Vermouth is the continuance of a very ancient tradition.

Vermouth Production

Inside the whitewashed walls of the Martini & Rossi estate in the village of Pessione just over the hills from Torino are the original cellars now housing an extensive wine museum, a villa used for entertainment, numerous warehouses, separate winemaking facilities for both Asti Spumante and Vermouth, and a small, exotic garden where guests can see a selection of the herbs that make Vermouth unique.

Three main types of Vermouth are made: a sweet white called Bianco, a dry white called Extra Dry, and a sweet red labeled Rosso. All are created by adding herbs, spices, distillates and sugar to a light base wine, with the main differences arising from the grape varieties used, the herb flavorings selected, and the final sugar and alcohol levels.

Fine wine grapes are selected from numerous vineyards throughout the region, vinified under the supervision of Martini & Rossi technicians, and the base wines brought to Pessione where the Vermouth making process begins.

The blend of herbs and spices are different for each Vermouth and a carefully guarded secret. The essence infusions for Martini & Rossi's 15 world-wide facilities are all made in Pessione. The list of herbs available is long: bitter-tasting plants include aloe, angelica, blessed thistle, cinchoma, European centaury, germander, lungwort, lungmoss, quassia and rhubarb. Aromatic plants are anise, bitter almond, cardamom, cinnamon, clove, coriander, dittany of Crete, galingale, marjoram, nutmeg, Roman camomile, rosemary, summer savory, thyme, tonka bean, and vanilla bean. The bitter aromatic plants include allspice, elder, elecampane, gentian, juniper, bitter orange, sweet orange, saffron, sage, sweet flag, speedwell, wormwood, and yarrow.

The quality of herbs and spices is extremely important. Thus, only the best wild herbs and imported spices are purchased from reliable suppliers to ensure their freshness and full flavor. An "infusion" is then made from the herbs and spices either through distillation or maceration.

Distillation of herbs takes place in a mixture of alcohol and water heated to 80°C. Volatile aromas are recovered at the same time as the alcohol in which they are dissolved. The distilled extract is then drawn off, herbs pressed, washed to recover the alcohol, pressed again, removed and burned. The resulting liquid is amber in color with a strong bouquet but has practically no taste.

Aromatic and bitter plants are introduced to the wine in the form of an extract created by maceration. This part of the infusion both fortifies the wine and gives it a distinctive rich, bitter flavor. Fixed stainless steel pipelines lead through the immaculate cellars into large blending tanks where the various ingredients are added to the base wines. Martini & Rossi's world-wide reputation for quality is no doubt based on their commitment to using only the finest ingredients. Absolutely no artificial flavors or extracts are used. To the base wine is added cane sugar, the distilled aromatic alcohol, the bitter tasting maceration extract, and finally to the Rosso only, caramel. Made from sugar heated and cooked until it becomes a brown, viscous mass, caramel is the only coloring allowed by government laws. It gives Rosso its deep amber hue and imports a special flavor, extra body, and smoothness to the red Vermouth.

The blend is mixed thoroughly then aged for three to six months. After aging, the Vermouth is cold stabilized to remove natural impurities, tartrates and salts. A final sterilizing filtration ensures the wine's purity and stability after it reaches the more than 200 export markets of Martini & Rossi.

In taste and style, each Vermouth is distinctive as the result of variations during its creation. The quality of herbs and spices used for dry Vermouth is lighter and much different than for sweet. The portions of base wine used in the blends are 70% for the Extra Dry and 75% for the sweet types, Rosso and Bianco. The final sugar and alcohol levels also vary. Rosso and Bianco have an average residual sugar of 16% and alcohol of 16%;

Extra Dry has an average of 2% residual sugar and 18% alcohol.

Martini & Rossi's success is based upon its reputation as the finest Vermouth in the world — one well earned and carefully preserved. The entire facility at Pessione reflects their preoccupation with quality. Although it has grown from an old company, it has been modernized into a model of organization and efficiency. The workers have been trained to consider it a food facility and that cleanliness is essential throughout.

10 R 10

¾ oz. MARTINI & ROSSI EXTRA DRY VERMOUTH
¾ oz. Dry Sherry
dash Bitters
Stir. Add lemon twist.

ACCURATE

¼ oz. MARTINI & ROSSI ROSSO VERMOUTH
¼ oz. Saki
1¼ oz. Cognac
Stir. Serve on the rocks.

AMERICANO

¾ oz. MARTINI & ROSSI ROSSO VERMOUTH
¾ oz. Campari
Club Soda
Build Campari and Martini & Rossi Rosso Vermouth in tall glass. Fill with club soda. Add twist.

CARDINALE

²/₅ oz. MARTINI & ROSSI EXTRA DRY VERMOUTH
²/₅ oz. Bombay Gin
¹/₅ oz. Bitters
Add ice and serve.

CARUSO

½ oz. MARTINI & ROSSI EXTRA DRY VERMOUTH
½ oz. Bombay Gin
¼ oz. Hiram Walker Green Creme de Menthe
Stir. Serve on the rocks.

CONTINENTAL COOLER

2 oz. MARTINI & ROSSI ROSSO VERMOUTH
4 oz. Soda
splsh Rose's® Grenadine
Stir. Serve on the rocks.

FAITHFUL JACK

½ oz. MARTINI & ROSSI EXTRA DRY VERMOUTH
½ oz. Bombay Gin
¼ oz. Hiram Walker Triple Sec
¼ oz. Asbach Uralt
Shake. Serve on the rocks with a cherry.

FRENCH KISS

1 part MARTINI & ROSSI ROSSO VERMOUTH
1 part MARTINI & ROSSI EXTRA DRY VERMOUTH
Serve over ice in rocks glass.

GOLDEN BOY

½ oz. MARTINI & ROSSI EXTRA DRY VERMOUTH
½ oz. Bombay Gin
¼ oz. Grand Marnier
Stir over the rocks.

GRAPE ESCAPE

1 part MARTINI & ROSSI EXTRA DRY VERMOUTH
1 part Bombay Gin
1 part Asbach Uralt
2 parts Bacardi Rum
splsh Rose's® Lime Juice
Stir well on the rocks.

INTERLUDE

¼ oz. MARTINI & ROSSI EXTRA DRY VERMOUTH
½ oz. J&B Scotch
¼ oz. Grand Marnier

Prepare in a mixing glass with ice cubes. Pour into double cocktail glass and decorate with slice of orange.

INVERTED MARTINI

3 oz. MARTINI & ROSSI EXTRA DRY VERMOUTH
1 oz. Bombay Gin

Add an olive or lemon twist.

LEMONTINI

3 oz. MARTINI & ROSSI EXTRA DRY VERMOUTH
 Lemonade

Fill with lemonade, add a slice of lemon.

LUCIEN

1 part MARTINI & ROSSI ROSSO VERMOUTH
1 part MARTINI & ROSSI EXTRA DRY VERMOUTH
2 parts Cognac
2 parts J&B Scotch

In a tall glass with ice.

MANUELA

⅓ oz. MARTINI & ROSSI EXTRA DRY VERMOUTH
⅓ oz. MARTINI & ROSSI ROSSO VERMOUTH
⅓ oz. Bombay Gin
2-3 drps Cognac
2 drps Bitters

Prepare in a mixing glass. Pour into cocktail glass.

MARTINI & ROSSI "007" COCKTAIL

2 parts MARTINI & ROSSI EXTRA DRY VERMOUTH
2 parts Orange Juice
 splsh Rose's® Grenadine

Stir. Serve on the rocks.

MARTINI SWEET

⅓ oz. MARTINI & ROSSI ROSSO VERMOUTH
⅔ oz. Bombay Gin

Prepare in a mixing glass with 4-5 ice cubes. Serve in a cocktail glass.

NEGRONI

½ oz. MARTINI & ROSSI EXTRA DRY VERMOUTH
½ oz. Bombay Gin
½ oz. Campari

Serve in rocks glass over ice.

NUMBER ONE

½ oz. MARTINI & ROSSI ROSSO VERMOUTH
½ oz. Bombay Gin
½ oz. Liquore Galliano
½ oz. Campari

Shake. Serve on the rocks.

PERFECT MANHATTAN

¼ oz. MARTINI & ROSSI ROSSO VERMOUTH
¼ oz. MARTINI & ROSSI EXTRA DRY VERMOUTH
1½ oz. Wild Turkey 101
1-2 dshs Bitters

Stir. Serve straight up or on the rocks.

PIE-IN-THE-SKY

1 part MARTINI & ROSSI ROSSO VERMOUTH
1 part Bacardi Rum
4 dshs Asbach Uralt
1 part Rose's® Lime Juice
2 dshs Rose's® Grenadine

Shake. Serve on the rocks.

RAY'S BEST

¾ oz. MARTINI & ROSSI ROSSO VERMOUTH
¾ oz. Asbach Uralt
   dash Bitters
   dash Rose's® Grenadine

Stir over the rocks.

RED RABBIT

¼ oz. MARTINI & ROSSI EXTRA DRY VERMOUTH
½ oz. Bombay Gin
¼ oz. Hiram Walker Cherry Flavored Brandy
   dash Campari

Shake with ice. Serve over rocks.

RED ROSE

1 part MARTINI & ROSSI ROSSO VERMOUTH
1 part Hiram Walker Sloe Gin
2 dshs Bitters
   Club Soda

Stir. Add club soda.

RIVERSIDE

½ oz. MARTINI & ROSSI EXTRA DRY VERMOUTH
½ oz. MARTINI & ROSSI ROSSO VERMOUTH
½ oz. Bombay Gin
½ oz. Orange Juice

Shake. Serve over ice.

ROSSO SUNSET

1½ oz. MARTINI & ROSSI ROSSO VERMOUTH
½ oz. Hiram Walker Triple Sec
3 oz. Orange Juice
   splsh Rose's® Grenadine

Shake. Serve over ice.

ROYAL ROSSI

¼ oz. MARTINI & ROSSI ROSSO VERMOUTH
1 oz. Bombay Gin
¼ oz. Liquore Galliano
½ oz. Campari

Shake. Serve on the rocks.

RUM MARTINI

dash MARTINI & ROSSI
    EXTRA DRY
    VERMOUTH
1¼   oz. Bacardi Rum

Stir on the rocks or strain into cocktail glass. Add olive or lemon twist.

SHINING APPLE

½   oz. MARTINI & ROSSI
    ROSSO VERMOUTH
½   oz. Asbach Uralt
¼   oz. Hiram Walker
    Cider Mill
    Schnapps

Shake. Serve over crushed ice.

SWEET & DRY

¾   oz. MARTINI & ROSSI
    ROSSO VERMOUTH
¾   oz. Bacardi Rum
3 dshs Asbach Uralt
1 dash Rose's® Grenadine
1 oz. Lemon Juice

Shake. Serve on the rocks.

SWEET ROCKS

2   oz. MARTINI & ROSSI
    ROSSO VERMOUTH

Serve on the rocks with a lemon twist.

TEN TON COCKTAIL

1 tbs. MARTINI & ROSSI
    EXTRA DRY
    VERMOUTH
1¼ oz. Seagram's V.O.
1 tbs. Grapefruit Juice

Combine with ice. Shake well. Strain and add ice. Add a cherry.

THE PRINCESS

1 part MARTINI & ROSSI
    ROSSO VERMOUTH
1 part Bacardi Rum

Stir over ice.

THE SWING COCKTAIL

1   oz. MARTINI & ROSSI
    ROSSO VERMOUTH
1   oz. MARTINI & ROSSI
    EXTRA DRY
    VERMOUTH
3   oz. Orange Juice
1 tsp. Powdered Sugar

Shake well with ice. Serve over the rocks.

THE TONIC TWIST

2   oz. MARTINI & ROSSI
    EXTRA DRY
    VERMOUTH
4   oz. Tonic

Add a twist of lime.

VERMOUTH CASSIS

2   oz. MARTINI & ROSSI
    EXTRA DRY
    VERMOUTH
½   oz. Hiram Walker
    Creme de Cassis
    Soda

Fill with soda, ice and add lemon twist or wedge.

VERMOUTH COCKTAIL

2 oz. MARTINI & ROSSI ROSSO VERMOUTH
1 dash Bitters
1 dash Cherry Juice

Stir well. Serve on the rocks.

VERMOUTH COOLER

2 oz. MARTINI & ROSSI EXTRA DRY VERMOUTH
  dash Rose's® Grenadine
  Club Soda

Serve in large glass with ice. Fill with club soda.

VERY DRY

2½ oz. MARTINI & ROSSI EXTRA DRY VERMOUTH

Serve over ice. Add lemon twist.

WESTERN ROSE

¼ oz. MARTINI & ROSSI EXTRA DRY VERMOUTH
1¼ oz. Bombay Gin
¼ oz. Asbach Uralt

Shake. Serve in rocks glass with ice.

ROSE'S® LIME JUICE

Rose's® Lime Juice . . . a remarkable brand with an adventurous heritage and a robust history: sailing ships, warm West Indies Isles, trenches of World War I, Africa's Gold Coast, the London Blitz . . . all part of the colorful legend of this unique product.

Lauchlin Rose (1829-1885), a descendent of a prominent family of Scottish ship builders, founded L. Rose & Company in Leith, Edinburgh in 1865. Describing himself as a "lime and lemon juice merchant," he combined a keen business sense with his knowledge of the sea. Scurvy, caused by a deficiency of Vitamin C, had been the scourge of sailors since the early days of sailing ships. To prevent "this most terrible of the diseases of maritime life," a supply of lime or lemon juice, preserved with 15% of rum, was generally boarded for long voyages. In 1867, Mr. Rose developed and patented a process that effectively prevented fermentation and preserved fruit juice without alcohol. The same year, the Merchant Shipping Act was passed, whereby all vessels, Royal Navy and Merchant, were required to carry lime juice for a daily ration to ship's company. It was this enactment that resulted in British sailors being called "Limeys" and brought about a sales volume boost for this new L. Rose & Company business . . . Rose's® Lime Juice, from Cape Town to Singapore, from Bombay to Belize, now literally sailed the seven seas.

In 1875, the head office was moved from Scotland to England. From the first days of the brand, the classic Rose's® bottle, with the embossed "lime leaves & fruit" design, has been the container. Many of the earlier versions of this are today considered choice collector items. At the new base in London, business prospered and three of Lauchlin Rose's nine children entered the firm. In 1885, the company bought the Bath Estate on Dominica in the Caribbean's Windward Islands. The estate produced an abundant lime crop, and additionally there was considerable cocoa acreage. Some fresh limes from the island were annually shipped to North America, but it was not until 1901 that the first bottled Rose's® Lime Juice arrived in the U.S. from the U.K.

The early years of the new century were successful for the growing Rose's enterprise, and in 1919 Lauchlin Rose, grandson of the founder, entered the business. By 1924, he was General Manager and that year established a lime industry in the Gold Coast, now Ghana. That new venture really had its start in the Summer of 1916. Just prior to the Somme Battle, Lauchlin Rose was assigned to the Royal Engineers of the ill-fated British 8th Division, serving under the Engineers' Commander, Sir Gordon Guggisberg. After the war, Sir Gordon became Governor of the Gold Coast. On a chance meeting with Mr. Rose, their discussion led to the proposal of developing Ghana as an alternate supply source of lime.

Depression years of the early 30's were tough for the company as they were for all world trade. By 1930, India and the USA were the company's two leading overseas sales areas. From 1935 until the outbreak of WWII, the business enjoyed steady expansion and increased prosperity. As war threatened, there was growing concern that the location of the company's facilities placed it in a probable target area. An alternate site was located and the move was completed to St. Albans, northwest of the city. On September 7, 1940, three days after the onset of the Blitz, L. Rose & Company's London premises were almost completely bombed out.

The business in the post-war period was marked by steady, perhaps spectacular growth. The firm joined with Schweppes in 1957 and became a part of Cadbury Schweppes in 1969. Rose's® brand Grenadine was introduced through the U.S. operation in the 1970's. Rose's® expanded distribution and consumer preference in retail outlets, bars, clubs, and restaurants, has continued to increase volume.

CREAMY LIME FIZZ

1 oz. ROSE'S® LIME JUICE
1¼ oz. Bombay Gin
2 oz. Cream
2 oz. Milk
2 tsp. Sugar
2 oz. Schweppes Club Soda or Seltzer

Combine Rose's® Lime Juice, gin, cream, milk and sugar with ice; shake. Strain into a tall glass filled with ice. Top with soda.

ROSE'S® BLOODY CAESAR

½ oz. ROSE'S® LIME JUICE
1¼ oz. Absolut Vodka
6 oz. Mott's Clamato Juice

Combine in a highball glass filled with ice cubes; stir.

ROSE'S® BLOODY MARY

½ oz. ROSE'S® LIME JUICE
1¼ oz. Absolut Vodka
6 oz. Mr. & Mrs. "T" Bloody Mary Mix

Combine in a highball glass filled with ice cubes; stir. Garnish with a stalk of celery.

ROSE'S® CAPE CODDER

½ oz. ROSE'S® LIME JUICE
1¼ oz. Absolut Vodka
6 oz. Cranberry Juice

Combine in a tall glass filled with ice; stir.

ROSE'S® CLASSIC DAIQUIRI

1 oz. ROSE'S® LIME JUICE
1¼ oz. Bacardi Light Rum
½ tsp. Powdered Sugar

Blend for 20 seconds and pour over ice.

ROSE'S® COLADA

1 oz. ROSE'S® LIME JUICE
1¼ oz. Bacardi Light Rum
1 oz. Coco Casa Cream of Coconut
3 oz. Pineapple Juice

Combine in a blender with 8 - 10 ice cubes. Blend until thick and smooth. Serve in a tall glass.

ROSE'S® FOGHORN

½ oz. ROSE'S® LIME JUICE
1¼ oz. Bombay Gin
6 oz. Schweppes Ginger Ale

Pour Rose's® Lime Juice and gin into a highball glass filled with ice. Top with ginger ale; stir.

ROSE'S® GALA PUNCH

1 oz. ROSE'S® LIME JUICE
1¼ oz. Bombay Gin
2 oz. Orange Juice
2 oz. Grape Juice

Shake with ice. Strain into a tall glass filled with ice.

ROSE'S® GIM-LITE

1 oz. ROSE'S® LIME JUICE
1 oz. Absolut Vodka
6 oz. Schweppes Club Soda or Seltzer

Combine Rose's® Lime Juice and vodka in a large stemmed glass with ice cubes. Fill with soda; stir. Garnish with lime wedge (optional).

ROSE'S® GIN & TONIC

½ oz. ROSE'S® LIME JUICE
1¼ oz. Bombay Gin
6 oz. Schweppes Tonic Water

Pour Rose's® Lime Juice and gin into a highball glass filled with ice. Fill glass with tonic; stir.

ROSE'S® GIN GIMLET

1 oz. ROSE'S® LIME JUICE
1¼ oz. Bombay Gin

Stir with ice to chill. Strain into cocktail glass.

ROSE'S® KAMIKAZE

1 part ROSE'S® LIME JUICE
1 part Absolut Vodka
1 part Hiram Walker Triple Sec

Shake with ice and serve over ice in an old-fashioned glass.

ROSE'S® MARGARITA

½ oz. ROSE'S® LIME JUICE
1¼ oz. Sauza Conmemorativo Tequila
¼ oz. Grand Marnier

For a frozen Margarita, place all ingredients in blender with 6 ice cubes. Blend until slushy. Pour into a salt-rimmed glass. Or, simply shake well with ice and strain into glass.

ROSE'S® MEXICAN ZINGER

½ oz. ROSE'S® LIME JUICE
1¼ oz. Sauza Conmemorativo Tequila
¼ oz. Hiram Walker Triple Sec
2 scps. Vanilla Ice Cream

Combine all ingredients in a blender. Blend until smooth and creamy. Serve in a brandy snifter.

ROSE'S® PASSION PUNCH

½ oz. ROSE'S® LIME JUICE
1 oz. Bacardi Dark Rum
2 oz. Pineapple Juice
2 oz. Orange Juice
2 oz. Schweppes Ginger Ale

Pour all ingredients into a tall glass half filled with ice. Stir gently and garnish with an orange slice and cherry.

ROSE'S® PINEAPPLE DAIQUIRI

¾   oz. ROSE'S® LIME
      JUICE
1¼   oz. Bacardi Light Rum
¼   oz. Hiram Walker
      Triple Sec
3   oz. Pineapple Juice

Combine in a blender with 8 - 10 ice cubes. Blend until thick and smooth. Serve in a tall glass.

ROSE'S® PLANTER'S PUNCH

1   oz. ROSE'S® LIME
      JUICE
½   oz. ROSE'S®
      GRENADINE
1¼   oz. Bacardi Dark Rum
2   oz. Pineapple Juice
2   oz. Orange Juice
1   dash Bitters

Shake with ice. Strain into a hurricane glass filled with ice. Garnish with pineapple wedge.

ROSE'S® STRAWBERRY MARGARITA

1   oz. ROSE'S® LIME
      JUICE
¾   oz. Sauza
      Conmemorativo
      Tequila
½   oz. Grand Marnier
½   cup Strawberries
      (Fresh or Frozen)

Combine all ingredients in a blender with 4 ice cubes. Blend until thick and smooth. Pour into a large, sugar-rimmed margarita glass.

TEQUILA ROSE

1½   oz. ROSE'S® LIME
      JUICE
¼   oz. ROSE'S®
      GRENADINE
1¼   oz. Sauza
      Conmemorativo
      Tequila
6   oz. Grapefruit Juice

Combine ingredients. Pour over ice in a tall glass.

NON-ALCOHOLIC RECIPES

CLAMATO COCKTAIL

1   oz. ROSE'S® LIME
      JUICE
6   oz. Mott's Clamato
      Juice

Stir together in a highball glass filled with ice.

COCO CRANBERRY SMOOTHIE

2   oz. ROSE'S® LIME
      JUICE
6   oz. Cranberry Juice
2   oz. Coco Casa Cream
      of Coconut
1   med. Banana

Place all ingredients and 4 ice cubes in a blender. Blend until smooth and thick. Serve in a large stemmed glass.

DAISY MAE'S SNOW CONE

½ oz. ROSE'S® LIME JUICE
¼ oz. ROSE'S® GRENADINE
1 oz. Strawberry Syrup
4 oz. Schweppes Club Soda or Seltzer

Fill a goblet with shaved ice. Add all except Rose's® Grenadine. Float Rose's® Grenadine on top.

DUST CUTTER

¾ oz. ROSE'S® LIME JUICE
6 oz. Schweppes Tonic Water

Serve over ice in a tall glass.

FROZEN STRAWBERRY DELICIOUS

½ oz. ROSE'S® LIME JUICE
4 oz. Pineapple Juice
½ cup Strawberries (Fresh or Frozen)
1 tbs. Sugar

Combine all ingredients in a blender with 4 ice cubes. Blend until smooth. Serve in a tall, stemmed glass.

KONA COAST

1 oz. ROSE'S® LIME JUICE
¼ oz. ROSE'S® GRENADINE
5 oz. Mott's Apple Juice
2 oz. Schweppes Ginger Ale

Stir together and serve over ice in a tall glass.

NEW YEAR'S SNIFTER

½ oz. ROSE'S® LIME JUICE
½ oz. ROSE'S® GRENADINE
1 tsp. Sugar
4 oz. Schweppes Bitter Lemon
4 oz. Pink Grapefruit Juice
2 oz. Schweppes Club Soda or Seltzer

Combine Rose's® Lime Juice, Rose's® Grenadine and sugar together in a large snifter. Add ice cubes, bitter lemon, grapefruit juice and soda; stir.

ROSE'S® LIMELIGHT

¾ oz. ROSE'S® LIME JUICE
6 oz. Schweppes Club Soda or Seltzer

Serve over ice in a tall glass.

ROSE'S® TROPICAL BREEZE

1 oz. ROSE'S® LIME JUICE
3 oz. Cranberry Juice
3 oz. Schweppes Club Soda or Seltzer

Pour Rose's® Lime Juice, cranberry juice and soda over ice in a collins glass; lightly stir.

SHIRLEY TEMPLE

1 oz. ROSE'S® LIME JUICE
1 oz. ROSE'S® GRENADINE
6 oz. Schweppes Ginger Ale

Pour over ice in a tall glass. Garnish with a cherry.

STRAWBERRY PUFF

1 oz. ROSE'S® LIME JUICE
4 oz. Milk
½ cup Strawberries (Fresh or Frozen)
1 oz. Coco Casa Cream of Coconut

Combine all ingredients in a blender with 4 ice cubes. Blend until thick and creamy. Serve in tall, stemmed glass.

THE GRECIAN

1 oz. ROSE'S® LIME JUICE
¼ oz. ROSE'S® GRENADINE
4 oz. Peach Nectar
2 oz. Orange Juice

Blend juices with 4 ice cubes for 30 seconds. Pour into a goblet. Add Rose's® Grenadine and garnish with fresh fruit.

THE ISLANDER

1 oz. ROSE'S® LIME JUICE
¼ oz. ROSE'S® GRENADINE
1 oz. Orange Juice
1 oz. Grapefruit Juice
1 oz. Pineapple Juice
3 oz. Schweppes Club Soda or Seltzer

Shake the juices with ice. Strain into a goblet filled with ice, top with soda and Rose's® Grenadine.

SAMBUCA ROMANA

Talent spotters in "show biz" are always on the look-out for rising stars with obvious talent and the potential to draw crowds. IDV (International Distillers and Vintners) too, constantly keeps a corporate eye open for brands with potential to add to its evergrowing portfolio of success stories.

Back in 1983, the company spotted a rapidly rising star — known in the jargon of the US beverage alcohol industry as a "hot brand." Hot brands are the fastest growing wines, spirits and beers in the business and last year's list named 27, out of which 21 were imported and two of those were liqueurs — both Italian.

One of those liqueurs had originally been introduced to Americans back in 1967. Sales built up gradually and by 1975 had reached 27 thousand, in just two states. Not bad for a relative beginner. Within less than ten years the scene had changed dramatically, with sales shooting up to 220 thousand cases — and still mainly in New York and New Jersey.

Sambuca Romana, one of Rome's favorite liqueurs had, most definitely been "discovered." IDV's talent scouts signed it up, gaining world distribution for the brand, so that its full potential could be developed on a truly international scale. The successful US sales strategy has been led by a clever up-market advertising campaign evoking the glamour and romance associated with Rome. Recipes encourage adventurous young sophisticates to try Sambuca Romana in Italian style "Con Mosca" with three coffee beans floated on the top, briefly flamed before drinking. Now, Sambuca Romana is one of Metro New

York's most widely known, popular liqueurs, served in most restaurants and bars.

IDV's new acquisition will continue to be distilled in Rome by Pallini Liquori, a family company steeped in the timeless Italian tradition of liqueur production.

That Italian tradition goes back considerably further than most people realize. Pilny, the Roman historian and naturalist, who died almost 2000 years ago in the eruption of Vesuvius, wrote about the art of distillation and the blending of herbs. By medieval times the distiller was the magician of his day, attempting to produce cures and elixirs, love potions and aphrodisiacs. Most of these distillers were monks and as few people could read or write, their secret recipes usually remained undisclosed. Retaining this knowledge provided them with an excellent means of making themselves indispensable to such powerful families as the Borgias and the Medicis, rulers of Florence. Catherine de' Medici, who by marrying Henri II, became Queen of France, possessed recipes for herbal elixirs, originally obtained by her great grandfather Lorenzo the Magnificient. She used them to restore the King and their seven children whenever they were unwell. She also received medical advice from her confidante famous for his herbal plague cures — Nostradamus the Jewish physician and astrologer, whose predictions are still published today. It was he, who predicted with spine-chilling accuracy, King Henri's untimely death; while jousting, a lance would pierce his armour and be driven through his eye. Catherine de' Medici, also as predicted lived to be almost 70, during a time when few lived beyond 40 years of age. The secret restorative that she used most frequently was discovered to contain brandy, sugar, cinnamon, liquorice and sambuca.

Sambuca, which is the Latin name for elder, is one of the ingredients in Sambuca Romana. A shrub which grows prolifically in Rome, elder has a fascinating history. The leaves, the pretty white flowers and purple berries of the elder contain volatile oils which for centuries have been used in lotions and potions.

Nicholas Culpeper, the London apothecary, born in 1616 wrote the *Complete Herbal*, which still remains one of the best reference books available. Culpeper considered that amongst many other beneficial effects a "decoction of elder, cured the bite of adders and mad dogs, and purgeth the 'tunicles' (whatever they might be) of the brain, taketh away headache, and is greatly beneficial to the eyes."

The Medici family, whose strategic power and wealth spanned several centuries, obviously knew exactly how to use their herbs, as well as their heads.

Whoever it was that said "history repeats itself" must have known that a modern version of the old Roman elixir was to become one of today's favorite liqueurs. Whether it's served in New York with the traditional three coffee beans or on the Via Veneto, transforming a cup of espresso coffee into Cafe Roman, Sambuca Romana captures the spirit of history, romance and enchantment of Rome — the Eternal City.

ALESSANDRO

¾ oz. SAMBUCA ROMANA
¾ oz. Bombay Gin
¾ oz. Cream

Shake with ice. Strain into cocktail glass.

BLUE CLOUD

1 oz. SAMBUCA ROMANA
½ oz. Hiram Walker Blue
  Curacao
  Club Soda

Fill large snifter with crushed ice. Pour blue curacao and Sambuca Romana. Fill with club soda. Garnish with cherry, lemon and orange slices. Serve with short straws.

BLUSHING BRIDE COCKTAIL

¾ oz. SAMBUCA ROMANA
¾ oz. Hiram Walker Sloe
  Gin
1 tbs. Rose's® Lime
  Juice
1 Egg White

Mix all ingredients in a blender. Pour into chilled cocktail glass. Garnish with fresh peach slice, dipped in Sambuca Romana.

BUCA ALMA

¾ oz. SAMBUCA ROMANA
¾ oz. Absolut Vodka
¼ oz. Hiram Walker
  Amaretto

Stir and pour over crushed ice.

CHOCOLATE CHIP SAMBUCA

1 oz. SAMBUCA ROMANA
¾ cup Chocolate Chip
  Ice Cream

Blend and serve or freeze until serving.

CON MOSCA

1 oz. SAMBUCA ROMANA
3 Roasted Coffee
  Beans

Float coffee beans on top.

CREMA CAFFE

¾ oz. SAMBUCA ROMANA
¾ oz. Kahlua
¾ oz. Cream

Shake with ice. Strain into cocktail glass.

ERMINE TAIL

1 oz. SAMBUCA ROMANA
½ oz. Cream
  Instant Espresso
  Coffee Powder

Pour Sambuca Romana in liqueur glass. Add cream, pouring over back of spoon so it floats. Dust with espresso powder.

FOREIGN AFFAIR

¾ oz. SAMBUCA ROMANA
¾ oz. Asbach Uralt

Stir with ice and strain into cocktail glass. Twist lemon peel over glass, drop in.

GLADIATOR

¼ oz. SAMBUCA ROMANA
¾ oz. Bombay Gin
½ oz. Campari

Shake with ice. Strain into cocktail glass. Garnish with orange wedge.

HEATHER'S DREAM
½ oz. SAMBUCA ROMANA
½ oz. Heavy Cream
½ Canned Peach or
½ Ripe Peach,
Peeled

Combine in blender with ¼ cup crushed ice. Mix at high speed until smooth. Pour into chilled wine glass.

ITALIAN RUSSIAN
½ oz. SAMBUCA ROMANA
1 oz. Absolut Vodka

Pour over ice cubes in small old-fashioned glass. Stir well. Twist orange peel over glass, drop in.

O'BUCA
1 oz. SAMBUCA ROMANA
3 oz. White Wine
3 oz. Orange Juice

Pour into tall glass over ice.

REUNION
½ oz. SAMBUCA ROMANA
½ oz. Absolut Vodka
6 Fresh
Strawberries

Mix in blender with crushed ice until smooth.

ROMAN BLITZ
1½ oz. SAMBUCA ROMANA
1½ oz. Hiram Walker
Creme de Cassis
½ oz. Martini & Rossi
Vermouth
Club Soda

Pour into highball glass over ice. Fill glass with club soda and stir lightly.

ROMAN MARTINI
½ oz. SAMBUCA ROMANA
1½ oz. Bombay Gin
Twist of lemon if desired.

ROMAN SHAKE
1 oz. SAMBUCA ROMANA
3 oz. Milk
Pour in a glass with ice and shake.

ROMAN SNOWBALL
1 oz. SAMBUCA ROMANA
Fill wine glass with shaved ice and mound top. Add Sambuca Romana. Drink turns milky, like a snowball. Serve with short straws.

ROMAN STINGER
½ oz. SAMBUCA ROMANA
½ oz. Hiram Walker
White Creme de
Menthe
1 oz. Cognac
Shake with ice. Strain into cocktail glass.

ROMANA CAFFE
½ oz. SAMBUCA ROMANA
¾ cup Hot Coffee
Add Sambuca Romana to a cup of hot, black espresso or regular coffee. Top with sweetened whipped cream. Dust with nutmeg. Garnish with cinnamon stick.

ROMANA ROYALE

1 oz. SAMBUCA ROMANA
6 oz. Cappucino

Add Sambuca Romana to a steamy cup of cappuccino. Top with nutmeg.

ROMANA SOUR

1½ oz. SAMBUCA ROMANA
1 oz. Lemon Juice
  Club Soda

Shake Sambuca Romana and lemon juice with ice. Strain over ice into old-fashioned or sour glass. Add a splash of soda and garnish with cherry and orange slice.

ROMANHATTAN

¼ oz. SAMBUCA ROMANA
1½ oz. Seagram's V.O.
¼ oz. Martini & Rossi
  Rosso Vermouth
  dash Bitters

Stir with ice. Strain into cocktail glass. Squeeze lemon wedge into glass and drop in.

SANTABUCA

2 oz. SAMBUCA ROMANA
6 oz. Egg Nog

Serve in tall glass. Garnish with cinnamon stick.

SILVER SPLINTER

½ oz. SAMBUCA ROMANA
1 oz. Bacardi Dark Rum
2 oz. Heavy Cream

Serve over crushed ice.

SNOW MELTER

1 oz. SAMBUCA ROMANA
½ oz. Bacardi Rum
½ oz. Hiram Walker
  White Creme de
  Cacao

Mix. Pour over ice and serve.

SUNNY SAM

½ oz. SAMBUCA ROMANA
1 oz. Absolut Vodka
  Orange Juice

Pour over ice in 7 oz. goblet.

THE LAVA

1 oz. SAMBUCA ROMANA
2 oz. Cranberry Juice
1 oz. Club Soda

Pour into highball glass over ice. Add a twist of lemon.

WHITE CLOUD

1 oz. SAMBUCA ROMANA
  Club Soda

Pour over ice in tall glass.

WHITE VELVET

1½ oz. SAMBUCA ROMANA
1 Egg White
1 tsp. Lemon Juice

Mix in a blender with ½ cup crushed ice or shake very well. Strain into large, chilled cocktail glass.

SAUZA

The World's Top-Seller, Has Spirited Tradition.

A Tequila Backgrounder

Whether sipped in a frothy concoction, savored with a bit of salt and a bite of lime, or tempered with fruit juice, tequila is today's consuming passion.

In an era of plenty and, for many, prosperity, a corresponding spurt in the spirit's sales isn't hard to swallow. But beyond its contemporary appeal, tequila has a centuries-old, quality tradition.

Natural History

As early as 200 A.D., Mexico's highly-advanced Aztecs recorded their liking for a mild alcoholic beverage made from a plant. However, its tendency to spoil rapidly earned it an Aztec epithet, octili poliqhqui. When Spain's conquistadores arrived in Mexico in the 16th Century, they took that phrase for the soured brew and called it pulque. Pulque has survived the centuries and still is consumed in Mexico today.

Linking their own distillation experience with a desire for a more potent, and palatable spirit, the Spaniards experimented with other varieties of the plant from which pulque was derived. The Aztecs called the plant metl; the Spanish renamed it maguey, adapting an Aztec term once again.

The Spaniards did find that other plant varieties yielded stronger spirits, which they collectively called mezcal, from a native word metl-calli, meaning "stew" or "concoction."

Mezcal also survives as a popular Mexican drink today; but don't confuse it with tequila!

Out of the Blue

Mexico's mezcal production thrived over the next two

centuries. In the nineteenth century, however, Don Cenobio Sauza began producing his own variety of mezcal, called "vino Tequila," or wine from Tequila after the town where he lived. Tequila is a hillside hamlet situated at the foot of a dormant volcano in the state of Jalisco in Central Mexico. In fact, "tequila" means "lava hill," showing the reverence and awe the townspeople felt toward their "monument."

With the advent of species classification, botanists began to classify the Mexican maguey plant, which was named agave, from the Greek word meaning "admirable" or "noble."

They identified some 400 species of the agave plant, which, incidentally, is *not* a cactus, nor is it related to the cactus, despite its profusion of sharp, pointed leaves.

Only one species of agave was markedly different — the one found in and around the town of Tequila and used by Don Cenobio Sauza to produce his vino Tequila variety of mezcal. Although similar in character to other species of agave, this plant had blue-hued leaves, not the usual green leaves common to most agave varieties.

What these naturalists discovered became the cornerstone of a truly unique positioning: only the blue agave, found in a desert-like area of Central Mexico, can produce tequila.

That puts tequila in some rather exclusive company, with Cognac, from France's Cognac region; and sherry, derived only from Spain's "Sherry Triangle" in and around Jerez.

Today, Mexico's Tequila territory not only includes the namesake town 40 miles northwest of Guadalajara, but also encompasses portions of adjacent states such as Guanajuato, Nayarit, Michoacan and Tamaupilas. All provide an ideal climate for the blue agave's growth.

Industrial Age

Don Cenobio Sauza, due to his pioneering of the blue agave-based spirit, is credited with transforming this quirk of nature into a major industry — the making and the marketing of tequila. In the late 19th Century, Don Cenobio bought two distilleries and began to exhibit his "product" at fairs throughout Mexico. He also started an export business, sending tequila northward to New Mexico, according to Sauza family records, over 100 years ago.

He named his product Tequila Sauza.

His son, Eladio, took over the business as the new century began. He continued the tradition of expanding the market by exhibiting the product at fairs in Mexico, and he added several new brands to the Sauza line.

Now, Eladio's son, Don Javier Sauza, carries on this family tradition, while looking to the future. Continuing to expand distribution to markets in Europe, the Far East and Canada, Don Javier also has created a research center to study the long-term management of the blue agave.

Through three generations, Tequila Sauza has become the best seller, not just in Mexico, but throughout the world.

Heart to Heart

Precision and tradition are the hallmarks of the tequila-making process. Unlike many distilled spirits, tequila spends more time on land than in bottles or barrels.

To say the blue agave is a slow-growing plant is an understatement: it matures, on average, in eight years. As the plants mature, seedlings are planted to yield new offspring. In fact, some 1 million blue agave, all at various stages of growth, dot the tequila-producing landscape at any one time.

At "birth," the blue agave, with its spiked, sword-like leaves and greenish pineapple-like center, is about the size of an onion. But when mature, the heart (called the "pina," Spanish for pineapple, due to its similar shape) weighs some 50 to 150 pounds. It is the heart which is cultivated and distilled for tequila.

Using a "coa," a long pole-like instrument with a sharp cutting edge, workers called "jimadores" strip away the outer leaves, uncovering the "pina," which is sent to the distillery. At the distillery, the "pinas" are shredded, then cooked in special steel ovens, called "autoclaves." This cooking transforms the natural starches into sugars. When "done," the cooked "pinas" yield a rich, golden juice called "aguamiel," or honey syrup.

That juice is transferred to vats where it ferments for about 48 hours with the help of yeasts that have been specially developed by the tequila producers over the years. These yeasts are carefully preserved for proprietary use, as they directly influence the character and style of each producer's tequila. The yeasts that the Sauza family uses have been carefully developed over the last 100 years.

Once fermented, the "wine" of the blue agave is piped into stills, where tequila's double distillation process begins.

The Process

First distillation yields an "ordinario" — a 40 proof spirit that requires a second distillation. During each distillation, the first and the last samples ("heads and tails") are removed because they contain most of the impurities and lack the finesse to develop into quality tequila. The "heart" or middle part of the spirit is then distilled a second time to produce a 110- to 120-proof spirit.

Period of Aging

The best quality tequilas are then aged for at least 3 to 6 months prior to bottling. The popular gold and silver tequilas like Sauza Gold and Sauza Silver are included in this aging category.

The next level of aging given to quality tequilas is from 6 months to 1 year in stainless steel vats. Tequilas in this group are given the name "reposado" or rested. Sauza Hornitos is a "reposado" tequila. This resting period is important as the tequila takes on its mature character and settles down.

Both Sauza's super-premium quality Conmemorativo and Tres Generaciones tequilas are of the "anejo," or aged, variety. Conmemorativo is allowed to age for four years before bottling and has a natural golden hue and distinct, smooth and mellow agave taste. Unlike other tequilas, Sauza Conmemorativo gets its golden color as a result of the aging process in oak barrels. Other tequila producers like Cuervo simply add caramel to their silver tequila to obtain gold tequila. Sauza's rare Tres Generaciones ("3-G's") ages in oak for eight years. This smooth tequila, which is aged longer than any other tequila available in the United States, offers rich subtle flavors which should be savored and sipped like a fine cognac.

Before bottling occurs, tequila is passed through charcoal filters to remove any remaining impurities. It is then adjusted to the desired proof — usually 80 proof for U.S. distribution; 90 to 96 proof for Mexico's consumers.

To be Tequila

Mexico's Bureau of Standards requires that for a spirit to be named tequila, it must contain at least 51% of spirits from the blue agave plant, grown only in the official Tequila territory in and around the town of Tequila in the State of Jalisco. In addition, the distilled spirit can be diluted by no more than 49% with neutral spirits.

Blending with neutral spirits has the effect of mellowing the pungent agave taste in the same way that malt whiskeys are blended with neutral spirits to obtain the lighter blended scotch whiskeys, which are flavored.

A special few tequilas such as Sauza Hornitos contain no neutral spirits and are unblended, or 100% blue agave. Hornitos is the favorite tequila for numerous "aficionados" of the pure, distinctive blue agave taste.

A Cultivated Taste

Associated with leisure, luxury and a festive, fiesta mood, tequila's new-found popularity reflects a carefully-cultivated reputation for quality and consistency which spans the centuries.

SAUZA'S "QUICK STUDY" OF TEQUILA

Category	Brand(s)	Aging	% Agave	Tasting Notes/Comments
Special Reserve Limited Edition "Añejo"	SAUZA Tres Generaciones (3-G's)	8 yrs. in oak	51%	Notably the longest-aged tequila produced; naturally golden—hued due to the years in oak (no artificial coloring). Akin to VSOP Cognac in character.
Super Premium "Añejo" Natural Gold	SAUZA Conmemorativo	4 yrs. in oak	51%	The flagship brand of the SAUZA line, its richness derives from the all-natural ingredients and oak aging. So smooth, it is the essential ingredient of ·the "Ultimate Margarita," served on the rocks.
"Reposado"	SAUZA Hornitos	1 yr. in stainless steel vats	100%	The preference of tequila purists, who appreciate the distinct 100% agave taste.
Premium	SAUZA Gold SAUZA Silver	6 mos 3 mos	60-70% 60-70%	SAUZA Gold is the perfect choice for lovers of the smooth, distinct "gold" style. SAUZA Silver, for traditionalists, is the leading-selling tequila in Mexico.
Popular "Ordinario"	SAUZA Giro Gold SAUZA Giro Silver	1-3 mos 1-3 mos	51% 51%	Giro has more of the distinctive agave flavor than other popular priced brands. An outstanding value for on-premise usage.

AMOR

1 oz. SAUZA CONMEMORATIVO TEQUILA
½ oz. Hiram Walker Orange Curacao

In an old-fashioned glass filled with ice.

BERTHA

1¼ oz. SAUZA CONMEMORATIVO TEQUILA
½ tsp. Red Wine
1¼ tsp. Superfine Sugar
1 tbs. Fresh Lemon or Lime Juice

In a chilled highball glass filled with ice. Twist lemon peel over drink and drop in. Garnish with maraschino cherry.

BLOODY MARIA

1½ oz. SAUZA CONMEMORATIVO TEQUILA
Tomato Juice
dash Worcestershire Sauce
dash Celery Salt
Pepper to taste
Salt to taste

In a double old-fashioned glass with ice, fill with tomato juice. Garnish with celery stalk and a squeeze of lemon.

BLUE SHARK

¾ oz. SAUZA CONMEMORATIVO TEQUILA
¾ oz. Absolut Vodka
1-2 dash Hiram Walker Blue Curacao

Combine with ice; shake well. Strain and add ice.

BLUE SMOKE

1¼ oz. SAUZA CONMEMORATIVO TEQUILA
1 dash Hiram Walker Blue Curacao
4 oz. Orange Juice

In a 10 oz. chilled wine glass with finely crushed ice, add tequila and orange juice and stir. Float blue curacao on top.

BRAVE BULL

1 oz. SAUZA CONMEMORATIVO TEQUILA
½ oz. Kahlua

In an old-fashioned glass with ice.

BUNNY BONANZA

1 oz. SAUZA CONMEMORATIVO TEQUILA
¼ oz. Apple Flavored Brandy
½ tsp. Hiram Walker Orange Curacao
2 tsp. Lemon Juice
1 tsp. Sugar Syrup

Combine with ice; shake well. Strain, add ice and decorate with lemon slice.

CHARRO

1 oz. SAUZA CONMEMORATIVO TEQUILA
1⅓ oz. Evaporated Milk
⅔ oz. Strong Coffee

Combine in a shaker with crushed ice. Strain into a chilled old-fashioned glass with ice.

COCO LOCO
(CRAZY COCONUT)

1½ oz. SAUZA CONMEMORATIVO TEQUILA
3 oz. Pineapple Juice
2 oz. Coconut Syrup Mix
Grated Coconut

Blend with crushed ice and pour into a tall glass. Garnish with a pineapple spear. If available, serve in a coconut shell.

COCONUT TEQUILA

1¼ oz. SAUZA C0NMEMORATIVO TEQUILA
2 tsp. Lemon Juice
2 tsp. Cream of Coconut
1 tsp. Maraschino

Combine in a blender with ice at a low speed for 15 seconds. Strain and serve straight up in a cocktail glass.

COMPADRE

1 oz. SAUZA CONMEMORATIVO TEQUILA
¼ oz. Hiram Walker Cherry Flavored Liqueur
⅓ oz. Rose's® Grenadine
4 drps Bitters

In a shaker combine with crushed ice. Strain into 4 oz. chilled cocktail glass.

CONCHITA

1¼ oz. SAUZA CONMEMORATIVO TEQUILA
½ oz. Lemon Juice
6 oz. Grapefruit Juice

In a chilled highball glass, fill with grapefruit juice and stir.

DORADO COCKTAIL

1¼ oz. SAUZA CONMEMORATIVO TEQUILA
1½ oz. Lemon Juice
1 tbs. Honey

Combine with ice; shake well. Strain in a tall glass filled with ice.

DUKE'S DAISY

1¼ oz. SAUZA CONMEMORATIVO TEQUILA
2 tsp. Raspberry Liqueur
2 tsp. Rose's® Lime Juice
Club Soda

Combine all ingredients except soda in shaker, shake. Strain into 8-oz. chilled wine glass. Fill with club soda.

DURANGO

1¼ oz. SAUZA CONMEMORATIVO TEQUILA
2 tbs. Grapefruit Juice
1 tsp. Almond Extract
Spring Water

Combine all ingredients except spring water with ice, shake well. Strain into a large tumbler, add ice and fill with spring water. Garnish with mint sprigs.

EARTHQUAKE

1¼ oz. SAUZA CONMEMORATIVO TEQUILA
1 tsp. Rose's® Grenadine
2 Strawberries
1-2 dshs Orange Bitters

Combine in a blender with crushed ice at a high speed for 15 seconds. Strain straight up with a lime slice and a strawberry.

EL TORITO

1 oz. SAUZA CONMEMORATIVO TEQUILA
½ oz. Hiram Walker Dark Creme de Cacao

In an old-fashioned glass filled with ice. For an after-dinner variation, serve in a snifter glass with no ice.

FROZEN TEQUILA

1¼ oz. SAUZA CONMEMORATIVO TEQUILA
¾ oz. Sugar Syrup or
1½ oz. Superfine Sugar

Combine in a blender with ice until smooth slush. Pour into chilled champagne glass. Garnish top with lime slice and cherry.

GENTLE MARIE

1 oz. SAUZA CONMEMORATIVO TEQUILA
½ oz. Hiram Walker Dark Creme de Cacao
½ oz. Cream

In a shaker with ice, combine all ingredients. Strain into brandy snifter with crushed ice.

GOLD SUNSET

1 oz. SAUZA CONMEMORATIVO TEQUILA
¾ oz. Grand Marnier
3 oz. Sweet & Sour Mix
¼ oz. Orange Juice
¼ oz. 7-Up
splsh Rose's® Grenadine

Stir all together over ice; top with a splash of grenadine.

GORILLA SWEAT

1½ oz. SAUZA CONMEMORATIVO TEQUILA
½ tsp. Sugar
1 pat Butter
    Hot Water

Pour tequila into an old-fashioned glass and fill with hot water. Add sugar and stir in butter. Garnish with a cinnamon stick and sprinkle of nutmeg.

GRAND MARGARITA

1 oz SAUZA CONMEMORATIVO TEQUILA
½ oz. Grand Marnier
1 oz. Lemon or Rose's® Lime Juice

Rub lime or lemon peel around rim of chilled cocktail glass and salt-frost rim with coarse salt. In shaker, combine ingredients. Strain into prepared glass.

HAND GRENADE

1 oz. SAUZA CONMEMORATIVO TEQUILA
3 oz. Unsweetened Cranberry Juice

Combine in a mixing glass, stir well. Strain into 4-oz. chilled cocktail glass. Twist orange peel over drink and drop in.

HORNY BULL

1¼ oz. SAUZA CONMEMORATIVO TEQUILA
    Orange Juice

In a chilled highball glass filled with ice. Fill with orange juice.

LA BAMBA

1 oz. SAUZA CONMEMORATIVO TEQUILA
¾ oz. Hiram Walker Hazelnut Liqueur
1½ oz. Banana (blender mix)
3 oz. Orange Juice
    7-Up

Blend with one scoop crushed ice. Serve in tulip glass topped with a splash of 7-Up.

LATIN LOVER

1 oz. SAUZA CONMEMORATIVO TEQUILA
½ oz. Hiram Walker Amaretto

In an old-fashioned glass.

MARGARITA

1 oz. SAUZA CONMEMORATIVO TEQUILLA
½ oz. Hiram Walker Triple Sec
1 oz. Rose's® Lime or Lemon Juice

Rub lime or lemon peel around rim of chilled cocktail glass and salt-frost rim with coarse salt. Shake ingredients. Strain into prepared glass.

MATADOR

1½ oz. SAUZA CONMEMORATIVO TEQUILA
2 oz. Pineapple Juice
1 oz. Rose's® Lime Juice
½ oz. Rose's® Grenadine

Blend all ingredients with crushed ice and strain into a large cocktail glass.

MEXICAN BANGER

1 oz. SAUZA CONMEMORATIVO TEQUILA
½ oz. Kahlua
   Orange Juice

In a tall glass with ice, float Kahlua on top.

MEXICAN FLAG

1¼ oz. SAUZA CONMEMORATIVO TEQUILA
1 tbs. Sugar Syrup
2 tsp. Rose's® Lime Juice
1 Green Grape
1 scp. Vanilla Ice Cream

Combine tequila, sugar and juice with ice; shake. Strain into champagne glass with hollow stem and add plenty of ice. Top with the grape, vanilla ice cream and a cherry.

MEXICAN MIST

1¼ oz. SAUZA CONMEMORATIVO TEQUILA
2 oz. Pineapple Juice
1 oz. Orange Juice
½ oz. Cranberry Juice

Serve on the rocks.

MEXICAN STINGER

1 oz. SAUZA CONMEMORATIVO TEQUILA
½ oz. Hiram Walker White Creme de Menthe

In an old-fashioned glass filled with ice.

MEXICAN SUNRISE

1¼ oz. SAUZA CONMEMORATIVO TEQUILA
½ tsp. Hiram Walker Creme de Cassis
1 tsp. Rose's® Grenadine
1 tbs. Fresh Lime Juice
   Club Soda

In a chilled highball glass filled with crushed ice, stir gently.

MEXICO MARTINI

1½ oz. SAUZA CONMEMORATIVO TEQUILA
1 tbs. Martini & Rossi Extra Dry Vermouth
2-3 drps Vanilla Extract

Combine with ice; shake well. Strain into old-fashioned glass and add ice.

MEXICO ROSE

1½ oz. SAUZA CONMEMORATIVO TEQUILA
1 oz. Rose's® Lime Juice
½ oz. Rose's® Grenadine

In an old-fashioned glass filled with ice.

MOCKINGBIRD

1¼ oz. SAUZA CONMEMORATIVO TEQUILA
2 tsp. Hiram Walker White Creme de Menthe
1 oz. Fresh Lime Juice

Combine in a shaker, shake vigorously. Strain into a 4-oz. chilled cocktail glass with ice.

NATURAL GOLD MARGARITA

1 oz. SAUZA CONMEMORATIVO TEQUILA
1 oz. Grand Marnier
½ oz. Sweet & Sour Mix

Serve blended with crushed ice or on the rocks.

NUMERO UNO

1 oz. SAUZA CONMEMORATIVO TEQUILA
½ oz. Hiram Walker Triple Sec

Serve on the rocks with a large squeeze of lime.

PINA

1½ oz. SAUZA CONMEMORATIVO TEQUILA
3 oz. Pineapple Juice
1 oz. Rose's® Lime Juice
1 tsp. Superfine Sugar

Combine in shaker with ice. Strain into chilled tall glass filled with ice.

PINATA

1¼ oz. SAUZA CONMEMORATIVO TEQUILA
1 tbs. Banana Liqueur
1 oz. Rose's® Lime Juice

In a blender with crushed ice, blend at medium speed until smooth. Pour, unstrained, into chilled whiskey sour glass.

ROSITA

1 oz. SAUZA CONMEMORATIVO TEQUILA
¼ oz. Martini & Rossi Extra Dry Vermouth
¼ oz. Martini & Rossi Rosso Vermouth
1 oz. Campari

In an old-fashioned glass filled with ice, add ingredients and stir gently. Twist lemon peel over drink and drop in.

SILK STOCKINGS

1 oz. SAUZA CONMEMORATIVO TEQUILA
¼ oz. Hiram Walker White Creme de Cacao
1½ oz. Evaporated Milk
1 tsp. Rose's® Grenadine

In a blender combine all ingredients and blend at medium speed until smooth. Pour, unstrained, into an 8-oz. chilled wine glass. Sprinkle with cinnamon and garnish with maraschino cherry.

SLOE TEQUILA

1 oz. SAUZA CONMEMORATIVO TEQUILA
2 tsp. Hiram Walker Sloe Gin
2 tsp. Rose's® Lime Juice

Combine in blender at a low speed for 15 seconds. Strain into a cocktail glass; add ice to fill the glass. Decorate with cucumber peel.

SUNSET

1 oz. SAUZA CONMEMORATIVO TEQUILA
1½ oz. Orange Juice
1½ oz. Pineapple Juice

Combine in blender and blend at medium speed about 30 seconds. Pour, unstrained, into an 8-oz, chilled wine glass with sugar-frosted rim.

T'N'T
aka
TEQUILA N' TONIC

1¼ oz. SAUZA CONMEMORATIVO TEQUILA
Tonic Water
½ oz. Lemon or Rose's® Lime Juice

In a chilled highball glass filled ¾ with ice. Fill with tonic and twist lime or lemon peel over drink and drop in.

TEQUILA BLOODY BULL

1¼ oz. SAUZA CONMEMORATIVO TEQUILA
3 oz. Tomato Juice
3 oz. Chilled Beef Boullion
1 dash Tabasco
1 dash Worcestershire Sauce

If desired, salt-frost rim of chilled tall glass using celery salt. Combine all ingredients with crushed ice and stir.

TEQUILA COLLINS

1¼   oz. SAUZA
      CONMEMORATIVO
      TEQUILA
1   oz. Sugar Syrup
1   oz. Fresh Lime or
      Lemon Juice
      Club Soda

In a tall glass ¾ filled with ice. Top with soda and stir. Garnish with maraschino cherry and thin orange slice.

TEQUILA DUBONNET

1   part SAUZA
      CONMEMORATIVO
      TEQUILA
1   part Dubonnet

Combine in old-fashioned glass; stir well and add ice. Garnish with slice of lemon.

TEQUILA FIZZ

1¼   oz. SAUZA
      CONMEMORATIVO
      TEQUILA
      Orange Juice
      Sour Mix
      Sprite

In a shaker with ice, all ingredients except Sprite. Strain into a chilled collins glass and fill with Sprite. Garnish with orange slice.

TEQUILA FLIP

1¼   oz. SAUZA
      CONMEMORATIVO
      TEQUILA
½   splsh Simple Syrup
1   splsh Half & Half
1   Egg

Shake and strain into chilled champagne glass. Garnish with nutmeg/allspice.

TEQUILA GHOST

1¼   oz. SAUZA
      CONMEMORATIVO
      TEQUILA
¼   oz. Pernod
2   tsp. Lemon Juice

Combine with ice; shake well. Pour into old-fashioned glass and add ice.

TEQUILA JULEP

1¼   oz. SAUZA
      CONMEMORATIVO
      TEQUILA
1   tsp. Superfine Sugar
      Club Soda

Crush 3 mint sprigs with sugar and add to chilled highball glass filled with ice. Add tequila and stir. Top with club soda. Stir gently until glass is frosted. Garnish with 1 mint sprig.

TEQUILA MIST

1¼   oz. SAUZA
      CONMEMORATIVO
      TEQUILA

In an old-fashioned glass with crushed ice. Twist lemon peel over drink and drop in.

TEQUILA NEAT

1¼ oz. SAUZA
CONMEMORATIVO
TEQUILA
1   Lime Wedge
Coarse Salt

Lick back of left hand between thumb and index finger and sprinkle with salt. Lick salt from back of hand, drink tequila, and bite into lime wedge—all in one quick sequence.

TEQUILA OLD FASHIONED

1¼ oz. SAUZA
CONMEMORATIVO
TEQUILA
½ splsh Simple Syrup
1   dash Bitters

Muddle cherry and lime slice, add simple syrup and bitters. Pour into old-fashioned glass filled with ice. Add tequila and twist lemon over drink and drop in.

TEQUILA RICKEY

1¼ oz. SAUZA
CONMEMORATIVO
TEQUILA
1   tsp. Rose's® Lime Juice
Club Soda

Pour tequila and lime juice into a highball glass; add ice and stir well. Fill with club soda. Twist in slice of lime. Sprinkle a little salt over the drink. Garnish with orange slice.

TEQUILA SLAMMER SHOOTER

⅔ shot SAUZA
CONMEMORATIVO
TEQUILA
1 splsh Sour Mix
1 splsh Sprite

In a cordial glass. Cover glass with hand and slam on table. Shoot drink while fizzing.

TEQUILA SUNRISE

1½ oz. SAUZA
CONMEMORATIVO
TEQUILA
½   oz. Rose's® Grenadine
Orange Juice

Pour grenadine into a tall glass first; then add tequila and fill with ice and orange juice. Garnish with slice of orange.

TEQUINI

1½ oz. SAUZA
CONMEMORATIVO
TEQUILA
½   oz. Martini & Rossi
Extra Dry
Vermouth

Stir in a mixing glass with ice. Strain into a prechilled cocktail glass and garnish with a lemon twist.

TOREADOR

1 oz. SAUZA CONMEMORATIVO TEQUILA
¼ oz. Hiram Walker White Creme de Cacao
½ oz. Cream
1 tbs. Whipped Cream
  pinch Cocoa

Combine all ingredients except whipped cream and cocoa in a shaker. Strain into a 4-oz. chilled cocktail glass. Top with whipped cream, and sprinkle sparingly with cocoa.

TROMBONE

1¼ oz. SAUZA CONMEMORATIVO TEQUILA
½ oz. Rose's® Grenadine
1 oz. Lemon Juice
1 oz. Pineapple Juice
1 oz. Orange Juice
  Ginger Ale

Combine all ingredients except ginger ale in mixing glass with crushed ice and stir. Pour, unstrained, into chilled tall glass. Top with ginger ale.

VIVA VILLA

1¼ oz. SAUZA CONMEMORATIVO TEQUILA
1 tbs. Hiram Walker Triple Sec
1 oz. Grape Juice
1 tsp. Rose's® Grenadine

Combine in blender with crushed ice, blend at low speed 15 to 20 seconds. Strain into chilled whiskey sour glass.

WHITE EL TORITO

1 oz. SAUZA CONMEMORATIVO TEQUILA
½ oz. Hiram Walker Dark Creme de Cacao
  Cream or Half & Half

In an old-fashioned glass filled with ice, float cream or half & half on top.

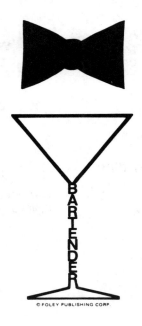

© FOLEY PUBLISHING CORP.

248

SEAGRAM'S V.O.

Seagram's V.O. was born early in the century as the "Very Own" treasure of the Joseph E. Seagram family of Canada. A special blend intended for the family's private consumption, V.O. was unveiled in 1911 at the wedding of Joseph E. Seagram's grandson, Thomas. The new Canadian whisky, first shared with the world in 1917, became the firm's flagship brand, and the standard bearer of integrity, craftsmanship and tradition that is Seagram.

This very special heritage has made Seagram's V.O. one of America's most beloved whiskies. When V.O. was introduced to the United States in 1934, its clean, mild flavor soon won for the brand a vast and loyal following. Market research has shown that V.O. drinkers pass on their loyalty to the spirit from grandfather to father to son, establishing a distinguished lineage of V.O. devotees. And V.O. drinkers consider themselves among a growing cadre of whisky connoisseurs, that segment of consumers of premium spirits who prefer not to mix their whisky into cocktails, but to enjoy it with a splash of water or soda.

The consistently smooth, well-rounded taste of V.O. is a testimony to the art of blending whisky. Each bottle of the six-year old whisky is a product of more than 75 aged whiskies, carefully blended to its famous delicate balance by a team of master craftsmen.

Ideal conditions abound in and around the five Seagram distilleries where the ingredients for V.O. are produced. The finest grains, purest spring water, and time-honored distilling methods result in the highest quality whiskies which are laid down in select charred white oak barrels for aging.

It is then that the true artistry begins. With a "palate" of hundreds of whiskies to choose from, the master blenders set about creating the one-of-a-kind golden color and complex character which is Seagram's V.O. Guided only by years of experience, they may blend as many as 120 whiskies in their mission to match the very special V.O. heritage. Once achieved, they taste their finished product alongside a sample of the approved V.O. standard-bearer to ensure the accuracy of their blend.

Some exacting standards extend throughout the production process, until the flawed bottles laden with 80-proof Seagram's V.O. are tied with their distinctive yellow-and-gold ribbons. These proud banners of quality were derived from V.O.'s original black-and-gold ribbons, which echoed the racing-horse colors of Joseph E. Seagram.

The generosity of spirit first shown at a Seagram family wedding when the century was new has proven a landmark event in the annals of the history of fine whisky. And a gift for a grandson has become a gift to American whisky lovers who have responded with a resounding thank you for Seagram's "Very Own."

BARBARY COAST COCKTAIL
¾ oz. SEAGRAM'S V.O.
¾ oz. Bombay Gin
¾ oz. Hiram Walker
Creme de Cacao
½ oz. Fresh Cream
Shake well with finely cracked ice. Strain into cocktail glass.

BLACKTHORN COCKTAIL
1¼ oz. SEAGRAM'S V.O.
1 oz. Martini & Rossi
Extra Dry
Vermouth
3 dshs Hiram Walker
Anisette
Stir well with cracked ice. Strain into cocktail glass.

BLENDER
¼ oz. SEAGRAM'S V.O.
¼ oz. Hiram Walker
Creme de Cacao
Blend with crushed ice.

BLINKER
1¼ oz. SEAGRAM'S V.O.
2½ oz. Tropicana
Grapefruit Juice
½ oz. Rose's® Grenadine
Shake well with ice. Strain into old-fashioned glass.

BLOOD AND SAND COCKTAIL
½ oz. SEAGRAM'S V.O.
½ oz. Hiram Walker
Cherry Flavored
Brandy
½ oz. Martini & Rossi
Rosso Vermouth
½ oz. Tropicana Orange
Juice
Shake well with cracked ice. Strain into cocktail glass.

BOOMERANG COCKTAIL
1 oz. SEAGRAM'S V.O.
¾ oz. Martini & Rossi
Extra Dry
Vermouth
¾ oz. Hiram Walker
Cherry Flavored
Brandy
2 dshs Lemon or
Rose's® Lime
Juice
Shake with cracked ice. Strain into cocktail glass.

BOUNTY
1¼ oz. SEAGRAM'S V.O.
1 oz. Martini & Rossi
Rosso Vermouth
3 dshs Benedictine
Stir with cracked ice. Strain into cocktail glass. Serve with twist of lemon peel.

BROOKLYN COCKTAIL

1½   oz. SEAGRAM'S V.O.
¼   oz. Martini & Rossi
      Extra Dry
      Vermouth
1   dash Hiram Walker
      Cherry Flavored
      Brandy
1   dash Bitters

Shake with cracked ice. Strain into cocktail glass.

CABLEGRAM

1¼   oz. SEAGRAM'S V.O.
1   tsp. Powdered Sugar
      Juice of ½ Lemon
      Ginger Ale

Stir well with ice. Strain into 4 oz. cocktail glass. Fill with ginger ale.

CALIFORNIA SOUR #1

1¼   oz. SEAGRAM'S V.O.
3   oz. Sweet/Sour Mix
½   tsp. Sugar

Shake. Serve up or on the rocks. Garnish with orange slice and a cherry.

CALIFORNIA SOUR #2

1   oz. SEAGRAM'S V.O.
¼   oz. Hiram Walker
      Cherry Flavored
      Brandy
½   tsp. Sugar

Shake with ice. Serve up or on the rocks.

DUBONNET MANHATTAN

1¼   oz. SEAGRAM'S V.O.
1   oz. Dubonnet Rouge

Mix all ingredients with ice, shake. Pour into a chilled old-fashioned glass. Garnish with a cherry.

EARTHSHAKE

½   oz. SEAGRAM'S V.O.
½   oz. Bombay Gin
½   oz. Hiram Walker
      Anisette

Shake well with ice. Strain into cocktail glass.

FRISCO COCKTAIL

1¼   oz. SEAGRAM'S V.O.
¾   oz. Benedictine

Stir with cracked ice. Strain into cocktail glass. Serve with twist of lemon peel.

HOT TODDY

1¼   oz. SEAGRAM'S V.O.
1   lump Sugar
2   Cloves

Stir in 5 oz. glass with hot water. Decorate with twist of lemon rind.

HURRICANE COCKTAIL

½   oz. SEAGRAM'S V.O.
½   oz. Hiram Walker
      White Creme de
      Menthe
½   oz. Bombay Gin
      Juice of 1 Lemon

Shake with cracked ice. Strain into cocktail glass.

INK STREET

⅓   oz. SEAGRAM'S V.O.
⅓   oz. Lemon Juice
⅓   oz. Tropicana Orange
      Juice

Shake.

METS MANHATTAN

1¼ oz. SEAGRAM'S V.O.
¼ oz. Martini & Rossi Extra Dry Vermouth
¼ oz. Hiram Walker Strawberry Schnapps

Mix all ingredients with ice and stir well. Strain into a chilled cocktail glass.

MILLIONAIRE COCKTAIL

1¼ oz. SEAGRAM'S V.O.
¼ oz. Hiram Walker Triple Sec.
1 dash Rose's® Grenadine
1 Egg White

Shake well with cracked ice. Strain into large cocktail glass.

MONTE CARLO COCKTAIL

¾ oz. SEAGRAM'S V.O.
¾ oz. Dubonnet
1 dash Bitters

Shake well with cracked ice. Strain into cocktail glass.

NEW YORKER COCKTAIL

1¼ oz. SEAGRAM'S V.O.
    Juice of ½ Lime
2 dshs Rose's® Grenadine
½ tsp. Bar Syrup

Shake with cracked ice. Strain into cocktail glass. Serve with twist of lemon peel.

OLD-FASHIONED COCKTAIL #1

1¼ oz. SEAGRAM'S V.O.
1 tsp. Sugar or Bar Syrup
2 twists Lemon Peel
1-2 dshs Bitters

Put sugar, 1 twist and bitters to taste in glass; stir well. Add 1 oz. Seagram's V.O.; allow to blend thoroughly. Add ice cubes. Add remaining Seagram's V.O. and lemon peel. Serve with a small bar spoon and a cherry. If desired, serve with a slice of orange and stick of pineapple.

OLD-FASHIONED COCKTAIL #2

1¼ oz. SEAGRAM'S V.O.
1 lump Sugar
2-3 dshs Bitters
    splsh Club Soda

Splash bitters onto the lump of sugar in old-fashioned glass. Add soda and muddle thoroughly. Add 2 ice cubes, lemon peel, cherry and Seagram's V.O.

SEAGRAM'S V.O. COLLINS

1¼ oz. SEAGRAM'S V.O.
    Juice of 1 Lemon
1 tsp. Sugar

Shake well with cracked ice. Strain into a 12 oz. glass over 2 or 3 ice cubes. Fill with club soda and stir. Decorate with a cherry.

SEAGRAM'S V.O. HIGHBALL

1¼ oz. SEAGRAM'S V.O.

In a highball glass, pour Seagram's V.O. over ice. Fill with water, club soda or ginger ale. Stir.

T.N.T. COCKTAIL

¾ oz. SEAGRAM'S V.O.
¾ oz. Hiram Walker Anisette

Shake with cracked ice. Strain into cocktail glass.

V.O. COOLER

1¼ oz. SEAGRAM'S V.O.
¼ oz. Martini & Rossi Extra Dry Vermouth
¼ oz. Hiram Walker Amaretto
2 oz. Tropicana Orange Juice
1 oz. Lemon Juice

Mix all ingredients with ice in shaker or blender. Pour into a chilled collins glass. Fill with club soda.

V.O. DRY MANHATTAN

1 oz. SEAGRAM'S V.O.
¼ oz. Martini & Rossi Extra Dry Vermouth

Mix ingredients with ice; strain into chilled cocktail glass. Twist lemon peel over drink and drop into glass.

V.O. GOLD RUSH

1¼ oz. SEAGRAM'S V.O.
Ginger Ale

Pour Seagram's V.O. over ice in a tall glass. Fill with ginger ale and stir.

V.O. GOLD SPLASH

1¼ oz. SEAGRAM'S V.O.
Pour over ice in a rocks glass.

V.O. GOLDFINGER

1¼ oz. SEAGRAM'S V.O.
Club Soda

Pour Seagram's V.O. over ice in a tall glass. Fill with club soda and stir.

V.O. LEMONADE

1¼ oz. SEAGRAM'S V.O.
Juice of 1 Lemon
3 oz. Water
1 tbs. Sugar

Combine in shaker. Pour over ice cubes in highball glass. Garnish with fruit or mint as desired.

V.O. MANHATTAN DANE

1¼ oz. SEAGRAM'S V.O.
¼ oz. Kirschwasser
¼ oz. Peter Herring

Mix all ingredients with ice, shake. Strain into a chilled cocktail glass or serve on the rocks.

V.O. MANHATTAN ROSE

1¼ oz. SEAGRAM'S V.O.
¼ oz. Martini & Rossi Extra Dry Vermouth
¼ oz. Chambord

Mix all ingredients with cracked ice, shake or blend. Strain into a chilled cocktail glass.

V.O. PERFECT MANHATTAN

1¼ oz. SEAGRAM'S V.O.
2 tsp. Martini & Rossi Rosso Vermouth
2 tsp. Martini & Rossi Extra Dry Vermouth

Combine with cracked ice; strain into a chilled cocktail glass. Garnish with lemon peel or maraschino cherry.

V.O. SOUR

1¼ oz. SEAGRAM'S V.O.
¾ oz. Lemon Juice
1 tsp. Superfine Sugar

Combine ingredients in mixing glass, add ice, shake well. Place cherry and orange slice in chilled glass. Strain drink into glass.

WALDORF COCKTAIL

½ oz. SEAGRAM'S V.O.
½ oz. Martini & Rossi Rosso Vermouth
½ oz. Hiram Walker Anisette
1 dash Bitters

Shake well with cracked ice. Strain into cocktail glass.

WARD EIGHT #1

1¼ oz. SEAGRAM'S V.O.
4 dshs Rose's® Grenadine Juice of ½ Lemon

Shake with cracked ice. Serve in goblet with finely cracked ice. Serve with straws.

WARD EIGHT #2

1¼ oz. SEAGRAM'S V.O.
½ oz. Rose's® Grenadine Juice of ½ Lemon Juice of ½ Orange Club Soda

Shake with cracked ice. Pour unstrained into an 8 to 10 oz. tumbler. Fill with soda. Garnish with orange slice and cherry.

WHITE SAND COOLER

½ oz. SEAGRAM'S V.O.
¼ oz. Hiram Walker Triple Sec
½ oz. Hiram Walker Creme de Banana
½ oz. Lemon Juice
2 oz. Pineapple Juice

Whip in blender, strain into tall glass ¾ filled with crushed ice. Garnish with pineapple stick.

ZAZARAC COCKTAIL

1¼ oz. SEAGRAM'S V.O.
3 drps Hiram Walker Anisette
½ oz. Bar Syrup
1 oz. Water
5 drps Bitters

Add Anisette to a well chilled old-fashioned glass. Swirl it around to coat glass thoroughly. Add remaining ingredients and 1 ice cube. Stir to blend. Squeeze a twist of lemon over top for oil. Serve with lemon peel in glass.

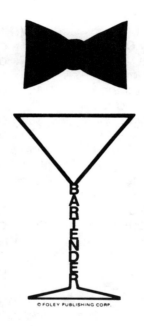

© FOLEY PUBLISHING CORP.

256

WILD TURKEY STRAIGHT BOURBON WHISKEY

8 Years Old, 101 Proof, Pure Kentucky

I'm very fond of water
I drink it noon and night
No mother's son or daughter
Hath therein more delight

But I forgot to mention
To give the glass its due
I add with due attention
Some Bourbon's amber hue!

The Wild Turkey Distillery, located in Lawrenceburg, Kentucky, is the official distiller of Wild Turkey Straight Bourbon Whiskey.

The making of Wild Turkey Straight Bourbon Whiskey begins with a mixture of grains, which include corn, rye and malted barley. All grain shipments are checked for ripeness, moisture content and purity before being shipped to Lawrenceburg. Once received, Wild Turkey rechecks the grain mix in its laboratories to ensure it meets the company's strict specifications. Following storage, the grain is ground into a meal, weighed and measured.

According to government specifications, at least 51% of the grain mix must be corn and the product must be distilled in the United States in order for a whiskey to be designated as a Bourbon. Corn, far sweeter than rye or barley malt, gives Bourbon its full flavor and rounds out the body of the spirit eliminating the hard edge often found in a whiskey. A better Bourbon, such as Wild Turkey, will contain more than just 51% corn, but each distiller's grain formula is kept a closely guarded secret so the Bourbon connoisseur may discover the distinctive pleasures of a finely made Bourbon.

Central Kentucky rests on a deep shelf of limestone, which serves as a perfect filter for the pure water, free of iron and other minerals, which is used to distill the Bourbon. It is no accident that Kentucky Bourbons are some of the best. The water in Blue Grass country is perhaps the single best natural resource for this purpose. The Wild Turkey 360-acre distillery is in close proximity to the Kentucky River, the source of the crystal clear water used in Bourbon making.

The six steps involved in producing Wild Turkey include mashing, malting, fermenting, distilling, aging and bottling. In the mashing and malting processes, grains are mixed with limestone-filtered water and cooked. The mixture is then cooled and malted barely is added. Diastases, an enzyme in barley, converts the starch of the corn and rye grains into sugar. After about three hours, the "mash" is transferred to a huge cypress vat, called a fermenter.

During the fermentation process, Wild Turkey's secret yeast formula is added to the mash. The yeast ferments the sugar and changes it into alcohol, or what is called "distiller's beer." Combined with other elements in the mash, the yeast also produces the aroma, body and taste that gives Wild Turkey its unique flavor. The important role that the yeast formula plays in the fermentation process accounts for the close secrecy by which it is guarded.

Following fermentation, the now yellowish liquid mash is pumped into a 40-foot high continuous still, where the alcohol content of the mash is vaporized under a precisely controlled temperature. The vapors, are changed into a liquid, called "low wine" condensers and flow through a second distilling process which produces a clear, colorless Bourbon. It is interesting to note that what was once considered a waste material — the grain residue from the first distillation — is now a high-protein by-product which the company sells as a supplement for livestock and poultry feeds.

Wild Turkey, after having distilled water added to

lower its alcohol content, is poured into new, charred white oak barrels. The expensive, deep layer, charred interior sides of the oak barrels contribute to Wild Turkey's mellow flavor and deep red color. The charred oak barrels makes "corn whiskey" into Bourbon imparting the smooth vanilla palate. This is perhaps the single most important ingredient to the aging.

After the barrels are filled, they are transferred to one of the distillery's 21 warehouses to mature. Wild Turkey's 101-proof Bourbon must mature for a full 8 years.

Bourbon ages best under changing temperatures. Because the distillery's warehouse temperature varies with the change of seasons, the barrels of Wild Turkey are continually rotated to different floors for exposure to various temperatures. This assures a consistency in aging and a uniformity in color and taste.

Because taste is most important, each day's output of Wild Turkey is taste tested before being placed into a barrel. After a barrel has aged for two years, it is sampled on an annual basis until maturity. Throughout the aging process, extensive notes are taken on the aging, aroma and proof of Wild Turkey.

As Wild Turkey comes out of its warehouses, distilled water is added to lower the proof gained during the aging process and another taste sampling is conducted prior to bottling. Following the bottling process, random samplings are conducted to ensure that Wild Turkey's high quality is preserved.

Eight years of care and quality are invested in the making of Wild Turkey. A premium spirit of this kind must be specially monitored and carefully crafted to ensure the smooth, fine flavor that makes Wild Turkey famous. The mysteries and intricacies of Bourbon making are many, varied and fascinating. This truly American, premium spirit is an example of craftsmanship indigenous to our country.

ANGELIC

1 oz. WILD TURKEY 101
½ oz. Hiram Walker
White Creme de
Cacao
2 oz. Half & Half
dash Rose's® Grenadine

Shake with ice and serve on rocks or strain into cocktail glass.

ATLANTA BELLE

1 oz. WILD TURKEY 101
¼ oz. Hiram Walker
Green Creme de
Menthe
¼ oz. Hiram Walker
White Creme de
Cacao
3 oz. Half & Half

Shake with ice and serve on the rocks.

BEEHIVE

1½ oz. WILD TURKEY 101
2 oz. Grapefruit Juice
¾ oz. Honey

Shake well and serve on the rocks.

BIG BOY NOW

1½ oz. WILD TURKEY 101
1 tsp. Hiram Walker
Cherry Flavored
Brandy
1 tsp. Lemon Juice

Stir in mixing glass. Pour over rocks glass half filled with ice.

BIONIC TURKEY

1 oz. WILD TURKEY 101
½ oz. Martini & Rossi
Rosso Vermouth
dash Yellow Chartreus
1 oz. Orange Juice

Shake with ice and serve on th rocks.

BOURBON AND COLA

1½ oz. WILD TURKEY 101
Cola

In a tall glass with ice, fill wit cola.

BOURBON AND GINGER

1½ oz. WILD TURKEY 101
Ginger Ale

In a tall glass with ice. Fill wit ginger ale.

BOURBON COLLINS

1½ oz. WILD TURKEY 101
4-5 oz. Sweetened
Lemon Mix
Club Soda

Shake with ice and pour into to glass with ice. Fill with club sodc

BOURBON DELIGHT

1 oz. WILD TURKEY 101
¼ oz. Martini & Rossi
Rosso Vermouth
¼ oz. Hiram Walker
Creme de Cassis
½ oz. Lemon Juice

Shake with ice and serve on th rocks.

BOURBON MANHATTAN

1¼ oz. WILD TURKEY 101
¼ oz. Martini & Rossi
Rosso Vermouth

Stir on the rocks or strain into cocktail glass. Add cherry.

BOURBON MILK PUNCH

1½   oz. WILD TURKEY 101
3   oz. Milk
1   tsp. Superfine Sugar
1   dash Vanilla Extract

In a cocktail shaker with ice, shake well. Strain into rocks glass and sprinkle grated nutmeg on top.

BOURBON OLD FASHIONED

1½   oz. WILD TURKEY 101
¼   tsp. Sugar
2   dshs Bitters

Muddle cherry and orange slice in bottom of old-fashioned glass. Add ingredients and stir well.

BOURBON SLOE GIN FIX

1   oz. WILD TURKEY 101
½   oz. Hiram Walker Sloe Gin
2   oz. Sweetened Lemon Mix

Shake with ice and serve on the rocks. Add slice of fresh or brandied peach.

BRASS KNUCKLE

1   oz. WILD TURKEY 101
½   oz. Hiram Walker Triple Sec
2   oz. Sweetened Lemon Mix

Shake with ice and serve on the rocks.

COLONEL "T"

1   oz. WILD TURKEY 101
½   oz. Hiram Walker Apricot Flavored Brandy
3   oz. Pineapple Juice

Shake with ice and serve on the rocks.

COMMODORE

1   part WILD TURKEY 101
1   part Hiram Walker Creme de Cacao
1   part Sweetened Lemon Juice
1   dash Rose's® Grenadine

Shake with ice and serve on the rocks.

CRANBOURBON

1½   oz. WILD TURKEY 101
   dash Bitters
½   oz. Lemon Juice
1   tsp. Sugar
   Cranberry Juice

In a shaker, shake all ingredients but cranberry juice. Strain into rocks glass filled with ice, top with cranberry juice.

DIXIE

1   oz. WILD TURKEY 101
¼   oz. Hiram Walker White Creme de Menthe
¼   oz. Hiram Walker Triple Sec
   dash Bitters

Shake with ice and serve on rocks with lemon twist.

DIZZY LIZZY

1½   oz. WILD TURKEY 101
1½   oz. Sherry
   dash Lemon Juice
   Club Soda

In a tall glass with ice, fill with club soda.

DUBONNET BOURBON MANHATTAN

1 part WILD TURKEY 101
1 part Dubonnet
  dash Bitters

Stir on the rocks or strain into cocktail glass.

FIVE-LEAF CLOVER

¾ oz. WILD TURKEY 101
¾ oz. Martini & Rossi
     Extra Dry Vermouth
1 tsp. Green Chartreuse
1 tsp. Hiram Walker
     Green Creme de
     Menthe

Stir with ice in mixing glass. Strain into cocktail glass. Garnish with green olive.

FLORIDA PUNCH

2 oz. WILD TURKEY 101
2 oz. Pineapple Juice
½ tsp. Sugar

In a tall glass with ice, fill with club soda.

HOT APPLE COBBLER

1½ oz. WILD TURKEY 101
     Hot Apple Cider

Fill with hot apple cider. Garnish with a cinnamon stick.

JOHNNY

1½ oz. WILD TURKEY 101
     Orange Juice
     dash Rose's® Grenadine

In a tall glass with ice, fill with orange juice.

KENTUCKY COCKTAIL

1 part WILD TURKEY 101
1 part Pineapple Juice

Shake with ice and serve on the rocks or strain into cockta glass.

KENTUCKY GENT

1 oz. WILD TURKEY 101
½ oz. Hiram Walker
     Peppermint
     Schnapps
2 scps. Vanilla Ice Cream

Blend with a little cracked ice a medium speed until smooth Pour into brandy snifter.

MACHO KAMACHO

1½ oz. WILD TURKEY 101
2 dshs Hiram Walker
     Peach Schnapps

In a mixing glass with ice, stir Strain over ice in a rocks glass Drop in one red grape.

MINT JULEP

1½ oz. WILD TURKEY 101
2-3 sprgs Mint
1 tsp. Sugar

In a tall glass, muddle mint, sugar, and 2 tsp. water. Fill with crushed ice and add bourbon. Stir until well frosted.

MINTY JULEP

1 oz. WILD TURKEY 101
½ oz. Hiram Walker
     Green Creme de
     Menthe

Add splash of water and stir or the rocks.

PERFECT BOURBON MANHATTAN

4 parts WILD TURKEY 101
1 part Martini & Rossi
    Rosso Vermouth
1 part Martini & Rossi
    Extra Dry
    Vermouth

Stir on the rocks or strain into cocktail glass. Add lemon twist.

PRESBYTERIAN

1¼ oz. WILD TURKEY 101
2 oz. Ginger Ale
2 oz. Soda

Stir together in a highball glass with ice cubes. Twist lemon peel over drink and drop in.

SHRAPNEL

½ oz. WILD TURKEY 101
¼ oz. Martini & Rossi
    Rosso Vermouth
¼ oz. Martini & Rossi
    Extra Dry
    Vermouth
¼ oz. Hiram Walker
    Apricot Flavored
    Brandy

Stir on the rocks. Add orange slice.

SLOE BIRD

1 oz. WILD TURKEY 101
½ oz. Hiram Walker Sloe
    Gin
½ oz. Lemon Juice
1 tsp. Superfine Sugar

Stir in mixing glass with ice. Strain into cocktail glass.

SOUR TURKEY

1½ oz. WILD TURKEY 101
1½ oz. Lemon Juice
½ tsp. Superfine Sugar

In a cocktail shaker with ice, mix well. Strain into a chilled sour glass and garnish with a lemon slice and a maraschino cherry.

SOUTHERN SOUR

¼ oz. WILD TURKEY 101
¾ oz. Southern Comfort
3 oz. Sweetened
    Lemon Mix

Shake with ice and serve on the rocks or strain into cocktail glass. Add cherry and orange slice.

STEVE'S SOUR

1½ oz. WILD TURKEY 101
1½ oz. Orange Juice
1½ oz. Sweetened
    Lemon Mix

Shake with ice and serve on the rocks.

TURKEY CRUSH

1½ oz. WILD TURKEY 101
4 oz. Orange Juice
    splsh Club Soda

Serve in a tall glass with ice.

TURKEY SHOOT

1¼ oz. WILD TURKEY 101
    Hiram Walker
    Anisette

In a pony glass; float anisette on top. Serve as a shot.

TURKEY SHOOTER

¾ oz. WILD TURKEY 101
¼ oz. Hiram Walker
White Creme de
Menthe

Shake in cocktail shaker. Strain into brandy snifter.

W.T. FIZZ

2 oz. WILD TURKEY 101
Club Soda

In a highball glass filled with ice; fill with club soda. Add a squeeze of fresh lemon, lime or orange. Garnish with a slice of the same fruit.

WARD 101

4 parts WILD TURKEY 101
1 part Orange Juice
1 part Sweetened
Lemon Mix
1 dash Rose's® Grenadine

Shake and serve on the rocks.

ANHEUSER-BUSCH, INC.

At Anheuser-Busch, Inc., the phrase "Somebody Still Cares About Quality" accurately depicts the philosophy of the world's largest and most successful brewing operation.

With 14 domestic brands and three imports, Anheuser-Busch, Inc., offers consumers the most diverse, high quality family of beers in the brewing industry.

Since its establishment as a small, South St. Louis brewery in 1860, the company has maintained key commitments to product quality, tradition and leadership. Through the years, the beer brands of Anheuser-Busch have become part of the American scene, quality products consumed responsibly by an overwhelming majority of American beer consumers.

History of Beer

The origins of beer are older than recorded history, extending into the mythology of ancient civilizations. Beer, the oldest alcoholic beverage, was discovered independently by most ancient cultures – the Babylonians, Assyrians, Egyptians, Hebrews, Africans, Chinese, Incas, Teutons, Saxons and the various wandering tribes that were found in Eurasia.

In recorded history, Babylonian clay tablets more than 6,000 years old depict the brewing of beer and give detailed recipes. An extract from an ancient Chinese manuscript states that beer, or "kiu" as it was called, was known to the Chinese in the 23rd century B.C.

With the rise of commerce and the growth of cities during the Middle Ages, brewing became more than a household activity. Municipal brew houses were established, which eventually led to the formation of the brewing guilds. Commercial brewing on a significantly larger scale began around the 12th century in Germany.

Although native Americans had developed a form of beer, Europeans brought their own version with them to the New World. Beer enjoys the distinction of having come over on the Mayflower and, in fact, seems to have played a part in the Pilgrims' decision to land at Plymouth Rock instead of farther south, as intended. A journal kept by one of the passengers – and now in the Library of Congress – states, in an entry from 1620, that the Mayflower landed at Plymouth because "we could not now take time for further search, our victuals being much spent, especially our beer..."

The first commercial brewery in America was founded in New Amsterdam (New York) in 1623. Many patriots owned their own breweries, among them Samuel Adams and William Penn. George Washington even had his own brew house on the grounds of Mount Vernon, and his handwritten recipe for beer – dated 1757 and taken from his diary – is still preserved.

Brewing at Anheuser-Busch

More than 100 years ago, Adolphus Busch created a beer that would become known for its uncompromising quality. The original Budweiser label guaranteed a beer brewed by a unique process, using only the highest quality ingredients.

Today Budweiser's label gives the same assurance of quality. On the label for all to see are the words: "This is the famous Budweiser beer. We know of no brand produced by any other brewer which costs so much to brew and age. Our exclusive beechwood ageing produces a taste, a smoothness and a drinkability you will find in no other beer at any price." Today, more than a century later, the quality is still there, still uncompromised.

The secret of fine, traditional brewing is really no secret at all – take the choicest, most costly ingredients, skillfully brew them allowing plenty of time for nature to work its wonders, age the beer slowly and naturally, and take intense pride and care in every step along the way. That's the way Anheuser-Busch has always brewed beer.

Ingredients

Beer is a food product made from barley malt, hops, grain adjuncts, yeast and water. The alcohol in beer results from the fermentation by yeast of an extract from barley malt and other cereal grains. In addition to alcohol, beer commonly contains carbohydrates, proteins, amino acids, vitamins (such as riboflavin and niacin) and minerals (such as calcium and potassium) derived from the original food materials.

All Anheuser-Busch beers vary in the type and mix of ingredients and in certain refinements in the brewing process to achieve their distinctive and unique characteristics. But all are alike in one respect – every Anheuser-Busch beer is completely natural without any artificial ingredients, additives or preservatives.

Superior ingredients are basic in the brewing of truly great beers. Anheuser-Busch uses only the finest, choicest, most costly ingredients available, selected through the most exacting requirements and specifications in the brewing industry. Again, nothing secret or mysterious, just the same basic ingredients that have been known for centuries as the way to make fine beers – barley malt, hops, rice or corn, yeast and water.

Malt — Malt is the soul of all great beers and Anheuser-Busch uses more malt per barrel than any other major brewer in the country. The malt it uses begins with the choicest golden barley selected from the finest fields in America – from the sweeping plains of Minnesota and the Dakotas and from the western states of Idaho, Washington, Wyoming, Colorado, Oregon, Montana and California.

There are two basic types of malting barleys. One produces two rows of kernels on each stalk, the other, six rows. The flavor of the two varieties differs, with two-row barley malt being a choicer ingredient because it produces a smoother-tasting beer. Anheuser-Busch beers contain a varying percentage of two-row barley malt. Michelob contains the highest percentage.

In a carefully controlled malting procedure, the barley is cleaned, steeped, germinated and kilned. Malt is a natural source of carbohydrates, enzymes and flavor compounds. Most of the enzymes are developed during the malting process. During brewing, the complex malt carbohydrates are broken apart by the enzymes. As a result, simple sugars are formed. These sugars are used by the yeast as an energy source during fermentation.

Hops – Hops, the cone-shaped clusters of blossoms from the vine-like hop plant, are the spice of beer, adding their own special aroma, flavor and character. Anheuser-Busch uses only the choicest imported and domestic hops, hand-selected by company agents from the world's finest fields in Europe and Washington, Oregon and Idaho.

Rice – Rice from Texas, Louisiana, Mississippi, Missouri, Arkansas and California adds lightness and crispness to Budweiser and Michelob brands, while Busch, King Cobra, LA and Natural Light are made with corn to produce a milder flavor. Anheuser Märzen is a European type all-malt brew without rice or corn.

Yeast – The brewer's yeast used in all Anheuser-Busch beers has been perfected and protected over decades, and all of the company's breweries are supplied from one carefully maintained pure-culture system.

Water – Pure water is also a key ingredient in brewing great beer. Water is checked just as rigidly as other ingredients and, when necessary, the water is treated to ensure conformity to Anheuser-Busch's exacting standards.

Brewing Process

Next comes the brewing process. Here, too, there is no secret – visitors have always been welcome to tour Anheuser-Busch breweries and witness the painstaking and exacting care it takes to produce its beers. As an example, following are the steps in the Budweiser brewing process.

Brewing at Anheuser-Busch is a long, natural process taking up to 30 days or longer. It may appear old-fashioned to brew beer principally the way they have been brewing it for more than 100 years but Anheuser-Busch has never found a better way to brew than by combining the finest ingredients with slow, precise steps which give nature the time it needs to create great beer. There are modern shortcuts such as forcing fermentation by mechanical agitation, using enzyme preparations for chillproofing or artificially injecting CO_2 into the beer for carbonation — but they don't create great beers.

Modern Technology

While it chooses not to use chemical advances to cut corners in brewing, Anheuser-Busch has always been

Alcohol Content

Through custom, the general public has come to refer to the alcohol content of American beers as either "3.2%" or "5%." The 3.2% designation refers to percent of alcohol by weight, and the 5% designation refers to percent of alcohol by volume. To clarify the real difference note that:

—3.2% (an alcohol by weight designation) is equivalent to 4% by volume;

—4% by weight is equivalent to 5% by volume.

Comparing the "by volume" numbers, it is clear that there is really only about a 1% difference in alcohol by volume between so-called 3.2% and 5% beers.

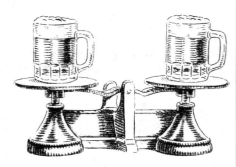

The Budweiser Brewing Process

Brew House

1. The barley malt and rice are coarsely ground in huge mills. Proportions are measured.

MILL

MILL

2. The ground malt and rice are mixed with water in separate tanks (malt in a mash tank and rice together with some of the malt in a cooker). Then the mixtures are combined in the mash tank. During mashing, enzymes in the malt break down starch into fermentable sugars.

MASH TANK

COOKER

3. The grains are strained, leaving a clear, amber liquid called wort.

4. The wort moves through the grant, which controls the rate of flow into the brew kettle.

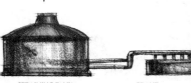
STRAINING TANK   GRANT

5. In the brew kettle, the wort is brought to a boil and natural hops are added.

NATURAL DRIED HOPS

BREW KETTLE

6. The spent hops are strained.

HOP STRAINER

Fermenting and Lagering

7. The wort is cooled to the right temperature to receive the yeast.

COOLING TOWER

8. As the cooled wort flows into primary fermentation tanks, yeast is added.

YEAST

9. For up to six days, the yeast converts the fermentable sugars to carbon dioxide and alcohol and the wort becomes beer.

10. At the desired state of fermentation, the beer is transferred to lager tanks. A portion of freshly yeasted wort is added and allowed to ferment and age. This is called kraeusening. This second fermentation matures the flavor. It is also the traditional, natural way of carbonating beer. (All Anheuser-Busch beers are naturally carbonated.)

Most brewers do not use a second fermentation. Since a single fermentation does not provide sufficient carbonation, these brewers add carbon dioxide to the beer before packaging.

Beechwood ageing is part of Anheuser-Busch's second fermentation. All of its beers are beechwood aged. A layer of beechwood chips is spread on the bottom of the lager tank. The chips have been cleaned and rinsed before use. The beechwood chips provide more surface area

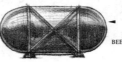

LAGER TANK

11. The beer is transferred to a chillproofing tank and natural tannin is added. The tannin combines with certain proteins, forming particles which settle to the bottom of the tank together with the added tannin. As the beer flows out of the tanks, the protein-tannin particles are left behind and removed from the beer. Chillproofing keeps the beer from becoming hazy when cooled to drinking temperature.

12. The beer is filtered.

13. Finished beer is sent to the packaging area.

for the action of the yeast. The yeast settles on the chips and continues to work until the beer is completely fermented.

Anheuser-Busch is the only major brewer in the world using the traditional beechwood ageing process to age and naturally carbonate its beer.

BEECHWOOD CHIPS

CHILLPROOFING

▼

FINAL FILTER

▼

BOTTLES   CANS   DRAFT KEGS

innovative in the use of science to promote quality. The company pioneered in the application of pasteurization in the brewing industry and developed the use of refrigeration railcars and a nationwide system of rail delivery.

Today, the Anheuser-Busch traditional brewing process is strictly maintained using modern technology in a rigorous program of quality assurance. Scientists and technicians use every skill available to ensure that each bottle, can or keg of beer is the very finest that can be produced, and to ensure that each Anheuser-Busch beer has its own great taste glass after glass, year after year.

Quality Assurance

Quality assurance at Anheuser-Busch begins with the testing of ingredients before brewing ever begins. Perfection is sought through close scrutiny extending down to the smallest detail of the packaging operation, including bottle crowns and can lids.

No scientific test, however, can replace tasting as the final judgement of quality. Numerous flavor panels meet daily at company headquarters and at each brewery to judge the aroma, appearance and taste of packaged, filtered and unfiltered beer. In addition, samples are flown into St. Louis from each brewery for taste evaluation.

Control of quality does not cease at the brewery. Anheuser-Busch's wholesalers play a key role in seeing that the quality that begins with the ingredients and continues through the brewing and packaging processes is preserved until it reaches the consumers. Anheuser-Busch wholesalers, at their expense, provide controlled environment warehouse systems that maintain beer freshness during storage.

In the marketplace, quality standards and beer freshness are maintained through a program of rotating beer stock on retail shelves. This rotation program includes a unique can coding system which electro-statically places a date code on every can. The code identifies the day, year and 15-minute period of production; the plant at which the product was brewed and packaged; and the production line.

The final result of all these efforts is a family of naturally brewed beers that the company believes is truly unique. And millions of consumers agree.

Anheuser-Busch remains firmly committed to quality, which it believes is, and has always been, the fundamental, irreplaceable ingredient in its successful performance.

Anheuser-Busch further believes that the consuming public will increasingly come to recognize and appreciate the natural quality and value that it has been brewing into its beers for more than a century.

History of Anheuser-Busch

It was 1852 and a tiny brewery on St. Louis' south side operated by George Schneider, opened for business. From 1857 to 1860, ownership of that brewery changed hands – three times. But it wasn't until 1860 that a great tradition of beer would begin.

His name was Eberhard Anheuser, a successful manufacturer turned brewery owner. And, in 1860, an expanded brewery re-opened its doors under the name of E. Anheuser & Co.

The following year, Eberhard's daughter, Lily, married a young St. Louis brewery supplier named Adolphus Busch. Enticed by his father-in-law's offer, Adolphus joined the brewery in 1864 as a salesman. In 1865, E. Anheuser & Co. produced 8,000 barrels of beer, featuring St. Louis Lager, the company's original flagship beer.

By 1873, Adolphus was a full partner in the brewery, serving as the company's secretary. And in 1876, with his close friend, Carl Conrad, Adolphus created a new beer — Budweiser Lager — which became the brewery's new flagship beer, and more than one hundred years later, still owns that title.

Upon the death of Eberhard in 1880, Adolphus became president and production of beer was up to 141,163 barrels, largely representative of an increase in the popularity of Budweiser Lager.

Michelob was introduced in 1896, and by 1901, production of Anheuser-Busch beer broke the million-barrel mark.

Adolphus Busch died in 1913 and August A. Busch, Sr. was named president – entering an era in which Anheuser-Busch was to face a variety of social and political changes: The First World War . . . Prohibition . . . and the Great Depression.

Intent on the survival of the company and protecting the jobs of its many hundreds of loyal employees during Prohibition, August focused the company's expertise and energies in new directions – including the production of corn products, baker's yeast, ice cream, soft drinks, commercial refrigeration units and truck bodies.

During this period, the company also introduced Bevo, a non-alcoholic malt-based beverage, as well as a number of carbonated soft drinks including chocolate-flavored Carcho; coffee-flavored Kaffo; Buschtee, flavored with imported tea leaves; Grape Bouquet grape drink; and Busch Ginger Ale. Each enjoyed various levels of success, but all were eventually discontinued when Prohibition ended and Anheuser-Busch could return to its core business — beer.

Baker's yeast proved to be another story — a long-term success story. This product, first manufactured in St. Louis in 1927, made great gains under the watchful eye of Adolphus Busch III, who became the company's president in 1934. Anheuser-Busch eventually became the nation's leading producer of compressed baker's yeast, a position it held until its Busch Industrial products subsidiary was sold in 1988.

August A. Busch, Jr., succeeded his brother as president in 1946 and served as the company's chief executive officer until 1975. He continued to serve as chairman of the board until 1977, when he was named honorary chairman. During his tenure, eight branch breweries were constructed; annual sales increased from three million barrels in 1946 to more than 34 million in 1974; Busch beer was introduced; and corporate diversification was extended to include family entertainment, real estate, can manufacturing, transportation and major league baseball. August Busch, Jr., died in 1989.

August A. Busch III became president in 1974 and was named chief executive officer in 1975, becoming the fourth generation of his family to serve the company in that capacity. In 1977, he was elected chairman of the board. Under his leadership, the company: opened two breweries, acquired one and is building the 13th; introduced Michelob Light, Natural Light, Michelob Classic Dark, Bud Light, LA, Michelob Dry, Bud Dry, Anheuser Märzen and Busch Light beers, King Cobra Malt Liquor and O'Doul's Non-Alcoholic Brew; acquired the nation's second-largest baking company; opened new family entertainment attractions; launched the largest brewers expansion projects in company history; increased vertical integration capabilities with the addition of new can manufacturing and malt production facilities; and diversified into container recovery, metalized label printing, snack foods, wines, international marketing and creative services.

Beer Brands

Anheuser-Busch has developed products to meet a wide range of consumer tastes and price preferences. And, although each brand is produced according to a time-honored Old World brewing method, using only the finest natural ingredients, all Anheuser-Busch beers have their own unique characteristics.

— Budweiser, the company's flagship brand, reigns as the top-selling beer brand in the world. Budweiser was introduced in 1876 when company founder, Adolphus Busch, set out to create the nation's first truly national beer brand – a beer that would be universally popular and transcend regional tastes.

Today, Budweiser leads the premium beer category – in fact, it outsells all the other domestic premium beers combined. With broad appeal among virtually all demographic consumer groups, the brand truly lives up to its reputation as the "King of Beers."

— In 1896, Anheuser-Busch developed another beer brand, Michelob. Considered a "beer for connoisseurs," Michelob was served only on draught in the finest retail establishments.

Michelob became available in bottles in 1961 and today, with its distinctive red ribbon and hourglass shaped bottle, the brand accounts for about 70 percent of all super-premium beer sales. It is brewed using the most expensive ingredients available.

— In 1978, Michelob Light was introduced as the industry's first super-premium light beer for consumers who prefer a full-bodied, rich tasting beer with reduced calories.

— Three years later, in 1981, the third member of the company's super-premium family – Michelob Classic Dark -- was introduced offering Michelob's smooth taste in a rich, dark beer.

— Bud Light is the company's premium entry in the light beer category and the industry's fastest growing light beer. Introduced in 1982, Bud Light now ranks as the number two light beer in the nation and the third best selling brand among all domestic beers.

- Michelob Dry was introduced in September 1988 and expanded into national distribution two months later. America's first super-premium dry beer, Michelob Dry, is produced using the exclusive DryBrew™ method of brewing. The longer brewing method produces a less sweet beer with no aftertaste.

- Based on the overwhelming consumer response to Michelob Dry, Anheuser-Busch launched Bud Dry in the Spring of 1989. This premium-priced dry beer represents a logical extension of the company's successful segmented marketing approach.

- Natural Light, the sub-premium priced beer, was unveiled in 1977, offering an excellent price/value for light beer drinkers seeking a quality product at an attractive price. It plays an integral role in the Anheuser-Busch three tier "Family of Light Beers" approach to the category.

- Busch, a popular priced beer, has also achieved strong growth in its markets. Introduced in 1955, the brand is now available in 41 states and ranks as the nation's fifth largest selling beer.

- In 1989, Anheuser-Busch introduced Busch Light, the light beer partner of its successful Busch brand, into selected Midwestern markets, and in 1990, expanded into national distribution.

- LA, introduced in 1984, is a reduced alcohol beer with a traditional beer taste. With about half the alcohol of regular beer, it offers a lighter alternative to consumers who choose to be more moderate in their consumption of beer and other alcoholic beverages.

- King Cobra is the Anheuser-Bush entry in the malt liquor category. First available in 1984, the brand is now sold in over 300 markets across the United States, offering a smooth, high quality malt liquor taste.

— Anheuser Märzen is an extra-premium, full-flavored beer brewed in small batches exclusively at the company's 119-year-old St. Louis brewery. It is an "all-malt" beer, meaning that no grain adjuncts are used. A distinctly American beer, Anheuser Märzen is available in select markets.

O'Doul's, a new, non-alcohol brew, was introduced by Anheuser-Busch in select test markets in March 1989. By January 1990, the brand reached national distribution. O'Doul's contains less than .5 percent alcohol by volume – about the same amount of alcohol found in soft drinks and fruit juices. O'Doul's is being marketed to consumers who want the great taste of Anheuser-Busch beer, but without the alcohol.

— Anheuser-Busch also imports and distributes three Danish-brewed beers in select United States markets: Carlsberg, the largest selling beer in Denmark; Carlsberg Light, the reduced calorie version of Carlsberg; and Elephant Malt Liquor, the largest selling imported malt liquor. All three are produced by United Breweries, Ltd. of Denmark.

Anheuser-Busch – dedication, quality and tradition – trademarks that have dictated the growth of the company and positioned it as the largest and most successful brewer in the world.

Beer Clean Glasses

Anheuser-Busch, the world's largest brewer, assures excellence in its draught beer from the brewery to the wholesaler. Likewise, Anheuser-Busch wholesalers take the necessary steps to make certain that the product is delivered to retail establishments in first-class condition. However, it's up to the Bartender to draw the best possible glass of draught beer for the consumer.

The first step is to serve the draught beer in a clean glass. . . a Beer Clean Glass. A glass may look clean, but is it near clean or beer clean?

Following are a few tips for obtaining a "Beer Clean

Glass," the eye-appealing glass filled with one of Anheuser-Busch's great beers with a clear, golden color and a good tight collar of foam.

A three or four-sink setup is ideal for getting glasses beer clean; a three-tank setup is most common. The first tank is for washing followed by two rinsing compartments.

A beer glass should be washed each time it is used — unless the customer requests that his glass be refilled. Proper cleaning and drying can be accomplished in four simple steps.

1. Used glasses should be emptied and rinsed with clear water to remove any foam or remaining beer which will cause dilution of the cleaning solution.

2. Each glass should be brushed in water containing a solution of odor-free and non-fat cleaning compound that will thoroughly clean the surface of the glass, and rinse away easily in clear water.

3. The glass must then be rinsed twice in fresh, clean, cool water – with the proper sanitizer in the last tank. Proper and complete rinsing is most important for a "beer clean" glass.

4. Dry glasses upside down on a deeply corrugated surface or stainless steel glass rack. Never towel dry glasses. Store air-dried glasses away from sources of unpleasant odors, grease or smoke that are emitted from kitchens, restrooms or ashtrays.

And, another secret to serving a perfect glass of beer. . .rinse the "beer clean" glass with cold, fresh water just before filling with Anheuser-Busch draught beer.

Dispensing Draught Beer

Obtaining a "beer clean" glass is just one step involved in the proper dispensing of perfect "brewery-fresh" draught beer. Equally important are proper refrigeration, cleanliness of dispensing equipment and proper pressures.

Since draught beer is perishable, it must not be exposed to warm temperatures. The retailer must preserve it by providing equipment that will maintain the temperature of the beer in the barrel between 38 - 42F. These temperatures should be maintained throughout the dispensing equipment so the beer in the glass as it is served to the consumer will also be 38 - 42 F. This range of temperature seems to satisfy the majority of tastes and is too small a variation to affect its flavor or quality.

Cleanliness is a most vital consideration. The beer faucets, tubing, hose, coils, taps and vents, including direct draw systems, must be thoroughly cleaned regularly. Glasses should be "beer clean," and no effort should be spared to keep the bar clean and bright.

Finally, proper pressure in the barrel is very important. To maintain the brewery fresh taste in the beer, its natural or normal carbonation must be preserved. The dispensing equipment through which the beer flows must have a pressure that corresponds to the normal carbonation of the beer at the temperature of the beer in the barrel. The size and length of the coil in the dispensing equipment will determine the pressure to be used.

With the dispensing equipment properly set up, you are ready to serve draught beer.

The right head of foam is important to giving a glass of beer that essential eye appeal. The size of the head is controlled by the angle at which the glass is held at the beginning of the draw. If the glass is held straight, so that the beer drops into the bottom, a deep head will result. If the glass is tilted sharply so that the beer flows down the side, the head of foam will be minimized.

For most beer glasses – and to please most customers – the head should be allowed to rise just above the top of the glass without spilling over, then settle down to a ¾" or 1" head of frothy white foam.

Remember, there are two key steps for serving a truly perfect glass of draught beer: — Use a "beer clean" glass, and before filling, rinse the glass in cold, running water.

SIGNATURE DRINKS FROM FROM ACROSS AMERICA

ABSOLUT ANNIE'S

1¼ oz. Absolut Vodka
4 oz. Cranberry Juice

ORPHAN ANNIE'S
Stirling, NJ

BACARDI STONE SOUR

1¼ oz. Bacardi Premium
Black Rum
Sour Mix
Orange Juice

Blend until frothy.
HOUSE OF DONG YUANG
Chicago, IL

BANANA BOGIE

2 parts Kahlua
2 parts Banana Liqueur
1 part Heavy Cream

Blend with ice and serve garnished with a cherry.
BOGIE'S
New York, NY

BANZAI

1¼ oz. Southern Comfort
1 oz. Absolut Vodka
½ oz. Creme de Noyaux

Mix in a tall glass and pour over ice.
KABUKI JAPANESE STEAK HOUSE
Roanoke, VA

BEETHOVEN'S BABY GRAND

1¼ oz. Absolut Vodka
¾ oz. Bombay Gin
¼ oz. Dry Vermouth

Add a twist of lemon, olives and cracked pepper on top.
BEETHOVEN'S LOUNGE
Fort Collins, CO

BEND ME OVER

1¼ oz. Absolut Vodka
¾ oz. Amaretto
1½ oz. Sweet and Sour

Chill. Serve straight up or on the rocks.
DAVID'S RESTAURANT & LOUNGE
Chattanooga, TN

BLUE LUI

¾ oz. Rum
½ oz. Blue Curacao
3 oz. Pineapple Juice
½ oz. Sour Mix
½ oz. Lime Juice

BAR LUI
New York, NY

BLUEBERRY TEA

¾ oz. Grand Marnier
¾ oz. Amaretto
Tea
Whipped Cream

YVETTE
Chicago, IL

BOP-A-RITA

1¼ oz. Tequila
¾ oz. Triple Sec
2 oz. Sweet & Sour - Lemon
1 oz. Pineapple Juice

BeBOP USA
Beaverton, OR

CAJUN MARTINI

1	btle. Absolut Vodka
	or
	Bombay Gin
6-7	Large Jalapeno Peppers
	Green Olives

Slice peppers and marinate in vodka/gin for at least 48 hours. Use 3 oz. for each martini. Serve in chilled glass. Garnish with olives.
ALLEGRO
Boston, MA

COPPER COVE
PEACH COBBLER

1	oz. Peach Schnapps
	dash Orange Juice
	dash Cream
	dash Peach Syrup
1	Fresh Peach

Combine with ice in a blender. Serve in a bucket with garnish of whipped cream and fresh peach slices.
THE COVE
Copperopolis, CA

DUST BUSTER

Vodka
Blackberry Brandy
Lemonade
In a tall glass with ice.
BUSTER'S DOWNTOWN
New York, NY

ELECTRIC WATERMELON

Equal parts:

½	oz. Vodka
½	oz. Rum
½	oz. Midori
½	oz. Triple Sec
	Orange Juice
	Grenadine
	Sprite

In a tall glass over ice.
RED ROBIN
Seattle, WA

EXTASE

½	oz. La Grande Passion
	Champagne
	(De Venoge)

LA PETITE MARMITE
New York, NY

FUZZY BUNNY

1¼	oz. Rum
½	oz. Peach Schnapps
¼	oz. Pineapple Juice
	splsh Rose's® Lime Juice
	splsh Ginger Ale

Shake well; garnish with orange and lime (or carrot and celery if available).
BUNNY'S SALOON
South Orange, NJ

GEMEAUX

Champagne
B&B
JACQUELINE'S
New York, NY

GUMBY & POKY
Light Rum
Dark Rum
Coconut Rum
Pineapple Juice
Orange Juice

Makes you extremely pliable.
LUCY'S
New York, NY

H.M.S. WICKET
1 oz. Grand Marnier
½ oz. Baileys Original
    Irish Cream

Fill with black coffee. Top with whipped cream. Dash of Chambord on top of whipped cream.
STICKY WICKET RESTAURANT & PUB
Hopkinton, MA

HARRY'S BERRY
1½ oz. Raspberry
     Schnapps
3   oz. Cranberry Juice

HARRY'S CAFE
Chicago, IL

HOT BLOND
½ oz. Bacardi 151 Rum
½ oz. Amaretto
½ oz. Liquore Galliano

Fill with orange juice in a ½ iced tall glass. Garnish with orange slice. Float Bacardi 151 Rum and flambe.
THE DUNGEON
Seattle, WA

JAMAICAN ROMANCE
1 oz. Dark Rum
½ oz. Chambord
    Liqueur
½ oz. Creme de Banana
    Pineapple Juice
    Cranberry Juice

Pour over ice in a tall glass. Garnish with a pineapple wedge.
BOBBY BYRNE'S PUB
Hyannis, MA

J.B. DANIGANS PUNCH
1   oz. Absolut Vodka
1   oz. Chambord
½   oz. 7-Up
½   oz. Orange Juice
½   oz. Pineapple Juice
½   oz. Cranberry Juice

Mix and strain over ice in a 10 oz. glass. Garnish with pineapple and orange slice.
J.B. DANIGANS
Poughkeepsie, NY

J.B.'S GROG
Gold Rum
Dark Rum
Grenadine
Sweet & Sour
Orange Juice

J.B. WINBERIE
Boston, MA

JOE'S GIMLET

1½ oz. Vodka or Gin
4 oz. Fresh Lemon
Juice
½ oz. Egg Whites
½ oz. Simple Syrup

*Blend egg whites and syrup.
Add lemon juice and liquor.
Pour over ice and shake.*
JOE'S STONE CRAB
Miami Beach, FL

LIVE WIRE

¾ oz. Baileys Original
Irish Cream
¾ oz. Frangelico
Chilled Expresso

Shake. Strain into a martini glass.
DUKES CHOWDER HOUSE
Seattle, WA

MARQUIS ROYALE

1 oz. Grand Marnier
1 oz. Half & Half
1 scp. Vanilla Ice Cream

*Blend with ½ cup crushed ice.
Pour into large champagne
glass. Top with whipped cream.
Float a few drops of Grand Mar-
nier. Garnish with a chocolate
orange stick.*
MARQUIS WEST
Santa Monica, CA

MAXIMILLIAN

Grand Marnier
Baileys Original Irish Cream
Kahlua
Creme de Grand Marnier
Steamed Milk

JACKSONVILLE INN
Jacksonville, OR

MOBY COCKTAIL

2/5 oz. Vodka
1/5 oz. Blue Curacao
1/5 oz. Peach Schnapps
1/5 oz. Rum
Cranberry Juice
7-Up

SPORTS
Indianapolis, IN

NUTTY IRISH COFFEE

¾ oz. Baileys Original
Irish Cream
¾ oz. Frangelico
Coffee

Top with whipped cream.
MUGS BUNNY
Chicago, IL

OPAL ALEXANDER

Opal Nera
Creme de Cacao
Heavy Cream

*Shake, strain and serve in a
chilled stem glass. Garnish with
nutmeg (optional).*
MARCELLO'S OF SCARSDALE
Scarsdale, NY

OTTO'S STINGER

1½ oz. Asbach Uralt
1 oz. Rumple Minze

*Shake with ice. Strain into
cocktail glass.*
OTTO'S BRAUHAUS
Horsham, PA

P.C.B. CONTAMINATION COCKTAIL

1   oz. Peach Schnapps
1   oz. Bacardi Light Rum
4   oz. Cranberry Juice

Add a splash of sour mix and shake well. Add an orange slice for color.

HARRY'S HIDEAWAY
East Hampton, Long Island, NY

PEACHE KEENE

1   oz. Peach Schnapps
3   oz. Pineapple Juice

Pour over ice in rocks glass.

DeSTEFANO'S
Chicago, IL

PJ LEI

1¼   oz. Bacardi Premium Black Rum
    Fill with Dole Pineapple Juice

In a tall glass over ice. Garnish with a pineapple spear.

CANTINA (PART OF DOBBS HOUSE)
Dallas/Ft. Worth Airport, TX

PRIVATEER'S ICE COFFEE

1½   oz. Kahlua
½   oz. Peppermint Schnapps

Fill 19 oz. tumbler with ice, add Kahlua and fill up ⅔ with fresh brewed iced coffee. Top with peppermint schnapps and garnish with whipped cream.

PRIVATEER TAVERN
Portsmouth, NH

PURPLE MOON

1   oz. Vodka
½   oz. Triple Sec
½   oz. Blue Curacao
    splsh Cranberry Juice
    dash Rose's® Lime Juice

Chill and serve straight up in a rocks glass.

FULL MOON NIGHTCLUB
Encinitas, CA

RECOVERY ROOM TRANSFUSION

    Vodka
    Grape Juice Concentrate
    Bacardi 151 Rum

The beer tap system is used mixing the vodka and grape juice concentrate. Once drawn into a glass it is garnished with a sugar cube and topped with Bacardi 151 Rum and flambed. Garnish with fresh grapes and orange slices.

THE RECOVERY ROOM
Morristown, NJ

RED FOX

½   oz. Southern Comfort
½   oz. Melon Liqueur
¼   oz. Amaretto
¼   oz. Sloe Gin
1   oz. Pineapple Juice
3   oz. Cranberry Juice

Pour in a 12 oz. glass with ice, shake well.

OCEANFRONT
Brigantine, NJ

RICK'S CAFE
Baileys Original
Irish Cream
Kahlua
Irish Whiskey
Vanilla Ice Cream

Top with hot coffee. Float ice cream on top.

THE STORE
Basking Ridge, NJ

RICK'S COOLER
Vodka
Lemonade
Grenadine

RICK'S
Clifton, NJ

ROJO'S COOLER
¾ oz. Hiram Walker
Creme de Banana
¾ oz. Bacardi Rum
2 oz. Orange Juice
2 oz. Pineapple Juice

Pour ingredients in a tall cocktail glass over ice. Shake. Garnish with fresh fruit.

ROJO'S
Corning, NY

SIDEWINDERS
1 oz. Blackberry Brandy
1 oz. Southern Comfort
1 oz. Rose's® Lime Juice
7-Up

Shake well; add a splash of 7-Up and serve in a tall glass or as shots.

CURVE INN
Springfield, IL

S.S. WESTMORELAND
1 oz. Cherry Marnier
½ oz. Vodka
½ oz. Kahlua
dash Salt
splsh Water

Serve on the rocks.

THE WESTMORELAND
COCKTAIL LOUNGE
Landing, NY

SCREAMING CLAM
2 oz. Vodka
4 oz. Clam Juice
Tomato Juice
dash McIlhenny's
Tabasco Peppar
Sauce
¼ tbs. Horseradish
½ oz. Fresh Lemon
Juice
dash Pepper
2 oz. Worcestershire
Sauce
dash Orange Juice

Shake and serve in 16 oz. Fou Fou glass with celery salt rim. Garnish with a clam with eyes, celery and lemon.

GLADSTONE'S MALIBU
Pacific Palisades, CA

STRAWBERRY FIELDS FOREVER
Hiram Walker Creme de Cacao
Amaretto
Frozen Strawberries
Vanilla Ice Cream
Blend.

BATCH'S RED ROOSTER
Orange, MA

STRAWBERRY SUMMER COOLER

1¼ oz. Apricot Brandy
½ cup Strawberries
1 oz. Orange Juice
1 oz. Pineapple Juice
1 oz. Grapefruit Juice

Blend with ½ scoop of ice, pour into 17 oz. snifter. Garnish with whipped cream and a strawberry.

REFLECTIONS
Leola, PA

SUMAC

1 oz. Apple Schnapps
1 oz. Peach Schnapps
1 oz. Strawberry Schnapps
1 oz. Banana Schnapps
½ tsp. Grenadine
4 oz. Orange Juice

Shake well, serve over ice. Garish with orange slice and cherry.

COLONIAL PIZZA & SPAGHETTI HOUSE
Easton, PA

SWEDISH PEACH

1 oz. Absolut Vodka
2 oz. Peaches & Cream Liqueur

Serve over ice in brandy snifter. Garnish with peach slice.

HOLIDAY INN
Omaha, NE

SWISS SUNRISE

1 oz. Kammer-Blackforest Kirschwasser
¼ oz. Grenadine Club Soda

In a tall glass with ice; top with club soda.

AUBERGE SWISS
Berkeley Heights, NJ

SYCAMORE SUNSET

1½ oz. Bacardi Rum
Orange Juice
7-Up or Sprite
Grenadine

Fill a tall glass with ice, pour in rum. Fill with half orange juice and half 7-Up. Dribble grenadine. Garnish with a cherry and orange slice.

SYCAMORE GREENS
Duanesburg, NY

THE BIG BOPPER

3 oz. Tequila
1 oz. Triple Sec
½ oz. Grenadine
3 oz. Orange Juice
3 oz. Sweet and Sour

Flash blend, pour over rocks. Garnish with orange, lime wheel and cherry.

STUDEBAKER'S
Rockville, MD

THE FLOWER STREET CODDER

½ oz. Absolut Vodka
½ oz. Peach Schnapps
½ oz. Chambord Cranberry Juice

FLOWER STREET BAR
Los Angeles, CA

THE GIGGLER

1¼ oz. Amaretto
Strawberries
Cream of Coconut

Blend with ice.

GIGGLERS RESTAURANT
Parsippany, NJ

THE MAD MONK

1 part Benedictine
1 part Kahlua
1 part Hot Coffee

Top with whipped cream, and a float of Cointreau.
FACETS
Seattle, WA

THE MAYFAIR TROPICAL COOLER

1¼ oz. Light Rum
dash Anisette
½ oz. Orange Juice
2 oz. Pineapple Juice
dash Grenadine

Serve over ice in a Collins glass. Garnish with a fan and a cherry.
THE MAYFAIR REGENT
Chicago, IL

TIFF'S TEMPTATION

¾ oz. Triple Sec
½ oz. Vodka
¼ oz. Chambord
¼ oz. Lime Juice

Mix and chill in glass mixing cup, one-quarter filled with ice. Serve in pony or liqueur glass.
SHERATON PLAZA
Chicago, IL

TROPICAL TREAT

½ oz. Absolut Vodka
½ oz. Bombay Gin
½ oz. Peach Schnapps
2 oz. 7-Up
1 oz. Pineapple Juice
¼ oz. Grenadine

Combine all ingredients in a large glass filled with ice, shake.
PARKERS' LIGHTHOUSE
Brooklyn, NY

WICKED STEPMOTHER

1½ oz. Absolut Peppar
1 oz. Amaretto

Serve over ice in an old-fashioned glass.
SUGARBUSH INN
Warren, VT

THE WINDY CITY

1¼ oz. Canadian Club Classic
dash Hiram Walker Triple Sec

In on the rocks glass packed with ice, fill with water. Add lemon twist.
HIRAM WALKER, INC.
Des Plaines, IL

CRICKET'S COFFEE

Granulated Sugar/Cinnamon
Lime Wedges
1½ oz. Grand Marnier
1½ oz. Amaretto
10 oz. Hot Coffee

In a bowl, mix together 2 parts sugar, 1 part cinnamon. Rim two stemmed glasses with lime wedge, dip in mixture. Hold a flame close to the sugar ring, turning the glass slowly until ring is crystallized all around. Pour ¾ oz. Marnier in each glass; light one. Holding the glass by the stem, pour flaming Marnier from one glass to the other, turning glasses slowly, and keeping it flamed at all times. Put out the flames. Add ¾ oz. Amaretto and Coffee to each glass. Top with Whipped Cream. Serves 2.

CRICKET'S COFFEE created by Joe the Bartender
CRICKETS
Chicago, IL

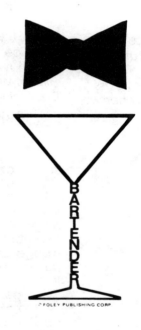

©FOLEY PUBLISHING CORP

POUSSE-CAFÉS

Pousse-Café, French for "after coffee" was and is the quintessential test of a Bartender's ability as a mixologist. Pousse-Cafés are French in origin and are layered specialty drinks. Bartenders in New Orleans first popularized Pousse-Cafés in the late 1840's and the drinks became a fad in bars and restaurants throughout the United States in the early 1900's.

A Bartender is really put to the "test" when making a Pousse-Café. One needs a steady hand and the knowledge of specific gravities of cordials, syrups and brandies. From three to twelve different types of the above-mentioned are poured over the back of a spoon into a cordial glass. The spoon brakes the fall of the liquids, enabling them to layer easier. By adding the ingredients in order of their specific gravities, they remain separate and the result is a colorful rainbow effect. Pousse-Cafés can be prepared ahead of time for use at a party or to end a special dinner. They will keep for at least an hour in the refrigerator before the layers start to blend. If brandy is your last ingredient, the "show" would go on further by flaming it when served, or even squeezing an orange peel on the lit brandy would heighten the effect.

THE ULTIMATE COCKTAIL BOOK is happy to present a listing of the Hiram Walker cordial line and their specific gravities. So grab your spoons and cordial glasses and "Pousse-Café the night away!!"

The Hiram Walker cordials, liqueurs and products shown below can be used in Pousse-Cafés. Be sure to pour slowly over the back of a spoon. For best results allow at least five units between each liqueur starting with the type having the highest number.

HIRAM WALKER
POUSSE-CAFÉ SPECIFIC GRAVITY INDEX

No.	Proof	Product	Specific Gravity	Color
1	40	Creme de Cassis	1.1833	Purple
2	25	Grenadine Liqueur	1.1720	Red
3	54	Creme de Cacao	1.1561	Brown
4	48	Hazelnut Schnapps	1.1532	Tawny
5	40	Praline	1.1514	Brown
6	50	Praline Liqueur	1.1514	Brown
7	54	Creme de Cacao	1.1434	White
8	56	Creme de Noyaux	1.1342	Red
9	48	Licorice Schnapps	1.1300	Clear
10	54	Chocolate Cherry	1.1247	Brown
11	56	Creme de Banana	1.1233	Yellow
12	54	Chocolate Mint	1.1230	Brown
13	48	Blue Curacao	1.1215	Blue
14	54	Swiss Chocolate Almond	1.1181	Brown
15	25	Haagen-Dazs, Peach	1.1160	White
16	60	Creme de Menthe, White	1.1088	White
17	60	Creme de Menthe, Green	1.1088	Green
18	60	Orange Curacao	1.1086	Tawny
19	34	Haagen-Dazs, Original	1.1037	Cream
20	34	Haagen-Dazs, Vanilla	1.1029	Cream
21	48	Cider Mill Apple Schnapps	1.0999	Tawny
22	48	Orchard Orange Schnapps	1.0998	Clear
23	60	Anisette, White and Red	1.0987	White/Red
24	48	Creme de Strawberry	1.0968	Red
25	48	Wild Strawberry Schnapps	1.0966	Clear
26	40	Juicy Grape Schnapps	1.0933	Purple
27	48	Red Hot Schnapps	1.0927	Red
28	60	Triple Sec	1.0922	White
29	60	Rock & Rye	1.0887	Yellow
30	40	Cranberry Cordial	1.0872	Cranberry
31	50	Amaretto	1.0842	Tawny

No.	Proof	Product	Specific Gravity	Color
32	48	Old Fashioned Root Beer Schnapps	1.0828	Tawny
33	84	Sambuca	1.0813	White
34	40	Country Melon Schnapps	1.0796	Pink
35	70	Coffee Flavored Brandy	1.0794	Brown
36	48	Red Raspberry Schnapps	1.0752	Clear
37	48	Snappy Apricot Schnapps	1.0733	Tawny
38	48	Cinnamon Schnapps	1.0732	Red
39	48	Spearmint Schnapps	1.0727	Clear
40	60	Shamrock Schnapps	1.0617	Green
41	60	Peppermint Schnapps	1.0615	Clear
42	48	Jubilee Peach Schnapps	1.0595	Clear
43	70	Raspberry Flavored Brandy	1.0566	Reddish
44	70	Apricot Flavored Brandy	1.0548	Tawny
45	70	Peach Flavored Brandy	1.0547	Tawny
46	70	Cherry Flavored Brandy	1.0542	Reddish
47	70	Blackberry Flavored Brandy	1.0536	Purplish
48	90	Peach Schnapps	1.0534	Clear
49	90	Root Beer Schnapps	1.0441	Brown
50	50	Amaretto and Cognac	1.0394	Tawny
51	60	Sol Y Sombra	1.0376	Tawny
52	90	Cinnamon Spice Schnapps	1.0358	Reddish
53	90	Peppermint Schnapps	1.0340	Clear
54	60	Sloe Gin	1.0241	Red
55	70	Ginger Flavored Brandy	0.9979	Light Brown
56	90	Kirschwasser	0.9410	Clear

INDEX BY DRINK NAME

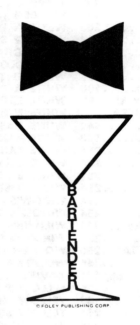

YOUR SPECIAL RECIPE

YOUR SPECIAL RECIPE

YOUR SPECIAL RECIPE

YOUR SPECIAL RECIPE

YOUR SPECIAL RECIPE

YOUR SPECIAL RECIPE

YOUR SPECIAL RECIPE